THE
RELUCTANT
POLITICIAN

Iskandar Erling Karlberg

Here's to a more mature

Malaysia

Taufik

Kuala Lumpur
February 2016

The **Institute of Southeast Asian Studies (ISEAS)** was established as an autonomous organization in 1968. It is a regional research centre dedicated to the study of socio-political, security and economic trends and developments in Southeast Asia and its wider geostrategic and economic environment.

The Institute's research programmes are the Regional Economic Studies (RES, including ASEAN and APEC), Regional Strategic and Political Studies (RSPS), and Regional Social and Cultural Studies (RSCS).

ISEAS Publishing, an established academic press, has issued more than 1,000 books and journals. It is the largest scholarly publisher of research about Southeast Asia from within the region. ISEAS Publishing works with many other academic and trade publishers and distributors to disseminate important research and analyses from and about Southeast Asia to the rest of the world.

THE RELUCTANT POLITICIAN

Tun Dr Ismail and His Time

OOI KEE BENG

INSTITUTE OF SOUTHEAST ASIAN STUDIES

Singapore

First published in Singapore in 2006 by ISEAS Publishing
Institute of Southeast Asian Studies
30 Heng Mui Keng Terrace
Pasir Panjang
Singapore 119614

E-mail: publish@iseas.edu.sg
Website: <http://bookshop.iseas.edu.sg>

This book is published under the Malaysia Study Programme funded by
Professor Saw Swee-Hock.

ISEAS Library Cataloguing-in-Publication Data

Ooi Kee Beng, 1955–
    The reluctant politician : Tun Dr Ismail.
    1. Ismail Dato Abdul Rahman, Tun, 1915–1973.
    2. Politicians—Malaysia—Biography.
    I. Title
DS597.15 I82O61   2006

ISBN-10:   981-230-424-X (soft cover)
ISBN-13: 978-981-230-424-7 (soft cover)
ISBN-10:   981-230-425-8 (hard cover)
ISBN-13: 978-981-230-425-4 (hard cover)

Typeset by Superskill Graphics Pte Ltd
Printed in Singapore by Utopia Press Pte Ltd

CONTENTS

Foreword by Tun Dr Haji Mohd Salleh bin Abas   vii

Message from the Director, K. Kesavapany   xi

Preface   xiii

Acknowledgements   xvii

About the Author   xxi

Chronology   xxiii

PART ONE
Merdeka or Medicine?

Chapter One   The Acting Prime Minister Dies   3

Chapter Two   Life before Politics   13

Chapter Three   UMNO and the Road to Merdeka   45

Chapter Four   Positioning Malaya in the World   86

Chapter Five   The Making and Partitioning of Malaysia   137

PART TWO
Remaking Malaysia

Chapter Six   Forced from Retirement   185

Chapter Seven   A Lack of Time   219

Chapter Eight   Nailing Things into Place   241

List of Abbreviations   277

Bibliography   281

Index   297

FOREWORD

I feel greatly honoured to write a Foreword for this very long awaited book on the life of the very famous son of Malaysia, the late Tun Dr Ismail bin Dato' Haji Abdul Rahman Yassin.

Undoubtedly this volume will become good source material for students of the modern history of Malaysia. I do not wish to repeat what is already written about the late Tun in this book — about his education, his well-known character as a man of integrity, his common sense approach to problems be they big or small, easy or difficult, and above all, his sacrifice, especially of his health for the country. All these are set out in details that leave no one with any doubt that the late Tun was not only a pragmatic and wise person but also one who was very meticulous, especially when it came to questions of law and politics.

I had the privilege of coming into contact with him when I joined the Attorney General's Chamber in Kuala Lumpur in 1963. I must have gradually won his confidence because he later constantly consulted me whenever law and politics came into conflict. He would want to know what the law was on any given problem that he had to deal with. The Attorney General then, the late Tan Sri Abdul Kadir bin Yusof, being a political Attorney General with membership in the Cabinet, was a very busy person. That was why the job of advising the late Tun fell on me as the Solicitor General for the country. Through constant interactions between me, him and Tan Sri Abdul Kadir, I came to enjoy the confidence of these two wonderful persons.

Subsequent to the May 13 riots, the late Tun Abdul Razak, the then Deputy Prime Minister, called me and my colleague the late Tan Sri Hashim Yeop Sani, to the Prime Minister's Office, the late Tunku Abdul Rahman Putra's residence at Jalan Dato' Onn. There were a few senior Ministers present. I need not repeat who they were, because these are mentioned in this book. The Ministers were discussing how to deal with the riots. From the top of Jalan Dato' Onn, we could hear gun shots being fired and we could see smoke bellowing from selected spots in the city and nearby suburban areas. The late Tun Dr Ismail, who had already retired from the Cabinet two years earlier, soon arrived wearing an expression of great concern on his face. He immediately joined in the discussion, and I still remember his words of caution to those present against the idea of a permanent suspension of the Constitution. He said, "If you should fail, then it will be like in many other coup d'etats, you will all end up being shot one by one." Because of this stern warning, the discussion changed direction and focussed instead on a declaration of emergency and on the establishment of the National Operation Council to run the country until normality had returned and Parliament could be recalled.

Another incident that showed the late Tun to be a pragmatic politician who would fight for what he thought to be the best solution irrespective of what happened to him personally was during the creation of the Federal Territory of Kuala Lumpur. The idea was conceived by him for stabilizing parliamentary democracy in Malaysia. He was convinced that with the new status for Kuala Lumpur, Malays and non-Malays would no longer have to be jealous of, and compete with, each other for control over the Selangor State Government, which then included the Federal

Capital. I advised the late Tun on the various legislative steps that the government needed to take to facilitate the separation of Kuala Lumpur from Selangor state. These included an agreement to be signed between the Selangor State Government and the Federal Government, as well as an Act of Parliament. While working with the late Tun on this undertaking, I heard him repeat several times words that showed his earnestness and sincerity: "I will do for the country what I will not do for myself and my family."

These words demonstrate the conviction and attitude of this great man when it came to making a choice between himself and the country. How greatly this contrasts with modern day politicians who shout eloquently at the top of their voice that they serve the people, and yet the truth is otherwise. The people whom they serve are, more often than not, themselves and their close friends.

Returning to this book, I recommend it to be read by all, especially by the generation of Malaysians who were born after the demise of the late Tun, so that they may attain a better understanding of the country, and gain an appreciation of the contributions this great man made.

Had he not died prematurely, Malaysia would have been different and the rule of law would not have suffered any reversal and would have continued to safeguard the freedom and liberty of all citizens, as indeed it is meant to do.

Tun Dr Haji Mohd Salleh bin Abas
Former Lord President of the Federal Court, Malaysia

MESSAGE FROM THE DIRECTOR

Growing up in Malaysia, I naturally knew about the achievements of the late Tun Dr Ismail Abdul Rahman, and about his reputation as a man of principle. When his private papers were kindly offered to ISEAS by his eldest son, Tawfik, my colleagues and I seized the opportunity to work on a properly researched book.

Tun Ismail bin Abdul Rahman funtioned as a pillar of strength under two late Prime Ministers, Tunku Abdul Rahman and Tun Abdul Razak, during a very difficult and challenging period in Malaysia politics. After completing his medical studies in Australia, he returned to his home state of Johor, only to be drawn into Malay national politics spearheaded by the United Malays National Organization (UMNO). He rose up in the party hierarchy as a result of his good work, dedication and loyalty. It is a truism to say that the Tunku would not have been able to hold UMNO together without Tun Ismail's support and loyalty. He became indispensable to UMNO and its leaders. Tun Ismail was not a politician in the normal sense of the term: He was much more a competent administrator on whom the Tunku and Tun Razak naturally came to depend. Tun Ismail was a man of principle and honesty and, above all, a person who clearly distinguished right from wrong.

During the difficult years of Malaysian politics, he was a "lone voice" against the growing tide of extremism and bigotry. Although he endorsed the concept of special rights, he made it known that they could only be temporary and not a birthright to suppress the rights of others. On the regional and international fronts, he worked assiduously for the formation of regional economic groupings, campaigned relentlessly to make Southeast Asia a zone free from big power politics, and revealed several times that relations between Malaysia and Singapore should be placed on a proper footing. He even envisaged the day when Singapore might re-merge with Malaysia. During the turbulence of the late 1960s and the early 1970s, both the Tunku and Tun Razak had to recall him from political retirement to serve the nation. Tun Ismail was a source of moderation and comfort to all Malaysians in the aftermath of the racial tragedy in 1969. It was he who gave confidence and hope to Malaysians to embark on a new phase in race relations. In Malaysian political circles, there is a unanimous view that Tun Ismail's greatest contribution was in ensuring that the country emerged intact and stable from the turbulence caused by the May 13 racial riots.

The Reluctant Politician will provide a glimpse of the man, the values he stood for, his public and private life, and his professional relationship with other prominent politicians of that era, both in Malaysia and Singapore.

This biography of Tun Dr Ismail is the first in a series of books that the Institute plans to publish on First Generation Southeast Asian Leaders. We believe that such books would help to throw light on their contributions to the making of modern Southeast Asia. Students and scholars of Southeast Asian politics might want to examine his thoughts in greater depth because he was well ahead of his time.

K. Kesavapany
Director
Institute of Southeast Asian Studies
Singapore

PREFACE

This work is based on the private papers of the late Tun Dr Ismail Alhaj bin Datuk Haji Abdul Rahman. These documents were found in somewhat scattered condition in his home after he passed away on 2 August 1973. His eldest son, Tawfik, understood that it was his inescapable duty to collect them and to care for them until such times when they could be used to tell his father's story, and to speak of the Malaysia he envisaged. The collection of Ismail's letters was in the keeping of one of his brothers, and came into Tawfik's care much later.

In March 2005, after lengthy discussions with his old friend Ambassador Verghese Mathews, a visiting research fellow at Singapore's Institute of Southeast Asian Studies (ISEAS), Tawfik decided to deposit these papers, which were in danger of physical deterioration, with ISEAS Library.

ISEAS Director Ambassador K. Kesavapany, who immediately decided that a biography about Tun Dr Ismail was long overdue, gave me the honour of writing it, and convinced Tawfik to be consultant and adviser for the project.

Perhaps because Tun Dr Ismail was a stickler for rules, hardly any official documents are to be found among his papers, with the exception of a Special Branch report from the early 1960s, the introductory page to which is missing. Being a hard-working and conscientious man, he tended to finish his work at his office, and seldom took important files home.

The documents that this biography relies upon most are, first, an unfinished and unpublished autobiography called "Drifting into Politics" that Tun Dr Ismail authored after he resigned from government work in mid-1967, to which he made only two additions in later years; second, the collection of correspondence he kept throughout his life, which though incomplete, provides intriguing information about his life, his friends and his character; and third, the series of reports that he wrote between September 1957 and January 1959 for the benefit of Prime Minister Tunku Abdul Rahman, when the former was Malaya's first Ambassador to Washington and first Permanent Representative to the United Nations in New York. These three constitute the "core" of his papers.

Tun Dr Ismail was a man of few words, even when he was recording his own life, and few embellishments are found in his writings. Much complementing research has therefore been carried out to provide illuminating backdrops for the sake of the average reader, to retrieve intimate details about his life, and to confirm events mentioned in the private papers.

A generous amount of relevant information was gathered from the archives of Malaysia's *New Straits Times Press* (*NSTP*), which host newspaper clippings about Tun Dr Ismail sorted in half-a-dozen medium-sized folders. Most of the pictures in this book are taken from there, and are used with the kind permission of *NSTP*.

Tun Dr Ismail graduated in medicine from Melbourne University's Queen's College in June 1945, and was the first Malay to do so. Altogether, he lived in Australia for six years, and if not for the letters he wrote home in 1940 and 1941, most details from that period would be unknown to us. Luckily these have been preserved. Some information on this period of his life can be found in the minutes of the bi-monthly meetings of Queen's College Sports and Social Club (QCSSC), from which several anecdotes are reproduced here. The present Master of Queen's College, Professor David Runia, kindly provided some pictures from that period for the book.

The National Archives at Kew, England, aided my work through the huge amounts of documents available about Malayan politics in the 1950s, and other relevant matters, including reports on a couple of Ismail's many visits to the United Kingdom.

Last, and certainly not least, a great number of useful and intimate details were gained through interviews with members of Tun Dr Ismail's family, friends, acquaintances, colleagues and staff.

My job has been to collect this information in order to weave together an easily readable and factually corroborated story. Although the tone of the book results from a balancing act between scientific writing and biographic narrating, I have tried as far as possible to resist dramaturgical temptations.

From start to finish, this journey has been awesome, to say the least. To write about the man, I had to understand the man, and I can confidently say that the more I understood him, the more he struck me as a rare and integrated soul. It is easy to understand him because he strove to be consistent, and it is easy to admire him because he strove to be fair.

The responsibility of writing the biography of such an important personage has been heavy. In many ways, this eased my job. The best strategy for an author in such a position to adopt is to allow the man's many facets to speak for themselves.

His life reflected Malaysia's early experiences, and his death in many ways also foreshadowed the waning of many early dreams. Of lasting significance is the fact that his actions and ideas remain a reminder to Malaysians of the hopes and aspirations of one of the country's most respected founding fathers, and one of the region's more far-sighted and practical thinkers.

He died on the evening of 2 August 1973, but his burial was postponed until 4 August in order to allow his eldest son Tawfik and Prime Minister Tun Abdul Razak to rush home in time for it. The *Malay Mail* (*MM*) proclaimed on the day of Ismail's funeral procession:

> Few men in the history of Malaysia have earned so much respect from the people or given so much of himself to their cause, as the late Deputy Prime Minister did. [...] For a man who insisted that he be judged not by his rhetoric but instead by his deeds, reputation and reality became one, a standard which is hard to emulate (*MM*, 4 August 1973).

This sense of loss was further expressed the day after the burial in the *Sunday Mail* (*SM*), which confidently stated: "The history books will record his full contributions both to the nation and the South-east Asian region" (*SM*, 5 August 1973). Strangely and sadly, this proved a false prophecy. There has in fact been a sorry lack of knowledge about Tun Dr Ismail and about his importance in the forming and reforming of Malaysia. This book is a humble attempt to help remedy that situation.

Ooi Kee Beng

ACKNOWLEDGEMENTS

This project could not have been completed without the able assistance of Encik Mohamed Tawfik bin Tun Dr Ismail. He was crucial to the project, and his generosity with his time, his memories, experiences, contacts, documentary sources and breadth of learning, has been overwhelming to say the least. The work he had earlier put into arranging his father's papers saved the project much valuable time. This wonderfully resourceful man arranged most of the interviews with prominent Malaysians done for the book.

Deep gratitude is also owed ISEAS Director K. Kesavapany for his trust in my ability to carry this project to its conclusion, and for arranging important interviews for me. He saw how important it was for Malaysia and Singapore, and indeed the whole region, to revisit their early history through the writing of biographies on chosen personalities. His decision to secure Tawfik Ismail as a consultant for the project was an inspired move, and turned the research process into an exciting experience for me.

Prof Saw Swee Hock provided generous financial and moral support through the Malaysia Study Programme at ISEAS. For this, I am deeply grateful.

I wish to express my warmest appreciation to the following for granting me exclusive interviews and for sharing their memories with me over the last two years:

Encik Daud Ahmad, Datuk Abdullah Ali, Tan Sri Zakaria Ali, Datuk Dr Hussein bin Tun Dr Awang, Datuk Seri Abdullah Badawi, Prof Tan Sri Maurice Baker, Mr Tom Critchley, the late Tun Ghafar Baba, Ungku Bakar, Leslie Eu Peng Meng, Tan Sri Aishah Ghani, Datuk Abdul Rahman Hamidon, Tengku Tan Sri Razaleigh Hamzah, Tun Musa Hitam, Encik Ariff bin Tun Dr Ismail, Cik Badariah binte Tun Dr Ismail, General Tun Ibrahim Ismail, Tan Sri Razali Ismail, Encik Tarmizi bin Tun Dr Ismail, Encik Tawfik bin Tun Dr Ismail, Cik Zailah binte Tun Dr Ismail, Encik Zamakhshari bin Tun Dr Ismail, Tan Sri G.K Rama Iyer, Prof Datuk Khoo Kay Kim, Mr Robert Kuok, Mr Lee Kuan Yew, Tun Lim Chong Eu, Dato' P.G. Lim, Tan Sri Lim Taik Choon, Datuk Haji Abdul Wahab Majid, Encik Din Merican, Tun Mohd Hanif Omar, Datuk Noordin Omar, Dato' Dominic Puthucheary, Mr Francis Puthucheary, Tengku Ahmad Rithauddeen, Tun Ghazali Shafie, Dato' Chet Singh, Brother Lawrence Spritzig, Tan Sri Abu Bakar bin Dato' Sulaiman and Puan Sri Sukarnya, Tunku Tan Sri Shahriman bin Tunku Sulaiman, Dato' A.S. Talalla, Dato' Tan Chin Nam, Datuk Abdullah Abdul Wahab, Prof Wan Arfah binti Tan Sri Wan Hamzah, Encik Wan Hussein bin Tan Sri Wan Hamzah, Encik Ismail Iskandar Wildun, Datuk Annuar Zaini, and Puan Sri Razimah Zakaria.

Thanks also to my researcher colleagues for being available when advice was sought, and to ISEAS' administrators, librarians and publishing staff who afforded me professional service with a smile. I am deeply indebted to ISEAS Library for allowing me full access to documents in its safekeeping.

I am also very grateful to the *New Straits Times Press (NSTP)* — and its Editor-in-Chief Dato Hishammuddin Aun — for allowing me to hunt through its archives. Not only did I find invaluable information there, I was able to countercheck details found in the Ismail papers and elsewhere. Many of the pictures in this book are used with the kind permission of *NSTP*. Thanks are also owed to Bernama News Agency and its chairman Dato Annuar Zaini for various forms of assistance that he rendered the project.

Others I wish to thank include the many who helped me throughout the research period. These include Dato' Dr Rais Yatim, Professor David Runia and Jennifer Bars from Melbourne University's Queen's College, Secretary of Parliament Datuk Abdullah Abdul Wahab, my friends John Liebmann and Maggie Fordham, Bert Tan, Kay Kuok, and Miranda Wong, as well as all the personal assistants and secretaries involved in arranging meetings and interviews. Thanks also to Bashir Basalamah for bringing several howlers to my attention. Finally, a warm hug is due to my loving wife Laotse Sacker for proofreading the final manuscript.

ABOUT THE AUTHOR

Dr OOI KEE BENG was born in Penang, and received his basic education at La Salle School and St Xavier's Institution.

He is presently a Fellow at Singapore's Institute of Southeast Asian Studies (ISEAS), where he coordinates its Malaysia Study Programme. His fields of interest include modern language philosophy, Chinese philosophy, nation building with a special focus on Malaysia, political economics and the philosophy of science. He has degrees in Public Administration and Chinese Language Studies, as well as a doctorate in Sinology, all from Stockholm University, Sweden, where he also lectured in Chinese Philosophy, Chinese History and General Knowledge of China between 1995 and 2004.

His books include *Chinese Strategists: Beyond Sun Zi's Art of War* (2006); *Era of Transition: Malaysia after Mahathir* (2006); *HRD for Developing States and Companies* (2005) in editorial collaboration with Abdul Ghani Pg Hj Metusin; *The State and its Changdao: Sufficient Discursive Commonality in Nation Renewal, with Malaysia as Case Study* (2001); *Chinese Studies of the Malay World: A Comparative Approach* (2003) in editorial collaboration with Ding Choo Ming; as well as translations of Chinese military classics into Swedish, such as *Wei Liao Zis krigskonst* (2001), *Wu Zis krigskonst* (2001) and *Sunzis krigskonst* (1997).

He also writes regular commentaries for regional newspapers about Malaysian politics and socio-economics.

CHRONOLOGY

Tun Dr Ismail Alhaj bin Datuk Haji Abdul Rahman

1915 — Born 4 November in Johor Bahru (JB) to Abdul Rahman bin Yassin (1890–1970) and Zahara binte Abu Bakar (?–1936).

1922 — Starts his education at Sekolah Bukit Zaharah and later goes to English College, both in Johor Bahru.

1936–39 — Does medical studies at King Edward College of Medicine, Singapore.

1939–45 — Studies medicine at Queen's College, Melbourne University.

1945–46 — Becomes the first Malay medical graduate from Melbourne University, and subsequently returns to Malaya. He joins the Medical Department in Johor, but leaves after a short stint.

1947–53 — Goes into private practice in Johor Bahru, and is moderately successful with a clinic called Tawakkal (Trust in God), named after his childhood home.

1948–54 — Nominated unofficial member of the Johor State Council, and then official member of the Johor Executive Council. He is elected into the Johor Bahru Town Council.

1950 — Marries Toh Puan Norashikin Seth (nickname Neno, born 17 January 1930 in Johor Bahru). The couple has six children, two girls and four boys (Mohd Tawfik, born 23 September 1951 in GH in JB; Zailah, born 2 May 1953 in GH in JB; Badariah, born 8 March 1957 in PJ; Mohamed Tarmizi, born 23 May 1960 in Bangsar KL; Zamakhshari, born 16 September 1964 at GH in KL, and Mohamed Ariff, born 25 October 1967 in KL).

1951 — Finally joins UMNO after Onn Ja'afar resigned and Tunku Abdul Rahman had gained control of the party.

1953 — Appointed in September as unofficial member of the Federal Legislative Council under Sir Gerald Templer. He becomes Member of Lands, Mines and Communication at Tunku Abdul Rahman's request. He moves with his family to Kuala Lumpur.

1954–55 — Becomes Member of Natural Resources.

1955 — Elected to the Federal Legislative Council for the Johore Timor constituency (to be re-elected in 1959, 1964 and 1969). Elected Minister for Natural Resources, and lays groundwork for Felda in May (see *The Star*, 26 March 2001).

1956 — The new Chief Minister Tunku Abdul Rahman appoints him Minister of Commerce and Industry.

1957 (September)–1959 (February) — Becomes Minister Plenipotentiary (without portfolio), and is sent as Malaya's first ambassador to Washington D.C., United States, and Malaya's first permanent representative to the United Nations in New York.

1959 — Returns from Washington and becomes Minister of Commerce and Industry.

1959 — Elected member for Johor Timor to the Dewan Ra'ayat and is appointed Minister of Foreign Affairs in August. He is Minister of Commerce and Trade from 20 September to 16 November, 1960.

1960 — Becomes Minister of Internal Security on 16 November, and also chairman of the Commission of the Enquiry into the Position of the Malayan Student Community in UK and the Republic of Ireland.

1961 — Given the additional post of Minister of Home Affairs on 22 February. Appointed Federal Representative to the Internal Security Council in Singapore, until 16 September 1963.

1962 — Leads delegation to UN general assembly 17th Meeting.

1963 — Becomes chairman of Malaysian Security Board.

1964 — Re-elected member of Johor Timor Constituency in April. Appointed Minister of Home Affairs and Minister of Justice. In September, he leads a Malaysian delegation to the UN Security Council to debate Indonesian aggression.

1965 — Makes trip to United Nations Headquarters in New York with his wife Neno, together with Philip Kuok and wife, then travels to Madrid, London and Beirut, before returning home end of November. In September, he receives the Grand Officer of the National Order of Vietnam from the South Vietnamese Government through a visiting delegation.

1966 — Ismail starts the year by visiting Manila to attend the presidential inauguration of Ferdinand Marcos. In April, he accepts an invitation from the South Korean Central Intelligence Service to visit Seoul for eight days, and is awarded the Order of Merit (First Class). He flies to London in May 1966 to attend the Conference of Law Ministers from the

Commonwealth. He becomes chairman of Malayan Banking after its financial collapse and subsequent nationalization. He becomes the first to be conferred the Seri Setia Mahkota (Grand Commander), which carries the title "Tun".

1967 — In June, he resigns from the Cabinet — though not as MP — for health reasons, and returns to private medical practice. He joins the Board of Malaysian Sugar Refineries and Guthries.

1967 — Undergoes successful treatment at the Royal Marsden Hospital in London for cancer of the naso-pharynx. Starts private practice in Kuala Lumpur with a group of doctors on his return.

1969 — Asked to return to government by Razak after 10 May elections. Becomes Deputy Director of Operations of the National Operations Council. On 12 June, he is appointed Minister of Home Affairs. In September, he makes a trip to Europe and the United Kingdom for medical treatment over three weeks. A medical check-up in 23–24 September gives him "a clean bill of health". His official golf handicap is certified by the Royal Selangor Golf Club on 21 October as 15.

1970 — Leaves for London on 3 March for heart consultation, and stays for nine weeks. In his absence, he is awarded the Republic of Indonesia Medal Second Class when President Suharto visited Kuala Lumpur. In September, the new premier Tun Abdul Razak bin Hussein appoints him deputy. He visits London between 4 and 11 October for a medical check-up on the way to New York for Twenty-fifth anniversary celebrations of the United Nations.

1971 — He visits Dubrovnik. In September, he travels to Singapore to study Singapore's low-cost housing schemes. While visiting

Sabah in May, he is awarded the Sri Panglima Darjah Kinabalu. He stays in London 24 October–28 November for medical check-up, returning to Malaysia *via* Paris, Belgrade and Cairo.

1972 — He receives the Honorary Fellowship Award from the Malaysian Institute of Management (MIM).

1973 — He takes on the portfolio of Minister of Trade and Industry on 3 January, and in March, visits Canberra, Sydney, Melbourne, Hobart and Armidale with his wife and daughter Zailah for talks regarding investments in Malaysia. He pays a visit to his alma mater, Queen's College, University of Melbourne, where he is conferred with an honorary degree of doctor of laws. He also visits the University of New England in Armidale to see his son Tawfik. On 9 June, he is awarded a similar degree by Universiti Sains Malaysia. Malaysia's Academy of Medicine makes him Honorary Member. On Thursday 2 August, he passes away of a heart attack at his home on Maxwell Road (renamed Jalan Tun Dr Ismail in early 1974) in Kuala Lumpur. On Sunday 4 August, after a huge state funeral procession the day before — the country's first — he becomes the first to be buried at the State Mausoleum.

Recreational activities: Regular nine-hole golf games and evening swims. Also involved in rugby, tennis, swimming, boxing, soccer and photography when he was a student in Australia.

PART ONE

Merdeka or Medicine?

Chapter 1

THE ACTING
PRIME MINISTER DIES

Tun Dr Ismail seemed fated to become the third prime minister of the country he helped free from colonial rule. Being the first Malay medical graduate from Melbourne University's Queen's College, he had imagined becoming a wealthy doctor in his hometown of Johor Bahru. The political fervour of the times overwhelmed him, however, and he was compelled to leave his private practice and enter reluctantly into politics. When he returned from Australia after World War II, he was convinced that the best strategy for intellectuals fighting for Malayan independence was to join an established mass movement. He found this in the United Malays National Organization (UMNO), but only after Tunku Abdul Rahman had become its leader in 1951. From that moment on, Ismail became a key player in the country's history until his premature death in 1973.

A faulty heart valve hounded him all his life, and he tried endlessly to remedy the condition through regular golfing and swimming. He was also plagued by recurrent neck cancer. In early 1967, with his wife pregnant with their sixth child, he felt that he had done enough in politics and decided to retire from his ministerial posts. His doctors were advising him to slow down, and he felt that his young family needed him more than ever.

The racial riots that followed the 10 May 1969 general elections pushed the country towards widespread chaos, and presented him with no other choice but to leave his comfortable retirement and return to the fray. With Prime Minister Tunku now sidelined, Deputy Premier Tun Abdul Razak Hussein and Ismail — who again became home affairs minister — became the true leaders of the country. For over four years, Razak and Ismail easily complemented each other in laying the foundations for a new Malaysia that would hopefully not see a repeat of inter-communal violence. Both died young and unexpectedly, however, and their programmes for nation rebuilding were continued by younger men whose goals were not always identical with theirs, nor as profound.

Razak was diagnosed with leukaemia already at the end of 1969. This secret was known only to him and Ismail, the medical staff involved, and a couple of Ismail's personal friends, who were all sworn to secrecy. This clandestine state of affairs could not but strongly affect policy formation as the two leaders discussed plans in the glaring light of Ismail's probable succession to the post of prime minister. The doctors told Razak that he had four years at most to live, although he managed to last six. Further pressure was exerted by the fact that Ismail, though not terminally ill, had recently suffered a recurrence of neck cancer, and his faulty heart valve was badly in need of surgery.

As fate would have it, the awe-inspiring and pipe-smoking Ismail was the first of the two to fall. On the evening of Thursday 2 August 1973, at the relatively young age of 57, he suffered a massive heart attack. He was alone in his study on the upper floor of his house on Maxwell Road — now Jalan Tun Dr Ismail — in Kuala Lumpur, resting after a light dinner and having checked on the younger children in their rooms. His wife was in hospital recovering from a tubal ligation operation, and Razak, for whom he was standing in, was away at the Commonwealth Heads of Government Meeting in Ottawa, Canada. That summit had in fact just started that same day.

Earlier that afternoon, Ismail officiated at the silver jubilee celebrations of the Peninsular Malaysia Malay Students Foundation (Gabungan Pelajar-pelajar Melayu Semenanjung — GPMS) at the Sultan Sulaiman Club in Kampung Bahru in the city. An explosion was included in the programme as a sound effect, but Ismail was somehow not informed of it. As a rule, after the racial riots of 13 May 1969, explosions were understandably not permitted. The sudden bang startled Ismail visibly. His 20-year-old daughter Zailah was watching the ceremony on television at home, and noticed that her father sweated profusely after the explosion. Annuar Zaini, treasurer-general of GPMS at that time, was in charge of the afternoon's arrangements. He did not register any sign that Ismail was not feeling well. What left a lasting impression on him, however, was how the many multi-coloured balloons released by Ismail as part of the celebrations were pounded to the ground by the sudden heavy downpour and kept from flying up into the sky like they were supposed to do. Many would come to see this as a bad omen (Annuar, interview 20 April 2006). Ismail then left the ceremony as planned, and with no further ado went off to visit his wife at Lady Templer Hospital. His press secretary, Wahab Majid, who had helped to prepare the speech for that occasion, was on leave, and so did not accompany Ismail, as would otherwise have been the case (Wahab, interview 6 July 2005).

Although Ismail had clearly been feeling frail lately, his golf had never been better. In fact, during a game the afternoon before at the Royal Selangor Golf Club, he scored an eagle, and was exhilarated by it (Leslie Eu, interview 9 September 2005).

Ismail had confided to his friend Robert Kuok about a month earlier that he had suffered three "quite serious" heart attacks in the space of two weeks.* Furthermore, he told Kuok that his wife, Norashikin (nicknamed Neno), was expecting their seventh child, which made him worry more than usual about his family. Ismail agreed with Kuok that he should go back into retirement once Razak had been on his trip to Canada. Interestingly, Kuok also noticed that Ismail's golf had improved phenomenally, and that he at least once actually managed to play par golf.

Ismail struggled with the fear that he might soon suffer a massive cardiac arrest, and therefore took the painful decision for his wife to terminate her pregnancy and undergo a tubal ligation. He was preparing the family for the possibility that he would not live long. The tragedy of his passing was therefore compounded for Neno by the fact that she had her fallopian tubes cut only two days before her husband's demise, and she was actually still in hospital recuperating from that operation when he passed away.

Both Razak and Ismail had for quite some time had the same doctor, the taciturn Scotsman Stewart C. McPherson. In a special check-up that Razak had with trepidation requested sometime at the end of 1969, the doctor discovered that the *de facto* premier was terminally ill. Razak quickly informed Ismail of this, and had the medical personnel privy to the information sworn to secrecy.

---

* These were probably cases of angina pectoris — chest pains — usually lasting two to ten minutes, and brought on either by physical exercise, psychological stress, extreme cold or a heavy meal. Heart valve problems can normally aggravate the condition <http://www.netdoctor.co.uk/diseases/facts/angina.htm>.

No one else was to know. As Razak and Ismail saw it, a serious problem of continuity now threatened the country's leadership and its reform policies. Ismail scribbled down some thoughts after learning of Razak's illness:

> With Tun Razak a doomed man, my heart operation became vitally important not only to myself and my family, but to the whole nation. Between the Tunku, Tun Razak and myself on the one hand, and all the other politicians on the other, there was a wide gap in leadership. With Tunku past his prime, Tun Razak a doomed man although unknown to the nation, everything seemed to depend on me (Drifting, 30 March 1970).

When chest pains came on the evening of 2 August 1973, Ismail's three youngest sons — 13-year-old Tarmizi, 9-year-old Zamakhshari and 6-year-old Ariff — were the only family members in the house. Neno was still in hospital and their two daughters — Zailah and Badariah — were out. Their eldest son, 22-year-old Tawfik, was away studying in Australia. The Chinese maid Ah Mui (Little Sister) was in the lower part of the house, as were Ismail's two bodyguards. Ismail's dog Tomo — named after a Japanese island — a boxer that lost a leg after being run over by one of his outriders, was in the courtyard. The Indian gardener had gone home.

Zailah remembers that just before leaving the house earlier that evening, she commented to her father that she had seen him on TV earlier, and had noticed how he was perspiring. Ismail, who was having dinner by himself, nodded in acknowledgement and complained that his steak was overly tough. As a rule, members of the family, at Ismail's request, often ate lunch together, and Ismail would try as far as possible to come home for the mid-day meal. Dinner-time, however, was a more relaxed occasion. Tarmizi, his second son, later reflected that his father "cut a very lonely figure eating his meal at the table" that evening (Interview 28 June 2005).

After finishing his meal, Ismail looked in on his young sons before going up to his study. Later, he rang the bell for Ah Mui, and asked for Zailah, who had not yet returned. He had by then suffered his heart attack and quickly told the maid that "I am going to die, please call my doctor and inform Gopal" (his private secretary) (*FEER* 13 August 1973). Dr McPherson, who resided in the neighbouring house, was away looking after Razak in Ottawa. Just before he left the country, Razak and Ismail decided that the doctor would accompany the prime minister on his trip instead of staying home to watch over Ismail (Tawfik, interview 28 April 2005). Ismail then dialled the telephone number of his other medical doctor, Dr Catterall, for the distraught maid (*FEER* 13 August 1973).

Tarmizi remembers being woken up by the maid and catching a glimpse of hectic activity upstairs in his father's room. Dr Catterall, who lived in Petaling Jaya, had already arrived, and was trying to resuscitate Ismail. The royal physician, Dr Pillai, who had been called after the bodyguards had reported to their superiors, had also turned up. Cabinet ministers started dropping in, and the atmosphere in the main room became somewhat chaotic. The prime minister was on the other side of the world, and the acting prime minister had just passed away. The country was leaderless for the moment.

As Tarmizi remembers it, there was no "team of doctors" on the spot that night, which contradicts later reports, for example in the *Far Eastern Economic Review* (13 August 1973) that there was. He was also disturbed by the fact that the ministers were discussing the future of national politics while the doctor was still doing his best to save his father. All in all, Dr Catterall laboured for five hours to revive Ismail, although the official time of death was later declared to have been 10 p.m. (Tarmizi, interview 28 August 2005).

On returning home later that evening after dropping off a friend, Zailah was surprised to find that all the lights in the building were on. Shocked by the news of her father's death, she set about making sure her younger brothers were all right. She remembers that one of the ministers called the Malaysian Embassy in Ottawa from the house, and she overheard Razak shouting at the distant end to remind his ministers that he was still the prime minister (Interview 23 April 2005).

In Canada, news of Ismail's death had arrived while High Commissioner Zakaria Ali was at a reception together with Razak and Dr McPherson. He was alarmed that he was to be the bearer of such terrible news. He steeled himself for the task and requested the doctor to tag along while he cornered Razak at an opportune moment. Just as Zakaria had feared, the prime minister was shocked and dazed by the news, and Dr McPherson had to take the frail man into an adjoining room to care for him. After some time, they re-emerged, and Razak, now clearly more in control of himself, set about organizing Ismail's funeral and other matters over the phone, losing his temper now and then and shouting down the mouthpiece (Zakaria, interview 12 April 2006). He gave orders for a state funeral, and for his friend to be buried in the Heroes' Mausoleum at the *Masjid Negara*. The Sultan of Johor had at the same time expressed a wish for Ismail to be buried in his home state.

The Canadian Government kindly put a special plane at Razak's disposal, with which he immediately flew to Copenhagen where he caught a commercial flight for home. Penang's Chief Minister Lim Chong Eu, who was also rushing home after receiving the same piece of bad news, met him en route (Lim, interview 9 January 2006). Razak was still in a "shattered state" when he arrived back in Kuala Lumpur on 4 August (G.K. Rama Iyer, interview 11 April 2006).

Back at Ismail's house, a discussion went on about how the widow was to be told. The burden was finally placed on her brother Ghazali Seth, Philip and Eileen Kuok, and Eileen's brother Leslie Cheah, who had been visiting Neno at the hospital at various times of the day. Neno was still under sedation when the group arrived. Badariah, her younger daughter, was there, and took the news about her father's demise calmly. The widow woke up at 5.30 in the morning, and Cheah went into her room to break the news. They then drove Neno back to the house in the early morning through the quiet streets of the city. On their arrival home, she went straight up to the bedroom where Ismail's body was lying (Kuok 1991, pp. 224–25).

In Armidale, Australia, the rugby team of the house that Ismail's eldest son Tawfik belonged to had just won a tournament. A series of knocks on his door at 3.00 in the morning — what he thought was the beginning of some customary victory prank by his Australian mates — brought him the sad news of his father's death. He was immediately struck by the fact that it was Thursday night, the most privileged time for Muslims to die, when followers of Islam all over the world prepare themselves for Friday prayers (Tawfik, interview 15 May 2006).

Back home in Kuala Lumpur, Ariff, the youngest of Ismail's children, woke up only at dawn. He remembers finding the furniture throughout the house covered with white textiles, and the boy wondered what festive day it could be (Ariff, interview 23 April 2005).

That day, Ismail's body was cleansed and then moved to *Masjid Negara* (National Mosque). Since the road from the house was considered too winding, the procession proper started from outside the Bank Negara Building. It moved along streets jammed with mourners taking part in Malaysia's first state funeral, and ended at *Masjid Negara* where Ismail's body was laid out in state.

Tawfik managed to reach home from Australia that night, while Razak arrived from Canada the next morning. The burial had been postponed for his sake.

The situation became confused and chaotic when the body was to be moved to the grave. Works and Communications Minister Sardon Jubir, who was the most senior cabinet minister after Ismail, had not followed the prime minister's definite instructions. Not only was Razak furious over the fact that Ismail's body was not laid out in state at the Parliament Building so that Malaysians of all faiths could view it without discomfort, as he had ordered, he had also wished for Ismail to be buried in the Heroes' Mausoleum. Sardon had instead prepared a plot just outside it (Tawfik, interview 15 May 2006). He had apparently consulted a mufti who claimed that a Muslim could not be buried under a roof (Ghafar Baba, interview 16 June 2005). The Tunku was also upset by Sardon's decision, and told Neno in exasperation: "My forefathers are all buried in a mausoleum under a roof!" (Kuok 1991, p. 225).

The proceedings were halted for several hours by Razak while soldiers in plainclothes armed with drills were brought in to break through the concrete and provide Ismail with a resting place befitting his stature. Apparently, Razak had greater trust in the army getting things done quickly than in the Public Works Department, whose workers had dug the first grave (Razaleigh, interview 28 June 2005). As those who had worked under Razak had learned, he would normally merely show some dissatisfaction when something did not go the way he had wished, but would then accept the situation and move on. On the matter of Ismail's burial, he was firm, and demanded that the fault be immediately remedied (Talalla, interview 30 March 2006).

Thus, Tun Dr Ismail Alhaj bin Datuk Haji Abdul Rahman became the first of Malaysia's national heroes to be buried in the Heroes' Mausoleum.

Not long before Ismail died, Madam Tang Mong Lan, the mother of his close friends Philip and Robert Kuok, had read his fortune and predicted that he would rise yet higher in his career. In a cruel way, fate proved her right. Ismail did not die as deputy prime minister, but as acting prime minister.

Chapter 2

LIFE BEFORE POLITICS*

Johor, despite being "longest and most intimately associated with the British", was the last of the Malay states to bow to pressure to accept a British adviser with wide-ranging political powers (Emerson 1937/70, p. 198). It was in fact only on 12 May 1914, on the very eve of World War I in Europe, that Sultan Ibrahim signed an agreement with the British allowing the General Adviser — a position created in Johor only four years earlier — to have the same powers as those enjoyed by British Residents in the rest of the Malay states. This fact testifies to the slow pace of colonization that the state of Johor went through during the nineteenth century, and to the late realization of direct British power there. Sultan Ibrahim's father, the energetic Sultan Abu Bakar, had encouraged migrant workers to develop estates along

---

* This chapter is based largely on Ismail's unpublished autobiography, on his letters home from Australia between 7 July 1940 to 1 May 1945, on the minutes of the Queen's College Sports and Social Club, Melbourne University, between 1939 and 1945, and on supplementary information supplied by his son, Tawfik, his daughter Zailah, his nephews Tan Sri Abu Bakar bin Dato Suleiman, Datuk Dr Hussein bin Tun Dr Awang, Encik Wan Hussein bin Tan Sri Wan Hamzah, and his niece Professor Wan Arfah binti Tan Sri Wan Hamzah.

Johor's many rivers, and had thus directed economic growth towards commercial agriculture (Winstedt 2003, pp. 134–35). He was also responsible for turning Johor into a constitutional monarchy in April 1895. Apparently, his budgetary sense was not the best. When he died, his son inherited "a working regime, a written constitution and an empty Treasury". What Johor managed to develop at the edge of British influence and pressure was a Malay bureaucracy "offering careers to local men which were much esteemed, both in terms of financial reward and high status in community" (Gullick 1992, pp. 110, 118). The relative independence of the royal family held great significance for the political thinking of Johor's elite, for the educational paths its upper class tended to take, and for the close ties that came to exist between the important families and the ethnic groups involved, and indeed between Johor and Singapore (Winstedt 2003, pp. 134–35).

Ismail was born within this setting on 4 November 1915 into an already illustrious family. His father was Abdul Rahman bin Yassin, "a stoutly built and dark man, almost morose in demeanour" (Robert Kuok, interview 10 February 2006). Abdul Rahman's sister, Anima, had died young, leaving him the only surviving child of Mohamed Yassin bin Ahat, a government officer and son of Orang Kaya Ahat of Padang Muar. Mohamed Yassin's wife was a daughter of Chinese convert Haji Mohamed Salleh bin Abdullah from Singapore, who was Johor State Treasurer, and his Malay wife from Mersing. When Mohamed Yassin's wife passed away, he married her younger sister.

The family lived in a huge house in Johor Bahru called *Rumah Tawakkal*. Abdul Rahman Yassin was employed by the Johor Land Office, and was married to his cousin Zahara binte Abu Bakar, "a vivacious woman, warm hearted and great", who was also "generous and stylish". Zahara belonged to the Orang Kaya Abu Bakar clan of Muar. She passed away in her early forties in 1936, and Abdul Rahman would go on to remarry twice. The couple had four sons — Suleiman, Ismail, Abdullah and Yassin — and five daughters — Khatijah, Esah, Rafeah, Zubaidah and Fatimah. Besides these children, the family also adopted many Chinese girls. These were generally given to them for adoption by their natural parents as thanks for help or advice that they had received from Abdul Rahman. Ismail remembered at least nine of them, all of whom were brought up no differently from the five daughters, and all of whom married well: "No one looking at them now could imagine that they were children of Chinese parents" (Drifting c1). Throughout his life, he remained protective of his many sisters.

Abdul Rahman Yassin attended the first English school in Muar — the Muar High School — and was among the few Malays at the time to pursue a secondary education by travelling across the Causeway to Raffles' College in Singapore. Despite proven success in his studies, the Johor government did not award him a scholarship to England. His ambitions to become a lawyer were therefore crushed. Nevertheless, in 1909, he joined Rodyk & Davidson, a law firm retained by the Johor government, and became Chief Clerk to the General Adviser and Commissioner of Lands the following year. After four years there, he left to become Deputy Registrar of Deeds at the Land Office. Between 1919 and 1924, he was Assistant Collector of Land Revenue for Johor Bahru and Segamat. He then became the first Malay to become Collector, and after eight years in that position, was made a Member of the Council of State. In August 1935, he was promoted to State Treasurer. His professional career taught him the wisdom of investing in land, and it was largely thanks to his properties and the rising price of rubber that he could afford to send his children overseas (Drifting c1; Abu Bakar Suleiman, interview 30 March 2006).

According to Ismail, Abdul Rahman Yassin was never made Mentri Besar of Johor because he was a "'lone wolf' and refused to indulge in intrigues". Nevertheless, the Johor State Assembly later elected him to independent Malaya's Senate, where he became its first president. He also became the first chairman of Malayan Banking when this was formed in 1960 (White 2004, p. 78).

When his wife Zahara passed away in 1936, Abdul Rahman Yassin was encouraged by Sultan Ibrahim, who as a rule sought to unite the aristocracy through marriage within the upper class, to take Kamariah, the daughter of the Mentri Besar of Johor and sister of Onn Ja'afar, who later founded the United Malays National Organization (UMNO), as his new bride.

Ismail's mother had often been sick, and his early upbringing had largely been at the hands of his paternal step-grandmother, who loved visiting her many married daughters whose husbands were posted in different corners of the state of Johor. The young Ismail was taken along on her many trips, "at the expense of my attendance at school". His earliest playmates were therefore his own distant relatives. The friends he eventually made in his first school years were all Malays, and it was only after he started secondary education at the English College in Johor Bahru that he had companions from other cultures. A "voracious reader", the teenage Ismail had a liking for "serious books" with philosophical content. His interests at this time were, however, not limited to these.

> [I]n those days the non-Malay girls especially the Chinese girls had more freedom than those of other races. I enjoy the company

of the opposite sex and since it was not possible to find them among my own race, I began to get closer and closer to my non-Malay friends. I am convinced that this early mingling with the other races during the most impressionable stage of my life had a lot to do with my non-racial outlook.

While at the college, he showed interest in sports and loved to read. He learned to admire English ways and he believed that it was the interpretations he formed about them that made him different from other Malays, "although I always got on well with the latter".

However, the uniqueness that he noticed about himself also had another cause. His family was different from those of most other Malays in those days in that his father was totally convinced that great financial sacrifices were worth making for one's children's education. This left each of them "possessing an insatiable ambition to get on in life".

Two of the four boys became lawyers, one became an economist and Ismail qualified as a medical doctor. In fact, in 1939, the British General Adviser W.E. Pepys publicly lamented that as far as he knew, "the only Johore Malay who has got a University degree is Inche Suleiman bin Abdul Rahman, the son of Dato' Abdul Rahman, State Treasurer, Johore. He is a BA (Cantab) and has been supported entirely by his father without a scholarship" (Winstedt 2003, p. 162).

What the daughters lacked in education, their father compensated for with gifts of land. Abdul Rahman Yassin owned a medium-sized rubber estate, and managed to give almost all his children a tertiary education. The two eldest daughters grew up at a time when it was not customary for Malay girls to be sent to school, let alone to an English institution. The third daughter was less lucky, and had her education cut short by the Japanese Occupation. She never went abroad for higher studies.

Johor's economy, which was founded on commercial agriculture and having Singapore as a captive consumer base, proved comparatively robust and stable even during the depression of the 1930s. Its population grew three-fold between 1911 and 1938, and its revenues increased by four times over the same period (Winstedt 2003, pp. 146–69).

Among the Chinese families in the culturally unique atmosphere of Johor Bahru were two that would play a central role in Ismail's life. One was the family of Cheah Tiang Eam, a golf-loving medical doctor who had practised in Foochow and Penang, and who moved his family and his practice to Johor Bahru in the mid-1920s. His wife was Emily Brockett, daughter of a successful English tea merchant based in Foochow, who was married to a Chinese lady. The Cheah family was therefore English-speaking and well trained in English manners.

Dr Cheah was a bosom friend of Abdul Rahman Yassin, and when it was time for the latter's eldest son Suleiman to be sent to England for law studies, it was decided that the boy should spend an hour or two each week at the Cheah house, having meals and learning etiquette appropriate to life in England.

The two families were therefore very close, and Ismail had an especial fondness for the Cheah children that would last throughout his life. The two youngest Cheah daughters — Eileen and Joyce — were to marry two of the Kuok brothers, Philip and Robert, respectively. Through the Cheah sisters, Ismail would later also become intimate friends with their husbands (Kuok 1991, pp. 87–109; Kuok, interview 10 February 2006). Leslie Cheah, the son in the family, remained a close friend of Ismail and his family throughout his life.

The second Chinese family in Johor Bahru with strong ties to Ismail's family was the Kuoks. The patriarch was Kuok Keng Kang, also from Foochow, a late immigrant to Johor Bahru, who had to face fierce competition from the dominant Teochews, and who attributed his subsequent success to the help he received from the Malay community. By 1920, Kuok's fortune was already made, and he was among the very few who could afford the new luxury of motorcars (Kuok 1991, p. 20). He and his wife, Tang Mong Lan, a devout Buddhist whom Ismail would sometimes go to for advice in later years, had three sons — Philip, William and Robert. William later joined the communist insurgency, and perished in an ambush in Pahang on 8 September 1953.

Another family with close ties to the Kuoks, the Cheahs and the Abdul Rahmans was that of Joseph Chako Puthucheary. His origins were Keralite, and he and his wife had five daughters and five sons, James, George, Anthony, Dominic and Francis, several of whom would become significant actors in Malaysian and Singaporean politics.

Joseph Puthucheary was the registrar of aliens and a teacher, and was actually Ismail's teacher of Latin. James, Puthucheary's eldest son, was very close to William Kuok, as was Onn Ja'afar, who later founded the United Malays National Organization (UMNO). When William Kuok, after being tipped off by Onn Ja'afar that the British were about to arrest him, left to join the guerrillas, Tang Mong Lan adopted James into the family. The fate of these few families from Johor Bahru would remain intertwined throughout the years. In fact, it was James Puthucheary who identified William's body after the ambush, and who broke the news to Tang Mong Lan (Puthucheary, interview 4 September 2006; Tawfik, interview 5 September 2006; Puthucheary 1998, p. 5).

Despite being given the best education available in Johor, Ismail was to find out to his disappointment, that he could not compete with students from Singapore, Kuala Lumpur and Penang. When he started medical school in Singapore in the late 1930s, he "did not even know what oxygen or friction meant". Furthermore, he learned that not only was progress within his new school based on merit, it was also limited to a definite number of students. What was worse was the attitude of schoolmasters who expected the medical students to "behave like school children". He remembered one amusing incident:

> It was my practice whenever I could afford it, to go with a few friends to a cabaret where we danced with the hostesses by paying with coupons. Invariably there was strong competition to dance with the currently popular hostesses. Clients were allowed to approach the hostesses only when the music began to play. Consequently at the first sound of the band playing there was a mad rush in the direction of the popular hostesses. One evening I was in the midst of one of these rushes. To my surprise I found myself standing directly in front of the most popular hostess. As I was dancing away I happened to look behind and saw a face red with anger. It was the face of one of my professors, who had expected me to step aside and give way to him to dance with the hostess. The next day happened to be the day on which I had to present myself to the professor for an oral examination of the anatomy of bones. He naturally gave me a difficult bone to identify and describe and when I could not, he made the sarcastic remark that if I were to concentrate more on bone anatomy rather than surface anatomy, I would make a success of myself as a medical student. This infuriated me so much that I retorted that as far as surface anatomy was concerned, I could give him a whole lecture on it. Needless to say this was held against me when the time came for me to sit for the annual examination in anatomy.

After doing dismally in his third annual examinations, Ismail had to appear before the state chief medical officer to explain himself, wherewith "a detailed history of my personal life, including the number of times I spent at the cabaret during the previous year", was read out to him alongside his academic results. Very much angered at this, he replied that he would not continue studying at "a college run by the Gestapo".

After failing to secure a spot in Hong Kong, Ismail nevertheless gained admission to Melbourne University, a turn of events he considered a "fortuitous one". Armed with acceptance papers from that institution's Faculty of Medicine, Ismail set sail from Singapore for Australia in May 1940. Along the way, he went ashore at "Batavia, Samarang, Soerabaya, Brisbane and Sydney". The shipping line agreed to take him despite his lack of immigration papers only after he promised to pay for the return journey should he be turned back at his final destination. He shared a cabin with an Indian magician who would eat his way through the menu for breakfast, lunch and dinner. This gentleman claimed himself to be the only person who could make Hitler laugh, a feat he had accomplished once by producing endless numbers of Deutchmarks from thin air when performing before the German leader. Hitler mirthfully wanted the man consigned to the national mint.

Luckily for Ismail, the registrar of the university, an elderly gentleman named Forster, had received his request for a landing permit and had managed to have it arranged and waiting. Ismail arrived on Thursday, 4 July 1940, to an Australia that had officially been at war for ten months. After swearing to obey the rules of the college — "the chief of which is never to bring alcoholic drinks into the College" — he moved the next day into a bedroom with an adjoining study room. This was to cost 130 guineas per year.

Sadly for him, his new school — Queen's College — would not credit the three years he had spent in medical school in Singapore, and the only benefit he managed to extract from the university was its permission to sit for his first-year examinations already in November 1940.

His first letter home was written around midnight the following Sunday, and provided his father with studious details about tuition and book costs, board and lodging costs, and sports and union fees, as well as suggestions about bank transfer procedures. Ismail would dutifully send a stream of letters to his father over the next eighteen months, often posting one every week or fortnight. Having arrived in the midst of the Australian winter, he found the low temperatures unbearable: "I shiver and my teeth chatter, because it is extremely cold to me". Within a week he was complaining of a "sore throat and slight temperature". He "did not feel normal", was lonely and homesick and often sought solace by the fire, longing for news from home.

Also at the college was Chan Chia Chow, the son of a family friend, who showed him around the grounds and provided him with information "on what to do and what to buy".

Everyone there worked hard as far as he could see, which he thought explained why no one did anything on Sundays except rest. At this early stage of his stay, he found the people friendly but "not as hospitable as those in Malaya", and "although they are nice [they] don't seem to ask any of their friends to their houses on weekends". Very sensibly, he thought his impressions unreliable at that juncture since he had newly arrived and was feeling unbearably lonely.

He encountered problems in getting a refund on the guarantee payment he had made to the shipping company, and this caused him great anxiety. He was already running late on his various payments, and these included fees for the coming term. He could not afford to buy a microscope for his Zoology class, for example, and felt greatly handicapped despite being able to borrow one occasionally, but "I could not do it too often". In great distress, he saw no other way out but to ask for more money from his father two weeks after arriving at Queen's: "I have a great fight before me and as you told me this is my last chance, I shall see that I will not abuse it."

The life of a medical student was not easy at Queen's, especially as he felt that he could not afford to fail the November examinations for fear that it would burden his family with an extra year of tuition fees.

> I have settled down to serious work. The Zoology is the same as in Singapore, but Chemistry and Physics, though they cover the same syllabus as in Singapore, yet we do more in detail. Most of the day I am in the University attending lectures and [doing] practical work but in the evening I attend tutorial classes in the College. We begin work at nine in the morning and stop at one for lunch, begin again at two and work until four in the University and from 5.15 to 6.15 tutorial work in the College. At 6.15 we have dinner and once a week on Thursday night we work in the College laboratory from eight o'clock until ten o'clock. It is the custom in the College for students to invite one another for supper in their rooms and this lasts for one hour and from eleven till one in the morning we study again.

He found things expensive in Melbourne, including cinema visits and even clothes and underwear. It took him a while to get used to imbibing huge amounts of beef: "We eat practically nothing but meat and potatoes and sweets".

By 4 August, he had received a remittance from home and could therefore buy himself a second-hand microscope and start taking private tuition in zoology. He soon received a letter from home, and also the deposit money from the shipping line. After accounting for all his costs, he thought he would have as much as £90 left for the coming term. This sum soon proved optimistic, and he later lowered it to £75. He continued to feel lonely and finally bought a radio from a fellow student, on which he managed to listen to the Malay news broadcast from Singapore. The laundry service was rather expensive, and fearing that his father might not believe him, he actually attached a laundry receipt in his next letter. Feeling that his education was costing his family too much, he requested of his father "to remind me now and then about my responsibilities because when one is away from home, one is apt to forget that one has responsibilities to those at home".

During the August break, Ismail stayed put at the college to complete some work. He went for a hiking trip to the Yarra Valley over a weekend, and was so enchanted and excited by the experience — which included the sighting of his first wild kangaroo — that he decided to trek regularly. He suspected that "most white people live to a long old age because they take a lot of exercise". Ismail, who had a muscular stature but measured not more than five-foot-six in height, was to exercise religiously throughout his life.

The weather got very cold that spring. Ismail lived through a day in late August that went on record as "the coldest day in the history of Melbourne". That September, the boiler broke down, and Ismail, seeing that the weather was not too bad, thought he would take a cold bath: "Well, I nearly freezed [sic] and I really could not breathe for a few seconds and I hope this experience will stand me in good stead in future."

It was during his time in Australia that he developed a strong liking for the books written by Arthur Conan Doyle about the clear-thinking Sherlock Holmes. His preference for the pipe and for deductive reasoning was derived from this exposure to the greatest of England's fictional detectives (Tawfik, interview 30 March 2006).

Records show that Ismail attended the Queen's College Sports and Social Club (QCSSC) bi-monthly meeting for the first time in the Common Room on 4 September. About fifty students turned up that day and the club publicly welcomed "Mr Ramaan" and "expressed the hope that he would soon adjust himself to our quaint customs". The meeting lasted from 7.30p.m. to 10.40p.m.

By October, the weather had grown decidedly warmer. Ismail went for another countryside hike, this time in the Warrandyke District, where he was dazzled by the open spaces and the endless hectares of fruit farms. His feeling of loneliness, however, did not leave him. He wrote on 7 October:

> I have never really got over my homesickness yet. Now and then, especially before I go to bed, my thoughts would carry me back to Johore and I visualize myself talking to you, Ma'Uda, Tok Ina and my brothers and sisters. Sometimes I really feel like crying and there is this emptiness in my chest, when I think of the number of years that must pass before I shall ever return to Johore. When these feelings overcome me, I always read the *Yasin*.*

That year, he spent his first *Hari Raya* — the Islamic festival marking the end of the fasting month fell on 2 November that year — away from home: "I shall be a sad man on that day when I should be happy. I think I shall spend the day in reading *Yasin*".

---

* The *Yasin* is the *surat* from the Koran most popularly used among peninsular Malays for meditative purposes. Ma'Uda was Ismail's stepmother.

At the end of the term, he provided his father with a detailed account of his past expenses, and asked to be allowed to keep the £25 left over as a reserve in case of an emergency, "if it is not asking too much and if it does not entail too much sacrifice on the family".

During the four-month summer vacation, no student was allowed to remain on campus. This posed a big problem for Ismail, since it meant that he would have to live elsewhere and pay for board and lodging. Ismail chose to stay away from Melbourne for economic reasons and because there would be fewer "temptations" elsewhere. He finally settled for a guesthouse called *Kia-Ora*, which cost £3 per day, in the seaside town of Lorne, which was 145 kilometres from Melbourne. He arrived on 14 November to find a one-street village set beside a long beach that seemed "to run on endlessly, and where surfing and sunbathing were popular pastimes". Ismail joined a hiking party a few days later, taking the longest route to Erskine Falls, which he thought to be "as pretty as the Kota Tinggi one". He wrote to his father:

> All the guests in the house are friendly and unassuming. Many of them are working people, who are on their fortnight's vacation. They all seem to be interested in Malaya and they all seem to like your pictures and mother's. The Australians are really wonderful people, devoid of snobbishness. They work hard and play hard, and no matter how poor they are, they [manage] to save for the holidays once a year.

He immediately sent a telegram home on receiving the good news that he had passed his first-year exams — "which speaks much for the teaching of Melbourne University", he humbly noted. He had nevertheless to return to Melbourne to take a re-examination for doing weakly not only in Chemistry, which he had expected, but also in Botany, which he had not. His schoolmate from Malaya failed, however, and was left without any idea what he was to do from then on: "When I compare my lot with that of Chia, Dr Chan Shu Lan's son, I thank God for being very kind to me."

Observing Australians on holiday, he was struck by how the rich and the poor, employers and employees, mingled unreservedly, "wealth and position being no barriers". Being a medical student, Ismail also observed that they had "such wonderful physique".

> The girls here could walk for thirty to forty kilometres without feeling tired and when I think what exercise has done for them, I begin to reflect on the sad fact [of] how sickly the Malay girls are. The chief trouble lies in the lack of exercise. Their grandmothers had wonderful physique and were free from sickness because in those days instead of sitting in comfortable cars, they walked. I wish something could be done to induce them to take such ladylike exercises as walking and playing badminton.

He had to leave Lorne on 21 December, since the guesthouse had been fully booked for Christmas. Besides, the tariff was considerably higher that whole week, which would have made it necessary for him to stay elsewhere in any case. He had seen enough of Lorne by then, and was sick of doing nothing. A family that he befriended in Lorne, the Smiths, took him to Melbourne in their car, where the man then drove him around looking for accommodation. After some trouble, Ismail managed to get a room at New Treasury Hotel, the same establishment he had stayed at on his first night in Melbourne six months earlier. Three nights later, on the advice of the Master of Queen's, he moved to Harcourt Guest House on Royal Parade. There he stayed for two months to prepare for the next term. His plan was to take a two-week break just before term start on 17 March in order to be able to return to class refreshed.

In the meantime, his father had been promoted to State Commissioner of Muar, and it seemed that some members of the family might have to move with him to that town. This caused Ismail some anxiety, and he asked repeatedly for information about how the family was divided between Muar and Johor Bahru.

New Year's Eve was spent with Chia Chow at St. Kilda Park. Ismail thought the fireworks display impressive, but "it is nothing compared to the ones I saw in Singapore during the Deepavali Festival". The crowded roads around the park reminded him of "the Ching-gay procession in Malaya".

He decided to move to another guesthouse in mid-January 1941. This new place was simply called "Fortuna" and stood close to the sea, which gave Ismail a chance to swim for exercise. He found the guests and the landlady's son "very interesting to talk to".

> I get up early in the morning, have a swim, breakfast and then work till lunch. In the afternoon I do a couple of hours' work and go for another swim. I feel very fit and can really work better. The tariff is somewhat expensive, about £3–10 a week, but I think it's worth it.

Ismail still suffered from homesickness and would seize every opportunity to talk to people who knew of Malaya "so as to alleviate my misery".

> Sometimes I really begin to be afraid of what this long absence from Malaya may do to me. I am afraid that I shall change so much that I shall find it difficult to fit into the old life again. It

is during such times when this feeling overcomes me that I turn to reading *Yasin* as you advised me to do. It really brings me relief.

He spent two nights at the end of January at Barwon Heads outside the city of Geelong, which is about seventy kilometres from Melbourne. He was house guest to a Mrs Lowson, a friend of the family, whose husband, a doctor, worked in Johor. She told Ismail that his father was "the most progressive Malay she had known".

Ismail enjoyed his weekend there, but was nevertheless homesick. The laughter of the Lowson children and their friends "brought sad memories of the time when I used to be among my sisters and brothers". Even when he peered over the Barwon River from the house, what he saw was "a coastline which strongly reminds one of that of the island of Singapore seen from Johore Baru".

A letter from his father, dated 31 January, informed him that he and Ma' Uda would be living alone in Muar without the children. This greatly upset Ismail who remembered that his father was prone to feel "lonely and dull" when away from the family.

He also received an allowance of £300 for the year, along with advice from his father to live within that amount. Ismail could now afford to buy a hiking outfit, "which consists of a rugger sack, a sleeping bag, a pair of shorts, 2 pairs of socks, enamelled plate and spoon and forks and mugs", and was further saving towards "a small tent and a pair of strong boots". The weather that month was highly unpredictable, going from "nice and warm" to "cold and icy". He joined a hike in early February to the Dandenongs which took him across an area known as "the patch". Again, Ismail became nostalgic, and noted that the terrain was reminiscent of Cameron Highlands back home.

On several occasions, he asked that the recently published book by Rupert Emerson, titled *Malaysia — A Study in Direct and Indirect Rule* be sent to him. It is not known if this influential work, now a classic in Malaysia studies, was ever delivered to him.

Later in February, Ismail noticed that a sizeable number of students from Malaya were arriving. Most of those he met before the term started were Chinese and all but one were girls between the ages of seventeen and nineteen. Ismail was twenty-five at this time. There were also two students from Singapore, a Chinese named Lim Chin Sen, who was to do medicine and an Indian named John Athisagam, who was from the Singapore College of Medicine, and who was at Queen's to finish his medical studies. Ismail helped Athisagam to find accommodation and arranged banking matters for the newcomer. In the process, he discovered that he would save on travel expenses into the city if he moved his account to the National Bank of Australasia, which had a branch on campus. This he did.

Just as the new term started, Ismail suffered a severe cold but was well looked after by the landlady, who also had a fever but who "has been kindness itself and has been offering me aspirin and a hot glassful of lemonade before I retire at night".

Ismail chose to do four subjects the coming academic year, including German, which all students had to pass by the third year to be allowed to go on to the fourth year. Ismail was "taking no chances and therefore I am trying to pass this year". His other subjects were Anatomy, Physiology and Biochemistry.

During the new term, he shared a study with an Australian fifth-year student. Ismail was happy about this because "this will give me the chance to know an Australian better". He was also impressed by the president of the QCSSC for reminding the seniors at the initiation of freshmen to treat Malayan students as guests: "This gesture of hospitality and kindness will remain long in my memory".

Ismail generally admired the Australians and found Melbourne University free of the bullying and colonial suppression that he had experienced in Singapore, and he considered the years spent in Australia to be "the happiest of my life" during which he found "ways and means to express myself".

These included relations with the opposite sex, although he thought it odd that his Australian friends "could treat sex as though it were the same as the act of eating".

> That they can do it without being emotionally involved seems quite practical to me and yet I cannot see it in this way. I regard sex as the finest expression of one's love for the opposite sex. Emotion plays a very important part.

He also made it a point to avoid seeking satisfaction from prostitutes: "What they want is money for goods delivered; I want some expression of love".

Nevertheless, it was in Australia that he "managed to get any sexual satisfaction" for the first time. His first affair with a "cultured vivacious girl from a middle class family" lasted a year until a fellow Malayan student, "a mutual friend", reported the matter to the girl's mother. Since the couple lacked the means to get married, they decided that the only thing to do was to separate. He then met a nurse with whom he had a relationship "which was not deep", and that soon ended without trauma. His third relationship was a much more satisfying one for him. This was with a German girl, and was carried out with the blessings of her parents. Ismail and the girl nevertheless finally decided to part "because we realized that mixed marriages do not often succeed".

On reminiscing about these women when writing his memoirs in 1967, Ismail realized that his relationship with them was educational as far as his ability to love was concerned.

> It was because of these happy episodes in my youth, when love was fulfilled for its own sake that my marriage owes its success. My wife was educated only up to secondary school level and was denied a higher education because of her marriage to me. We have been married for seventeen years and love never dims but rather becomes more bright as the years go on.

During the Easter break in April, Ismail went hiking with three other students. In five days, they travelled 110 kilometres over enchanting mountain terrain, singing songs and exchanging views by the nightly campfire, and staying at youth hostels run by the hiking association. Again, Ismail imagined possibilities for his own country.

> It occurred to me that probably this open air life with plenty of exercise must be the reason why Australians are such good soldiers and friends. I only wish they could have such an Association in Malaya so that people can see the country cheaply and at the same time get plenty of exercise. I am sure it will increase the quality of Malayan youth. Here during the holidays the students go for long hikes and work in the farms whereas in Malaya they loiter about towns, their idle minds thinking [of] what mischief to do.

This hiking trip was possibly the reason why he was not at the QCSSC meeting in the beginning of that month, at which attendance was obligatory. He had to apologize for his absence — along with a large group of others who had also stayed away — at the following meeting in June.

By the end of April, six weeks into second-year courses, Ismail, who had been able to study well, was feeling very confident that he would pass the year's examinations. At the same time, he learned that his brother Abdullah had failed his: "There is nothing I can do but to offer him my deepest sympathy and pray that he will get through his re-examinations."

Rumours were rife at that time that the university was planning to shorten the medical course from six to five years. This cheered Ismail up somewhat. Although his work remained up to expectations, he decided to remain at the college during the two-week May break "to do some study". Winter was again on the way and the air was often chilly. Ismail thought he was finally getting used to the low temperatures, but would occasionally suffer from colds.

Mrs Tan Soo Bin, a widow to whose house Ismail was often invited and whose three daughters had recently moved from Malaya to Melbourne to study, suddenly lost one of her children. The girl had been complaining about the severe cold, and suddenly passed away. Her mother was so distraught that she had to be moved to a nursing home, and refused to see visitors. Ismail was at the funeral: "As I watched [Mrs Tan] wailing beside the grave I could not help thinking that despite her millions, at that moment she was the poorest woman in the world".

Ismail feared the loneliness of school holidays: "The days are foggy and cold. The only thing to do is work and when you get tired of working you just look into the fire and dream of your home and your friends in Malaya". During the May break, practically only Malayan students stayed at the college. Those not doing medicine and who had a long vacation coming up were booking their flight home to Malaya early. Ismail admitted feeling envious of them. The fare was not inexpensive but these students feared, as Ismail did, that they might otherwise lose touch with "the Malayan way of life" if regular contact with their homeland was not maintained.

To add to his sense of alienation, Ismail was beginning to feel increasingly left out of developments within his family. He knew little about events happening back home and when informed in early June that his favourite sister, Esah, had been betrothed without his opinion being sought in advance, he conveyed his strong disappointment to his father: "If I go back at the end of the course a complete stranger to the family, would you blame me, seeing that everything I have heard from the family so far has been the barest of details?"

Rumours that the medical course would be shortened turned out to be true. This meant that while the second-year examinations would be taken in November, those for the third year would be held in August the following year. A third-year subject was subsequently moved to the second year, putting pressure on Ismail to study even more industriously. In the meantime, his father had started sending his allowance once every two months, and not quarterly as Ismail had expected. This did not suit his expenditure schedule and caused him difficulties in paying his college fees. Fearing that such worries would overly distract him from his studies, he quickly but apologetically asked his father for an extra sum to be forwarded to him. A telegraphic transfer of £25 was immediately sent from home. News also arrived that his brother Abdullah had failed in his final examinations.

The amount of studying Ismail was now required to do did not allow him to take time off for his beloved pastime — hiking. However, comfort came in the form of a tin of curry sent to a fellow Malayan. Ismail was happily asked to share the delicacy with him: "It's really nice to have a tasty dish such as a curry after having eaten so much tasteless food".

By the end of July, fear was palpably mounting among Malayan students in Melbourne that the war would spread throughout eastern Asia. Ismail felt the tension as well and was again exasperated that he, unlike many Malayan students he knew, was not receiving any news from his family. The start of the two-week winter break in August once again meant that students began leaving for home: "I felt more homesick than ever when I saw them going away, some driving home with their parents, others have either their sisters or brothers to take them away". On 10 August, he wrote to his father:

> I have always followed your advice that when despondent or in trouble to read a few verses from the Quran. At night just before retiring, I always read a few verses of the Quran."

Given the amount of work he had to go through, Ismail decided that he would throw himself into his work during the two cold weeks when the college would be empty. He received two surprise visits during the break. One was from a Mrs Robertson, who lived with her engineer son in Muar, and who had attended a few parties organized by Ismail's father. She confirmed that all was well with his family. The other was a family friend, a Mrs Smallwood, who bought him "a good lunch" and provided him with news about Johor.

When the new term began, Ismail received a letter from his sister Noi, informing him that their cousin Raja Tik, daughter of his late mother's only sister, had passed away. Ismail told his father that the girl had had a short and unhappy life, and that he was saddened by the thought of her demise.

The Victoria League — an organization founded in London in 1901 "to foster understanding between people throughout Britain and the Empire" (UC archives) — had lately been taking an interest in foreign students and had invited them to tea and dance. The wife of the governor of Victoria, Lady Dugan, also asked these students to Government House for refreshments.

On the evening of 27 August, "Mr Rahman" took time away from his studies to attend a QCSSC meeting. The student turnout on that occasion was large, and the gathering lasted a good four hours. Motions carried that evening included changing the butcher, and a request that "pineapple be not ruined by having melon added to it and served up disguised as pie". One concerned the club sending letters of appreciation to two lecturers who were leaving the college, and another for the club subscription fee to be fixed at £1 per term, and for more freshmen initiation rites to be held the following year. A motion concerning lights in the corridors was also raised, and carried:

> Mr W. Wilkinson said the shortage of lights in the East Wing made it dangerous in that quarter late at night. He urged that the Vice Master be approached [regarding] the leaving on of some lights. Mr Rahman endorsed this. He said that one night when he was sober, he couldn't find his way. The lights should be left on. Mr Byard said it would be better to leave the lights off, since Mr Rahman found his way better in the dark when he was drunk, and he was more often drunk than sober.

Ismail studied hard the following weeks. However, the fact that no news at all came during September from his family exasperated him: "If I who am alone here and busy studying could afford to write home every fortnight, surely *one* of the members of the family could write to me." This outburst led quickly to a guilty response from home. His father sent him two lengthy letters, for which he was very grateful. He learned that his sister Esah's wedding was to be held in Muar, but strongly discouraged his father from sending him money to fly home to attend it, preferring the money to be given to Esah as a gift instead.

The end-of-year holidays were to be shorter than they had been because of the shortening of the course. A military camp was being arranged for medical students, and Ismail hoped that that would provide him with something to do during his vacation. He had recently had a medical check-up and was found fit.

Ismail did not write for the next six weeks, during which time he "worked as I had never done before in my life". This paid off. He sent a letter on 29 November to inform the family that he was among the seventy or so students out of a total of 140 to160 who had managed to pass.

As it turned out, overseas students were not allowed to be included in the military camp. This upset Ismail's plans and greatly disappointed him. He had rashly thought that since he would not be spending any money at the camp, he could treat himself to items that he had theretofore avoided buying. This uncharacteristic extravagance now left him somewhat short of funds. It also meant that he had to find a place to stay until early February 1942. There was talk that the next term would run until the August examinations without a break. He therefore decided to stay and study in Melbourne until January and then move to Sydney before taking some time away from his studies.

By now, however, the war in East Asia was spreading. The Japanese military was marching beyond East Asia, moving south and east. An air attack on Singapore on 8 December, carried out about seventy minutes before Pearl Harbour was hit, signalled the start of the Pacific War. Things moved quickly, and already by February 1942, the Japanese had reached Singapore (Han, Fernandez and Tan 1998, p. 21). On 11 January 1942, Ismail wrote a short and anxious letter home.

All the Malayan students have received cables, letters, large sums of money to last for two or three years. I know you are not

as well off as the Chinese parents, but surely you could not be
so busy as not to be able to ask *one* in the family to write to me.
I tried to write to you but what could I say? It would be only
telling you how I am getting on.

Ismail was extremely fearful by this time that all money transfers
from Malaya would soon be stopped. As he was to find out four
years later, his father did make a final transfer, but this never
reached him. Not being called up for military camp training had
also left him feeling insecure about his own status in Australia.

No letter that he might have written and sent home after
the Japanese invaded Malaya in early 1942 has been preserved.
The next known correspondence from him to his father is dated
17 October 1945. There is therefore no record of any personal
reflection by Ismail on the Japanese Occupation, and very little
about his college experiences during that period. In the QCSSC
Minutes from 18 March 1942, under the heading "General
Business", some scarce information about him is found:

> Mr Rahman rose and moved that Mr Lim's photograph album
> be made available to the men of College. The album, he said,
> was a record of Mr Lim's four month's stay at Lorne. He had
> visited a certain fruitshop with Mr Lim and that he had been
> told that Mr Lim had grown much older. The latter had once
> been his protégé but was now cut off from his parent. It was
> the College's duty to look after Mr Lim. The motion was
> seconded by Mr Hargreaves. Mr Lim spoke strongly against the
> motion insisting that he could look after himself. The motion
> was carried. [The person referred to was apparently Lim Kean
> Chong, the younger brother of Lim Kean Siew, who was later
> a major opposition politician in Malaysia, and P.G. Lim, who
> became Malaysia's ambassador to the United States and to
> Yugoslavia in the early 1970s. What "fruitshop" refers to exactly
> is unclear].

Ismail also moved at this meeting for a vote of thanks "to the scrutineers for the election of table presidents", which had recently been held. Mr Lim seconded the motion, which was then carried. On 10 June 1942, the club held another meeting. The minutes state under the heading "Common Room Dance" that "Mr Rahman suggested that the Club economize by having a blackout dance. In this dance the lights should be switched out and a long record chosen. What happened in the dark didn't matter." It was not without reason that Ismail's schoolmates titled him "Tango King" already then, and later in life, he and his wife would become reputed in Kuala Lumpur for their flair and their love for dancing (Tawfik, interview 21 July 2006).

A further piece of information revealed in the club's continual records was that tobacco was always a hard item to come by throughout the war years.

The Wyvern, the college periodical, carried an article in its issue of October 1942, entitled "One Night When I Was Sober". The author is unknown, but it is written in a highly ironic fashion, and describes an encounter Ismail had with the wartime law of the land while visiting Tasmania.

So it happened, that Ish, the son of Abdul, on his first day in the Apple isle, becomingly attired in a large overcoat and scarf to match, with a blue felt pulled rakishly over one eye, and an expensive camera slung around his neck, in the approved Hollywood Secret Agent manner, slunk into a local chemist's establishment and enquired with an attractive accent for an expensive film for his expensive camera. The Chemist, a strong, silent, quick-thinking man-of-action, took in the situation at a glance, retired to the dispensary, and SOS'd the police department, and then engaged his would-be customer with more or less intelligent conversation until the "arm-of-the-law" arrived in plain clothes, to deal with the delicate and dangerous situation. The "arm-of-the-law" tactfully opened the conversation by delicately insinuating that Ish had probably just tethered his midget submarine to the jetty steps. "But Mon, I'm a British subject," objected Ish. "Yes, that's what they all say," artfully replied the "arm-of-the-law", doubtless referring to the twenty or thirty spies he had arrested the previous weekend. "You might also be a Jap spy, or a German agent, or a Thialandish (*sic*) fifth columnist, or a parachutist who has missed his plane, or a Philippino Quisling, masquerading as an aboriginal gum-leaf player"... "Wait a minute. Go easy, Mon" interrupted our Ish. "I'll come quietly with you; inspect my papers first." After some deliberation, the "arm-of-the-law" agreed to this, and they adjourned to the "arm-of-the-law's" place of business, where, after considerable difficulty he located someone who was able to read, and the suggested inspection was made — Ish helping out with the big words — and our hero's short but adventurous career as a spy was at an end (p. 21; IAR/11/3).

When funds stopped coming from home because of the war, Ismail managed "with a stroke of luck" to get in touch with the Johor Sultan's Representative in Australia, Keith G. Brooks, Member of Parliament for the state of New South Wales. With some help from the Master of Queen's, Brooks was persuaded to see the young man through the rest of his course. Ismail sought to keep a detailed account of payments, doubtless for his father's sake. He did not realize at that time that Brooks was actually lending him money from his own pocket, and had assumed that Brooks had access to Johor funds. By the time he realized the real situation, it was too late for him to change matters: "Had I known this from the beginning, I would not have accepted his offer to advance me the money." The final sum that Ismail's family would owe the MP amounted to an impressive £1,053.19.3.

Ismail finally graduated on 5 June 1945, and was immediately posted for twelve months as resident medical officer to Horsham Base Hospital in Victoria by the Medical Co-ordination Committee of Victoria. This was a body that exercised authority over all legally qualified doctors in Australia during the war and in the period immediately following it. News finally reached Ismail after the end of hostilities that all was well with members of his family. He responded without delay and sent his first letter home in three-and-a-half years, now assured that it would reach his father. This was dated 17 October 1945.

Abdul Rahman Yassin had in the meantime learned from the Sultan — who had finally managed to make contact with Brooks — that he was indebted to the latter for financial aid granted to Ismail. The Sultan informed Abdul Rahman that Brooks would appreciate a speedy refund. Ismail's father was relieved at being told that Ismail was in good health and had in fact graduated four months earlier. He immediately sent a letter to the Senior Civil Affairs Officer of the British Military Administration of Malaya, now the *de facto* government in Malaya, informing him of his financial difficulties.

> It is impossible at this juncture to raise this large sum whereas the advance so generously made should be paid without delay. Being in such an embarrassing position I cannot think of any other way except to venture to approach you and appeal to the Administration to see its way to grant an advance or loan of $7,500 to enable me to meet this liability — such advance or loan to be recovered from the coming Civil Administration to which I intend to apply for an appropriation from the Sultan Ibrahim Studentship Fund or, failing that, for advance payment against the gratuity for which I am eligible on retirement, due next year, or reduced pension, after 35 years' service. If necessary, I will put up security in the form of title to my house property.

Ismail did not receive any direct news from home until the end of February 1946. By then, he had been put in charge of the Horsham Base Hospital, where "my orders are final". He was obviously thrilled by this promotion.

> My colleagues treat me as an equal. Never by deeds or words have they ever discriminated me from the other Australian doctors. I have performed operations which no Asiatic doctors could ever hope to do under the old medical scheme in Malaya. [...] During my stay at the above hospital I never met a single person who took exception to me just because I am a Malay.

Ismail would tell his son Tawfik in early 1973 when visiting the latter in Australia that one of his many regrets was not having had the chance to meet as grown-ups any of the little babies he delivered during those months at Horsham, when he practised medicine for the first time as a full-fledged doctor (Tawfik, interview 28 April 2005).

Although Ismail was keen to return home after the war, he was apprehensive about how he would be treated as a doctor back in British Malaya. He had been informed that should he return, he would be "locally recruited", meaning that he would be considered inferior to his Australian doctor friends who were even then accepting positions in Malaya. Should that turn out to be the case, he planned instead to stay on in Australia and save enough to start a private practice when he did return home.

> Johore, I suppose, is still under Military Occupation. [...] When the Civil Administration takes its place again, the old order must go. People, irrespective of nationality and colour must be judged on their own ability and only then can peace be assured.

Even as he penned this, a political controversy was brewing back home regarding the Malayan Union proposed by the returning

British. His father, his brother Suleiman and his brother-in-law
Awang Hassan, along with four others, had been suspended from
their civil service positions for protesting against the Sultan
agreeing to the proposal. They claimed it to be beyond the ruler's
constitutional rights to do any such thing. While the British
argued that the Malayan Union would grant equality to the
Malayan population at large, Malays in general considered it an
insidious campaign aimed at abolishing the special position of
the Malays for good.

In his reply written on 2 April, Abdul Rahman Yassin informed
Ismail that the debt to Brooks had been paid after the Sultan had
phoned and worried him about it "as though the money was his
and not Mr Brook's". He also wanted Ismail to return home as
soon as he was released from his term of service. There was, he
advised his son, "plenty of scope for profitable private practice
now as there is scarcity of doctors in Malaya [...] and if you are
offered any colonial appointment please reject it".

Ismail had in fact been released by the end of March, when
wartime restrictions on doctors were suddenly lifted. He wrote to
his father on 16 April to say that he was on holiday but was
waiting for a reply from the Malayan Medical Service, and that
he was willing to accept a position "on identical terms to
Europeans". His father, on receiving his earlier letter, had quickly
sent him a telegram telling him to withdraw his application and
to go into private practice back home, which, he was convinced,
would prove much more profitable. To encourage Ismail further,
he promised to pay his travel expenses.

Ismail had in fact not applied for any position in Malaya
and had merely been making enquiries. He quickly sought a
passage home. It turned out that the first possible departure for
Malaya was not for at least another seven weeks, and he would
even then require a permit to enter Malaya from the south. This

need for an entry permit was soon waived, however, but Ismail learned that he could not sail earlier than in July. This would be on a boat leaving from Sydney. Coincidentally, the vessel was the *Marella*, the same one that had brought him to Australia exactly six years earlier.

While waiting, Ismail managed to do some *locum tenens* (temporary replacement work) to pay for his expenses and to pass the time. When he later arrived at the shipping office to book passage, he was pleasantly surprised to hear that it had been paid for. It turned out that the shipping agent was generously paying the home passage from Australia for all Malayans.

Ismail spent his final days in Australia buying drugs and instruments that he thought might be difficult to come by in Malaya, and choosing clothes for his sisters. He complained in his final letter from Australia — written on 14 July off Fremantle when he was already on the ship home — that his sisters had never bothered to write to him or he would at least have known what exactly to get for them. The home journey started on 7 July. The first week of the passage was very rough, and most of the passengers suffered seasickness. Ismail, however, was well equipped with appropriate medication, and was only mildly inconvenienced by the stormy seas. The trip lasted nineteen long days.

On 26 July 1946, Ismail the 31-year-old doctor, the first Malay to graduate from Melbourne University, arrived back in Singapore.

Chapter 3

UMNO AND THE ROAD TO MERDEKA

Ismail's immaculately dressed elder brother Suleiman met him on his arrival, and quickly briefed him on "the controversy over the Malayan Union". What immediately struck Ismail after being six years in Australia was how "political feeling engulfed Malaya as a fire engulfs a forest on a hot dry day".

Ismail's family was deeply involved in the resistance against the Malayan Union that the British, after the fall of Imperial Japan, were trying to impose on the whole peninsula. After the Sultan of Johor signed the MacMichael Agreement, a treaty with the British accepting the Malayan Union idea, seven men, led by Abdul Rahman Yassin and including his eldest son Suleiman as well as son-in-law Awang Hassan, issued a pamphlet criticizing the move. These men, all government servants, were consequently suspended for six months.

As many Malays understood it, the Malayan Union aimed to abolish the sultanates and the special position of the Malays. The opposition to this was strongest in the Unfederated Malay States, especially Johor, where the elite was also most active. At a meeting of forty-one Malay associations held in March 1946 in Kuala

Lumpur, the United Malays National Organization (UMNO) was born. UMNO's opposition to the Malayan Union proved highly successful, and the plan in effect never got off the ground, and was instead replaced on 1 February 1948 by the Federation of Malaya Agreement.

This later polity allowed for all seats in the federal and state legislature to be filled by nominees. Onn Ja'afar, the Mentri Besar of Johor and the founder of UMNO, offered Ismail a state seat, which he accepted. One of the first things Ismail did as Johor state councillor was to demand that his opposition to the establishment of the federation itself be duly recorded. He considered the federation illegal, especially with regard to the Johor constitution. Onn Ja'afar also offered Ismail a position in the Federal Legislative Council but only on condition that the latter joined UMNO. Ismail refused, telling Onn Ja'afar that he would give up his medical practice to go into politics only if the party was fighting for independence, which it was not doing. Despite his stand, Ismail did harbour respect for UMNO's official founder.

> He was the idol of the Johore people. Handsome, dashing and fearless, he was the envy of all. [...] He was a great man and the nation should be grateful to him for having mobilised Malay nationalism which was the spear-head to Malaya's Independence.

In the meantime, the Malayan Communist Party (MCP), having failed to capitalize on the period of chaos immediately following the fall of Japan, had adopted legal means to further their ends. It joined the Governor's Advisory Council in Singapore in 1945, maintained strong ties with the Malayan Democratic Union and the Malayan Nationalist Party, and soon established the General Labour Unions (GLU) in Singapore and later in other states. Although the powerful GLU did not have total control over the unions, its strikes and other activities caused sufficient anxiety among the British for them to take serious measures such as legally limiting those eligible to become union officials. Other British measures included the re-establishment of police authority in the countryside, and strict control of union accounts. These steps proved effective, and with the situation for workers significantly improved by 1947–48, the central union body lost much of its influence (Andaya and Andaya 1982, pp. 257–61). Within the MCP, those favouring armed struggle began gaining influence after Secretary-General Lai Tek was accused of being a double agent for the British, and subsequently disappeared. According to Chin Peng, Lai Tek was killed in 1947 in a botched kidnapping in Bangkok ordered by him (Chin 2003, pp. 189–90). Growing violence finally provided the British with sufficient excuse to declare a state of emergency on 18 June 1948. In April the following year, the British Parliament announced its intention to grant independence to Malaya. Communist activity increased around that time, to peak in the first week of September 1950 (Andaya and Andaya 1982, pp. 257–61).

Political consciousness among the Malays during this period was strongly configured by the fear of losing their special status, and Onn Ja'afar's popularity was built on his ability to defend that status. However, this agenda — best expressed by the slogan *Hidup Melayu* [Long Live the Malays] — existed in a tense relationship with the idea of independence — *Merdeka*. Mustapha Hussain of the Young Malays Union, a left-wing organization, claims in his autobiography the honour of being the man who injected the slogan of *Merdeka*, which was taken from the Indonesian context, into UMNO's programme at the March 1951 party general assembly. The word was officially adopted as the party slogan with the help of his protégé Garieb Raof, a Johor UMNO Youth leader (*Daily Telegraph*, 26 March 1951; Mustapha 2005, p. 368). Be that as it may, Onn Ja'afar seemed by this time to have realized that the British would not hand over power to a purely Malay organization. The conflict that had broken out between the British and their erstwhile allies, the MCP, had also radically changed the political equation, and may have forced Onn to take desperate action to widen UMNO's support base beyond the Malays.

His next move was to open UMNO to non-Malay citizens of the federation who were at least sixteen years old and who were willing to work for Malayan independence (Simandjuntak 1969, pp. 63–64). Mustapha Hussain believed that Onn Ja'afar nevertheless did not fully realize that independence could not be granted "unless the demand was unanimously made by the three major communities in Malaya" (Mustapha 2005, p. 342).

Resistance within the party to the change suggested by him proved too strong even for him, and he left UMNO on 26 August 1951 at the end of his term as party president. He formed the multi-racial Independence of Malaya Party (IMP) on 17 September, which in effect was to function like the reformed UMNO that he had failed to achieve.

Onn's departure from UMNO precipitated a crisis, as he had expected. But after his successor to the presidency, Tunku Abdul Rahman — reading the mood of the Malays correctly — adopted a platform for immediate and full independence, the party slowly gained new life and members. Mustapha claimed that he lost the presidency to Tunku Abdul Rahman Putra, and the deputy presidency to Abdul Razak, by only one vote in both cases. Sardon Jubir, a lawyer from Singapore who had moved to Johor, also vied for the presidency (Mustapha 2005, p. 342; CO 537/7297–17).

Ismail's reading of the times was that Malaya was undeniably bound for independence, with "the pace [being] dictated by the national leaders while the British would try their level best to thwart them". He also thought that Onn feared for the Malays should the British simply withdraw and felt the "wealth and the intellectual power" of the Chinese "would submerge the Malays" if independence was achieved too soon.

> At the time Malaya was under siege from militant communism, which was exploiting Chinese dissatisfaction for its own ends. Under pressure from the British, Dato Onn was at first forced to yield to Chinese demands on the issue of citizenship and language and later when this was not sufficient he was persuaded by the British to give in on the political field by opening the doors of UMNO to the non-Malays, especially the Chinese. When he failed to succeed in this objective he resigned on the mistaken premise that without him UMNO would fade away. He was also confident that with his stature he could form a non-racial party (Drifting c4).

Ismail thought that Onn Ja'afar, though "the man of the moment", was unsuccessful "because he did not believe in what he was doing" (Drifting c4). Onn's failure convinced most other parties for a long time to come, that the country was not ready for anything other than race-based politics. The Alliance formula created in 1952 — where parties representing all the major races formed a coalition — would prove to be the workable solution, at least in gaining independence.

For Ismail, the direction that his life was taking was not what he had intended for himself. As he would state later in life, he was a doctor who had "looked forward to being a millionaire" in his line of work, but who became a politician only reluctantly. Between 1947 and 1953, he ran a moderately successful private practice in Johor Bahru, calling his clinic Tawakkal (Trust in God), after his childhood home. Robert Kuok recalls that Ismail had his practice opposite the Kuok shop on Jalan Trus.

His patients were generally afraid of him, afraid of his no-nonsense style. He couldn't stand hypochondriacs, you see. We would send our truck drivers to him, and we made him our company doctor. Our drivers were not always happy about it (Interview 10 February 2006).

Musa Hitam, later deputy prime minister, recalls Ismail making house calls to his family home in Johor Bahru when he was a young boy (Interview 26 October 2005).

Soon after coming back from Melbourne, Ismail joined about half a dozen other returned students in forming a political discussion group called the Malay Graduates' Association. He learned the following from discussions with his peers:

It was impossible to influence people to support the independence movement merely by writing articles because time was against it and in any case all the newspapers that enjoyed a wide circulation were not anxious to do the wrong thing against the government in power. It was also impractical for the intellectuals to form their own party because such a party would not get mass support. The only alternative was to join a political party that already had mass support and which could be directed to fight for the independence of the country (Drifting c4).

UMNO was therefore always an option for these young activists. There is some uncertainty though, about the reasons behind the Tunku's decision to campaign for the party presidency. Many, including Mustapha Hussain, believed that Abdul Razak, being too young to contest the presidency, managed to convince the Tunku to run for the position instead (Mustapha 2005, p. 374). Shahriman Sulaiman, who was later Razak's aide, claims that Bahaman Samsuddin, a good friend of the Tunku and who was later health minister, was the one who persuaded the Tunku to take over UMNO (Interview 6 September 2005). The Tunku stated in one of his books that although many Malay leaders, including Razak, had asked him to be their leader, it was the promise of support from the Malay Graduates' Association, "led by the brothers Suleiman and Ismail", that decided the matter for him (Tunku 1981, p. 1). Suleiman was one of the Tunku's closest friends from their time together in Cambridge. The Tunku would remember with fondness in later years how the three Rahman brothers, Suleiman, Ismail and Yassin, were "the most dedicated workers in UMNO". Yassin was secretary-general for UMNO until independence (Tunku 1977, p. 311).

Ismail later said that it was after the Tunku had taken over UMNO that he decided to go into politics.

> I remember that one of my pastimes then was swimming and one day after swimming, Dato Sardon came to the beach in his sports car. We talked and he asked me to join UMNO. But I did not join UMNO until UMNO adopted Independence as its platform. I knew at that time the thinking of the Malays [was] that if Independence [were] achieved without Malay participation then there would be no meaningful place for the Malays after Independence. Thus when UMNO changed its stand and decided to fight for Independence, and with persuasion from Tunku Abdul Rahman, I drifted into politics (Letters and Speeches, 15 January 1971).

Interestingly, Henry Gurney reported to the Colonial Office on 29 August 1951 that the Tunku had confided in him that "while he had to talk about independence to satisfy some of his followers, he had no intention of making this a main feature of the new UMNO programme, which would aim rather at getting practical advantages for the Malays, such as land in the towns on favourable terms" (CO 537/7297–18). In light of how the Tunku soon led

UMNO to fight for independence, this piece of apparent misinformation seemed designed to appease the British.

Ismail and his wife Neno first met the Tunku when they were on their way to Penang for their honeymoon in 1950 — their respective families had paired them for marriage. A mutual friend of the Tunku and Ismail, Eugene Seow, had them both over at his flat in Kuala Lumpur. The first time Ismail saw the Tunku, the prince was sitting in a corner sipping gin: "I was struck by his friendliness, charm and unassuming ways". The older man invited the couple to the Kuala Lumpur Flying Club for the evening. However, he later shooed them out on discovering that they were in fact newlyweds: "In typical fashion he bundled us off telling us that we had no business being on the dance floor so late when we should be in bed enjoying our honeymoon" (Drifting c5).

The Tunku remembered this first meeting with Ismail, and in an article he wrote for *The Star* newspaper on 2 June 1975, he recalled how his friendship with Ismail grew from that moment on, "becoming very staunch indeed".

> [Ismail] was that type of man — short in temper and easy to take offence — but if he [were] allowed to reflect and calm down, he would recover his equilibrium as quickly as he had lost it. Above all, at heart he was a very loyal and faithful colleague (Tunku 1977, p. 170).

After becoming UMNO president on 25 August 1951, the Tunku asked the Malay Graduates' Association to nominate one of its members, preferably Ismail, to the party's Central Executive Committee (CEC). This was done, although Ismail cheekily suggested that the support he received from the group was given only because "the other members of the Association were not prepared to sacrifice their careers". Ghafar Baba from Malacca UMNO, who later became deputy prime minister, remembered that the Tunku was in fact overjoyed at getting Ismail over to his side (Interview 16 June 2005).

The first CEC meeting that Ismail attended was held at Kuala Lumpur's Majestic Hotel. The Tunku chaired it, and seemed to Ismail to be unfamiliar with conference procedures. Instead he was guided in protocol by party secretary Hussein Onn, the son of the former party leader. The most important point on the agenda that day was the question of loyalty among those supporters of Onn Ja'afar who had decided to remain in the CEC. Ismail insisted they could not serve two men at the same time, and therefore should resign or face expulsion. It was to take months before Onn's people, including the powerful Perak Mentri Besar Datuk Bukit Gantang, were fully purged.

In his first two years as leader, the Tunku had a hard time getting members engaged in party work. Ismail remembered that the Tunku on a long visit to Johor some months after he became president said that "the party was in disarray, there was no money and he had already started to sell his property to replenish the dwindling funds, and the members were apathetic" (Drifting c6). The Tunku would "rough it out" at Suleiman's house on his visits to Johor, sleeping at Suleiman's insistence in his host's bedroom (Tunku 1977, p. 164). The party was without resources at this time, and the Tunku had to sell his own property to finance it (Tan 2006, p. 165). The Tunku also recalled with warmth how Suleiman would, without his knowledge, give pocket money to the Tunku's two children, telling them that it was from their father (Tunku 1977, p. 164).

Ismail was fascinated by the Tunku, and found that his personality "evoked sympathy and loyalty wherever he went". The prince toured the country tirelessly, and managed to revitalize UMNO's journal, *Suara Merdeka*. The struggle against communist insurgents was still going on, and the Tunku would often draw attention to the plight of detainees. Ismail remembered: "He never approved of the violent methods adopted by those nationalists in their struggle for independence but he never failed to fight for them because they were inspired by nationalism":

> [The Tunku's] greatest asset was that he managed to be himself under all circumstances, no matter where he was, be it the palace or the kampong, in high or low society, whether among the rich or the poor. This quality of his is still with him. People thus began to know him as a person with faults as well as virtues. His blunders — of which there were many — used to shock people at first but as time went on, people got used to him and they forgave him because he was great enough to admit his faults in public and make his apologies in public. These lapses of his — the blunders and the mistakes — used to disarm many people who thought of him as a well-meaning leader with little brains. I remember people saying that Malcolm MacDonald [the United Kingdom Commissioner-General for South-East Asia, 1948–1955] once thought of the Tunku as an unstable leader. However beneath the superficiality, the unimpressiveness, lies a subtle brain which approaches political problems differently from others and whose answer to those problems appears so naïve that at first many people would laugh but which once acted upon proved effective and practical (Drifting c6).

The meetings that the Malay Graduates' Association held at this time were mainly attended only by Ismail and Mohamed Suffian Mohamed Hashim, the man who later became the country's chief justice and lord president. The two prepared drafts that were later discussed with the Tunku and other members. By now, Ismail was convinced after studying Kwame N'krumah's and Ghana's success in securing self-government — Ghana would incidentally gain independence six months before Malaysia —

that "the most important thing was to hold national elections and that if the pro-*Merdeka* party swept the elections, independence was a certainty" (Drifting c7).

Meanwhile, the Briggs Plan, named after Lieutenant-General Sir Harold Briggs who became director of operations in the Emergency in March 1950, had been implemented. This plan involved huge evacuations of rural Chinese, carried out to minimize communist contact with them. Within less than two years, 400,000 Chinese were moved into 400 New Village compounds. Gurney, though satisfied with the social welfare work carried out in these hastily created compounds by the Malayan Chinese Association (MCA) that he had encouraged into being in February 1949, was by now pushing for that organization to exercise greater political leadership and win over the Chinese working class (Heng 1988, p. 137). Interestingly, Ismail himself bluntly admitted to MCA leaders on 21 February 1953 that he had initially considered the MCA a social welfare association filled with members hoping to benefit from its party lottery (Heng 1988, p. 138).

On 6 October 1951, Gurney was ambushed and killed by communist guerrillas on Fraser's Hill. This may have contributed to the defeat suffered by the British Labour government in the 25 October elections in England. The following month, heavy casualties were inflicted on government forces in Malaya (Andaya and Andaya 1982, p. 260), and the secretary of state for the colonies informed the House of Commons on 14 November that the government's aim was to help colonial territories "attain self-government within the British Commonwealth. As far as Malaya was concerned, the promise of "eventual self-government" had already been proclaimed in the preamble to the Federation of Malay Agreement of 1948 (CO 1022/91, no. 23 — Stockwell II 1995, pp. 441–42).

After the new high commissioner, Sir Gerald Templer, was sworn in on 8 February 1952, the war against the communists "was waged with greater vigour" (Tunku 1986, p. 35). The communists had not been able to capitalize on their successes, however, and torn by internal conflicts, they decided to place political goals before military gains (Andaya and Andaya 1982, p. 260). This coincided with important changes in the governmental structure. In April 1951, the "member system" announced by Henry Gurney a year earlier became reality. Under this initiative, non-government members of the Federal Legislative Council were chosen to head various departments, which would give them the experience needed for eventual self-government (Oong 2000, p. 189). Templer began his term by eliminating the Federal War Council founded by Briggs two years earlier, and merging its responsibilities with those of the Executive Council, thus making the latter the only policy-making body in the colony. The British also decided in 1951 to start holding elections, but "at the village pump level". There were two reasons for UMNO not to agree to this, according to Ismail. First, these were suspected to be delaying tactics on the part of the British to postpone independence, and second, village level elections were notorious for their rate of failure. At the same time, the party could not let the elections take place uncontested, and realized that they provided an opportunity for it to test its own strength.

The first such elections were held in Malacca in November 1951, with disappointing participation from the public. MCA leader Tan Cheng Lock, while understanding that the lack of interest among the Chinese was due to discrimination against them on citizenship issues, nevertheless pleaded with them to vote in the Kuala Lumpur elections (Oong 2000, p. 190). The MCA had strong ties at this time with Onn Ja'afar's IMP, which stretched to such an extent that Tan was actually chairman of the

IMP's founding committee. Onn had expected a large group of non-Malays to join his new party. When this did not happen, he railed against the Chinese in his speeches, driving many to distance themselves even further from him. This supposedly helped to pave the way for certain MCA members to seek cooperation with UMNO (Simandjuntak 1969, p. 68). On 31 December, municipal elections were held in Penang, where the Chinese formed 73 per cent of the population. Penang UMNO formed a coalition with the Muslim League, and won only one of nine contested seats. The Radical Party, an ostensibly non-communal party that was nevertheless regarded as pro-Chinese, took six seats.

On 8 January 1952, the Kuala Lumpur Division of UMNO and the Selangor branch of the MCA announced that they would be contesting the Kuala Lumpur municipal election planned for 16 February as a coalition (Heng 1988, p. 161). This alliance had apparently been forged after discussions between Yahya Abdul Razak and H.S. Lee (the respective heads of the two organizations) in meetings arranged by Ong Yoke Lin and S.M. Yong. The fact that Ong and Yahya were both ex-pupils of Victoria Institution and that Ong was a classmate of Yahya's younger brothers, facilitated this unexpected initiative (Tjoa 1978). Ismail, however, told an alternate story regarding the genesis of this fateful coalition:

> Dato Onn had by this time started his IMP and his timing was such that it was in readiness for the Kuala Lumpur municipal election. One of the persons who Dato Onn disliked and who in turn disliked Dato Onn was Mr H.S. Lee. Their dislike of each other was so bitter and so personal that each was bound to oppose whatever the other did. Henry Lee at that time had control of the Chinese guilds in Selangor and as such he was in control of the MCA. Henry approached the local UMNO leader

Dato Yahya and after much discussion decided to form an
alliance of UMNO-MCA to contest the election to the Kuala
Lumpur municipality (Drifting c7).

Whichever the case may have been, "the Alliance trounced the
IMP", winning nine of twelve contested seats. The IMP secured
only two seats, putting central MCA leaders such as Tan Cheng
Lock in a bind. The close relationship between the MCA and the
IMP could not continue, and started unravelling from that point
onwards. By early 1954, Onn Ja'afar had disbanded his new party
in disappointment, and formed the effectually pro-Malay *Parti
Negara* (Malayan National Party).

Elections for the Johor Bahru Town Council immediately
followed those held in Kuala Lumpur, and the local committees
of both UMNO and the MCA adopted the proven Alliance formula.
Ismail was the man responsible for UMNO in Johor Bahru. He
was, however, suffering from "a severe infection of the valves of
the heart", and had to give his consent to the coalition from his
sick bed. He refused the doctor's advice to relax over the next few
months but instead, campaigned for the Alliance, "which nearly
killed him" (Abu Bakar Suleiman, interview 29 March 2006). The
reward for his dedication was a total victory, and the style of
politics that he exhibited at this early stage was to become typical
of him. He recalled in 1967:

> On the last day on which campaigning was allowed I made a
> broadcast as leader of the Alliance asking the electorate to elect
> either all the candidates on the Alliance ticket or none at all.
> This naturally caused a lot of alarm and consternation among
> the Alliance candidates who did not expect all of us to be
> elected and the most vociferous of those who opposed my line
> of action was a candidate who is now a minister of the 1964
> Alliance Government. The differences with the others reflect

the attitude which we took with regard to the election. I saw the election as a means of measuring our strength and popularity with the voters whereas some of my colleagues [...] were more interested in securing seats in the council for themselves. Luckily for me and for the party, we won all the contested seats" (Drifting c7).

Musa Hitam, then a young man becoming interested in politics, remembers Ismail's booming voice during this campaign. What struck him then, and later as well, was that Ismail would never beat about the bush, and would instead keep his speeches short (Interview 26 October 2005).

Ismail was by now convinced that the main tactic of the Alliance should be "to press for the election to be held at the national level as a means to gain independence" (Drifting c7). The MCA, because of the restrictive citizenship laws at the time, had not been especially enthusiastic about elections, fearing that such a process would merely make the Chinese political subordinates to the Malays. However, since the Alliance was proving to be highly successful, the Tunku and Tan Cheng Lock decided on 16 March 1953 to set up UMNO-MCA liaison committees throughout the federation in anticipation of federal elections. Onn Ja'afar continued showing his antagonism towards the MCA, which helped to strengthen Chinese support for the Alliance solution.

Ismail recalled once making a scathing attack on Onn, "dissecting him into four parts, all of which were anything but complimentary to him", and encouraging Tan Siew Sin to withstand pressure from his peers and instead push ahead with a motion on 6 May to censure Onn Ja'afar from making more "very inflammatory communal speeches attacking the Chinese" (CO 1022/86, no 26, enclosure C — Stockwell II 1995, p. 454; Drifting c8).

In early 1953, the fight against the communists was going very well, encouraging the high commissioner to make a sudden announcement on 15 July that a federal elections committee would be formed. This body was to suggest how a post-election government would be constructed. When formed, it consisted of a majority from outside the government, most of whom were supporters of Onn Ja'afar. The Alliance, despite being the winner of vast majorities in the local elections, was allowed only seven representatives. The Alliance decided nevertheless to play along for the time being. However, it demanded in April 1953 that elections should be held by the end of 1954 or their representatives would resign from the Federal Legislative Council. This stand was reiterated on 13 September at the UMNO general assembly in Alor Star. On the latter occasion, Ismail, speaking for himself and the absent Razak, told the gathering: "The $500 a month allowance to Councillors is a large sum, but we are prepared to give it up if it is for the good of the people" (*Straits Budget* 17 September 1953).

At this time, UMNO decided to introduce a uniform for its youth wing, consisting of "white shirt with red epaulettes, a red tie and a black cap". However, after it was paraded at Malacca UMNO's general meeting, the colonial government banned it. UMNO Youth members reciprocated by wearing pure white shirts and trousers instead, and were joined later by MCA Youth. The Tunku and Ismail reasoned with the British, arguing that the organization itself was "neither subversive nor unlawful". This was to no avail, and the uniform ban remained in place (Tunku 1981, p. 64).

In response to the growing strength of the Alliance, High Commissioner Templer decided to put the Tunku, who was already an unofficial member of the Executive Council of the Federal Legislative Council, in charge of a department. According to

Ismail, the Tunku "was too shrewd to fall into that trap: He knew that if he accepted, he would be tied down to the work of administering departments in his portfolio, leaving him little time for party work" (Drifting c8).

Instead, the Tunku nominated Ismail, despite complaints from some UMNO members that even that move would compromise the party's position. He prevailed, however, arguing that independence must be achieved constitutionally and not by force. Later he explained that he chose Ismail for the position because he was sure that the latter could be trusted to look after the interests of the Malays (Abu Bakar Suleiman, interview 29 March 2006). Thus on 29 September 1953, the Executive Council received two Alliance members — Ismail and H.S. Lee, the former as member for lands, mines and communications, and the latter as member for railways and ports. The Tunku remained an unofficial member.

> Thus one day [the Tunku] came to see me in Johore Baru and said that Templer wanted to see me. He gave me a letter, which I was not to read until after I entered the gates leading to King's House where Sir Gerald resided. Such was my loyalty and love for the Tunku that I never thought of protesting this unusual procedure. As soon as I entered the grounds of the King's House I read the note that the Tunku gave me... He said in the letter that when I saw Sir Gerald I would be offered a post in the administration. He did not want me to refuse, but to give a reply to the effect that I had to consult the party Central Executive Committee. I was thus placed in a difficult dilemma without much time to plan things out. When I was ushered into Sir Gerald's study I saw that Tun Sir Henry Lee was already there. Henry is not noted for his reticence and he straightaway blurted out that Sir Gerald had offered him the post of member of transport and that he would accept it only if Sir Gerald would agree to his drawing a nominal salary of £1 per month.

Unfortunately, he said, Sir Gerald would not hear of this and he was therefore compelled to accept the offer in the interest of the MCA and the country. It was obvious to me then that to delay the decision on the pretext of consulting the party executive would not work. [...] Faced by such a momentous decision I knew that I could not refuse without letting Henry and the MCA down and more important the Tunku down. Therefore I told Sir Gerald that I would accept on one condition, which was that if I should disagree on fundamental issues with him or with any majority decision of the Executive Council, he must promise to accept my resignation should I tender one. He agreed but added that he would be a fool to allow such a situation to arise.

Tunku Abdul Rahman's letter to Ismail reads, *ad verbatim*:

Dear Doctor,

I would like you to accept Templer's offer. I know it doesn't mean much to you and I also know that you would wish to remain as you are, but I also know what it would mean in the eyes of your pembesar-pembesar [superiors] *if you were taken on as a Member just now and because you are a leader of UMNO.*

I could not accept it myself because of the work I had to put in — here and there and everywhere almost at the same time, as otherwise UMNO would suffer. I told H.S. to accept for the sake of the Alliance. We will join you in one year's time, but in the meantime we got to bolster the name of the Alliance and the only way is for the government to recognise our strength. This is one of the ways. We put Alliance Members in the Exco as holders of portfolio.

I wish you luck.
Merdeka!

P.S. All that you to have say to him is that you would like to consult the UMNO Exco on the proposal and also Col. Lee.

The other three members of the Executive Council at that time were Onn Ja'afar, who was member of home affairs, Dr Lee Tiang King, a leader of the Penang Secession Movement, who was member of health, and E.E. Thuraisingham, chairman of the Communities Liaison Committee (CLC), who was member of education. [The CLC was the brainchild of the Commissioner-General for Southeast Asia, Malcolm MacDonald, who encouraged its birth at the end of 1948 at the start of the communist insurgency (Oong 2000, pp. 150–52)].

In his memoirs, Ismail generously remembered the various members of the Federal Legislative Council as "on the whole able men, and if it had not been for the fact that the contentious theme for the period was that of independence they would have served the country well" (Drifting c8).

Ismail's father was "very furious" at his decision to join the Executive Council, partly because he was informed only after the decision had been made, and partly because his son "had abandoned a profession which he took so much trouble and sacrifice to equip [him with]". The young man could only defend himself by saying that "any sacrifice which would advance the cause of independence for our country was never too great for me to offer". This did not appease the old man, and it was only after the Tunku personally came to his house to pacify him did Abdul Rahman Yassin agree to give Ismail his blessing.

In the Executive Council, road transport and natural resources were soon added to Ismail's responsibilities. He was thus involved in improving land administration, forming the Federal Land Development Authority (Felda), and resettling displaced landowners. Templer proved "a hard master but a wonderful man to work for". In the evenings, Ismail would join the Alliance Committee at the Miner's Club to work out policy details about an independent commission consisting of members from

Commonwealth countries to be entrusted with drafting a constitution for an independent Malaya.

> The Alliance had great faith in the Commonwealth and also felt that the experience of Commonwealth countries in regard to law, the civil service and the judiciary were almost identical. The Alliance also felt that the complexities of the multi-racial society such as that in Malaya could only be solved by an independent commission which would be unbiased (Drifting c9).

The Federal Elections Committee formed by Templer finally published its report in January 1954. The most controversial issue was whether elected members should form a majority or not, and if so by what margin. The majority report recommended 48 appointed and 44 elected members in the Federal Council. The Alliance minority proposed having 100 council members, three-fifths of whom were to be elected, and also demanded that federal elections be held by November 1954. The Conference of Rulers, which had veto rights on constitutional matters, soon produced a compromise solution proposing that 46 be nominated and 52 elected. The Alliance would not accept the rulers' initiative and stuck to their three-fifths formula.

At that year's UMNO general assembly, Ismail proclaimed:

> Election to the Federal Council is not an 'experiment' to the ordinary people in this country. It is an 'experiment' to those who fear the face of the electorate, to those who would prefer the *status quo* in order not to lose what they have, and afraid to fight for what they may not get, to those who could hinder the march of Malaya to Independence (von Vorys 1976; op. cit., p. 115).

Disappointed at how things were going, the Alliance decided to take matters into its own hands and send a delegation to England.

At a mass rally in Malacca, thousands of UMNO and MCA supporters spontaneously contributed towards the expenses of such a trip (Tan 1957).

On 21 April 1954, Tunku Abdul Rahman and T.H. Tan went off to London to see Oliver Lyttleton, the secretary of state for the colonies. Lacking resources, the two men had to share a single bed, the Tunku having to suffer the latter's propensity to snore heavily (Tan 2006, p. 165). Abdul Razak Hussein flew over from New York to join them. Lyttleton initially refused to receive them but was forced to relent by the public support accorded the trio by British members of parliament. He finally met the Malayan delegation on 14 May, but reported the "three worried little men" did not impress him (CO 1030/309, no. 53 — Stockwell III 1995, p. 28). The trip failed to gain the Alliance much headway (Oong 2000, pp. 204–12).

With encouragement from British leaders such as W.T. Proctor, Lord Ogmore, A. Creech Jones and Gilbert Brockway, the group laboured on and established the Merdeka Bureau in London to solicit support from the general public (Tan 1957).

On 25 May, an Alliance delegation consisting of the Tunku, Ismail, H.S. Lee and Leong Yew Koh — the latter two were founders of the MCA — handed over a resolution to Templer warning of a boycott if the recommendations of the Federal Elections Committee were accepted as law (CO 1030/310, no. 91 — Stockwell III 1995, p. 36). Soon after, on 13 June, UMNO and MCA officials released a press statement threatening to withdraw from government. They also explained that they were at the same time asking for a special independent commission — and not a royal one — to be formed to review the constitution.

On 18 June, all three Alliance members of the Executive Council resigned, as did twelve of the nineteen in the Federal Legislative Council. In their absence, the Council nevertheless passed the Federation of Malaya Agreement (Amendment) Bill on 24 June, which fixed the distribution between nominated and elected members at 46/52. The high commissioner was to be personally responsible for appointing five reserve members and two official members.

Ismail and his wife now decided to move back to Johor Bahru, with their three-year-old son Tawfik and one-year-old daughter Zailah in tow. Apparently, the mistake the Alliance had made in handling the elections issue was "in not seeking support from the Malay rulers whose consent was necessary for any change to the constitution" (Oong 2000, pp. 207–09). Its leaders quickly realized this, however, and on 2 July, a 2,000-strong Alliance procession was held in Johor Bahru that ended with a petition being presented to the Sultan of Johor to request the appointment of a special independent commission to review the constitution.

The boycott by the Alliance was a great worry to the British, who feared that the communists would make full use of the impasse and begin manipulating the electoral process. On 2 July, the new high commissioner, Sir Donald MacGillivray, sent Sir Michael Hogan, who was chairman of the Federal Elections Committee as well as attorney-general, to Johor Bahru to see the Tunku. The Tunku, Ismail and H.S. Lee met him at the residence of the British Adviser. The message Hogan brought was that MacGillivray wished to meet them on board the warship HMS *Alert*, which was then anchored off Singapore's Seletar Naval Base. The three thought it possible that they were being exiled and fearing the worst, started making plans about how the struggle would continue should that happen.

They were driven off at dusk in the adviser's car, arriving at Seletar Jetty at 11 p.m. that night (Tunku 1986, p. 50; Drifting c9). Hogan was also present at the meeting.

Sir Donald was there, waiting for us in the captain's cabin. He told us that he was going on a cruise for a fortnight up the east coast of Malaya and that he wanted to see us before we left. He said he was not at all happy at the turn of events and that the Alliance by its boycott of the Government was playing into the hands of the Communists who were already taking political advantage of it. He assured us that the six nominated seats reserved at the discretion of the High Commissioner would not be used to frustrate any political party which secured majority seats at the elections. We had to think fast and although the three of us had no time to meet to discuss matters we knew that if we did not offer some sort of compromise we might be taken away and exiled. If that were to happen, we knew the movement for independence would pass from the hands of the moderates to the hands of the extremists who because of the methods which they might employ would never achieve their goals. I therefore suggested that we were willing to show that we were responsible leaders by proposing that in exercising his discretion in nominating the six, the High Commissioner should do so only after consulting with the leader of the majority party. Sir Donald at first rejected this compromise because he said that this would fetter the discretion reserved for the High Commissioner. We said that was as far as we were prepared to concede and that we were prepared for the worst. Finally seeing that we could not be moved from our stand he agreed to think over our proposal during his voyage and would let us know his reply when he returned. It later turned out that the object of his voyage was to gauge the feelings of the East Coast Malays and if possible win them over to his side. When he found that the Malay support for UMNO was absolute and that he had failed to persuade them in spite of everything, he agreed to our compromise on his return to Kuala Lumpur.

To be exact, the high commissioner was actually charged with appointing five, and not six, reserve members. The next day,

MacGillivray made his report to Lyttleton, recommending that Ismail's suggestion be accepted. The Alliance also requested that MacGillivray use his position to make certain that state governments re-appointed Alliance members who had resigned. MacGillivray noted this but could not provide any guarantee. He was also very concerned that Parti Negara would resent the reinstatement of Ismail and H.S. Lee to the Executive Council: "It may be that they [Parti Negara] will carry their resentment so far as to submit their own resignations, but that is a risk which must, I think, be taken" (CO 1030/311, no. 125 — Stockwell III 1995, pp. 65–66). Interestingly, the compromise suggested by Ismail and accepted by MacGillivray is credited by Karl von Vorys in his book, *Democracy without Consensus*, to Mohammad Sopiee Sheik Ibrahim, who was not at the meeting (von Vorys 1976, p. 120).

On the strength of this new understanding, the Alliance ended its boycott on 7 July, and Ismail and H.S. Lee were reinstated on 1 August (*ST* 31 July 1954). Their coalition would now concentrate on winning the forthcoming elections at state and federal levels. The exact process of decolonization was still undecided, with the British claiming that the fight against the communists remained the main obstacle. By the end of 1954, however, the communist threat had significantly diminished, and there were also clear signs later in the year that the sultans were becoming more supportive of the Alliance demand for an outside commission to study constitutional change (CO 1030/174, no. 10 — Stockwell III 1995, p. 83; Oong 2000: 198, 211).

With the decision of the Malayan Indian Congress (MIC) to join the Alliance in April 1954 — after Parti Negara had demanded its disbandment as a condition for cooperation with its members — the concept of racial parties subsumed under a coalition party was completed and ready to be sold as such to the electorate (Tunku 1986, p. 51). In March 1955, nomination day for the federal elections was fixed for 15 July and election day was to be two weeks after that. The campaigning period was to be rather short.

The government of the day, in the form of High Commissioner MacGillivray, was unofficially backing Onn Ja'afar, and according to Ismail, telephone contact between the two men was continuous.

> As far as the Alliance was concerned, the main question was who was to challenge Dato Onn, who was standing in a Johore constituency. Tunku characteristically put up a trial balloon by spreading the rumour that Dato Sardon, the UMNO Youth Leader, was willing to sacrifice himself by taking on Dato Onn! When Sardon heard of it, he promptly denied the rumour because the fear of Onn was terrible and the shadow of Onn was dark. There remained only my brother Suleiman and I — members of my family were the only ones who could possibly take on Dato Onn — and so finally Suleiman offered to take on the challenge (Drifting c10).

Suleiman felt that he should be the one to accept the challenge since he was a Johor man himself. He also wanted the Tunku to return to Kedah to campaign there and throughout the country. The Tunku considered this "the most noble and selfless action" that Suleiman ever did. Suleiman could have contested in Batu Pahat and won hands down, and did not have to risk everything by taking on Onn Ja'afar. On 27 July, the coalition challenged all fifty-two electoral seats — thirty-five by UMNO, fifteen by the MCA and two by the MIC — and won fifty-one of these, losing only to a candidate from the Pan-Malayan Islamic Party (PMIP). Its main opponent, Parti Negara, which fielded thirty contenders, adopting a strong pro-Malay stance and demanding independence by 1960, a year later than the Alliance deadline, did not win a single seat. Suleiman — the "giant-killer"– won a landslide victory in Johor Bahru, gaining the highest number of votes returned in the whole election. Onn received only 2,802 votes out of the 11,547 cast in the constituency. (Tunku 1977, p. 164; Tunku 1981, p. 11; von Vorys 1976, p. 121; Tan 1957).

The voter turnout was impressive, averaging 80 per cent, but reaching as much as 89 per cent in one rural district in Negri Sembilan. There were 1,280,000 registered voters, about one million of whom were Malays and 180,000 Chinese. Why the issue of citizenship was such a controversial matter was borne out by the fact that Malays, comprising only half the actual population of the federation, made up 84 per cent of the electorate (CO 1030/225, no. 7 — Stockwell 1995, p. 149).

Other competing parties were the PMIP, which had 11 candidates; the National Association of Perak with 9 candidates; the Labour Party with 4 candidates; the Perak Malay League with 3 candidates and the Perak Progressive Party with two candidates. There were also 18 independents. Forty-three of the 77 candidates lost their deposit, a forfeit suffered by those failing to obtain at least one-eighth of the total valid votes (CO 1030/225, no. 4 — Stockwell 1995, pp. 145–49). In short, the Alliance formula proved a tremendous success. The Tunku could now form his own government. He was highly appreciative of the vital role played by the Rahman brothers, and would later recall:

> Right through the toil of rebuilding UMNO, forming the Alliance, and finally in the struggle for independence, [Ismail], like his brother, Datuk Suleiman, went all out to fight the rival party led by his step-mother's brother, Datuk Onn bin Ja'afar. Neither of them would give way; they went for one another hammer and tongs; and in the end Datuk Onn had to give in (Tunku 1975, p. 170).

The new cabinet comprised of the Tunku as chief minister as well as holder of the home affairs portfolio, H.S. Lee as transport minister, Ismail as minister for natural resources, Razak as minister of education, Leong Yew Koh as minister for health and social welfare, V.T. Sambanthan as labour minister, Suleiman as minister for local government, housing and town planning, Sardon Jubir as works minister, and Ong Yoke Lin as minister for posts and telecommunications. The portfolios of economic affairs and defence were reserved for nominated members (CO 1030/225, no. 3 — Stockwell 1995, pp. 143–44).

So it came about that Ismail and H.S. Lee — the two members from the Alliance — were joined in government by their Alliance colleagues two years after they had first agreed to be part of the Executive Council, one year later than the Tunku had promised in his earlier letter to Ismail asking the latter to accept membership.

Issues immediately facing the Alliance included the continued struggle against the communists, and the future school system and language use. But most important of all was *Merdeka*. The UMNO general assembly that year decided to accept UMNO Youth's suggestion that independence be achieved within two years and not four, as had been proclaimed during the electoral campaign (Tunku 1981, p. 13). Another hurdle to be overcome was the sultans' apprehension about their own future after independence especially with regard to the abolition of British advisers.

At the end of August, Alan Lennox-Boyd, the new Secretary of State for the Colonies, paid an official visit to Malaya. The Tunku's newly elected government quickly took the chance to ask for immediate top-level discussions about independence. This proved to be the right move, and the British Government later that year agreed to meet two delegations — one representing the elected Malayan Government and one appointed by the Malay rulers — in January the following year.

Before that, however, the communist problem needed to be curtailed. The MCP had been sending out feelers since June for negotiations to end the Emergency. These had been rebuked. On 8 September, an amnesty offer was announced — first by the director of operations and then by the Tunku (Tunku 1986, p. 64) — and meetings between representatives on both sides on 17 October and 19 November were secretly held to iron out details for a final rendezvous. The Tunku left it to Chin Peng, the secretary-general of the MCP, to decide the venue. Ismail was against the meeting, as were many other leaders within the Alliance.

> We were worried that in his anxiety to end the state of emergency, he might compromise himself to the extent that he might endanger the security of the country when Independence was achieved. He was steadfast in his desire to talk with [the Communists] and could not be dissuaded so the next best thing was to ensure that when the meeting took place, the Tunku was well briefed and his security not endangered. Tunku himself was adamant that a safe passage be guaranteed for Chin Peng and his aides. It says much for the trust that Chin Peng had in the Tunku that he accepted the invitation to meet the Tunku knowing full well that he was throwing himself at the mercy of the Tunku and the British (Drifting c11).

The historic meeting with the communists took place on 28 December 1955 in Baling, Kedah. A week earlier, UMNO had held its general assembly in Kuala Lumpur at which a resolution calling for full independence by 31 August 1957 was unanimously passed, although with two extra words added by the Tunku — "if possible". Apparently, those words convinced the MCP further that the British would find some way out of granting independence (Chin 2003, p. 371). The Tunku explained that he wanted the words added in case any delay due to technicalities or unexpected events should become necessary.

At the Baling talks, Chin Peng as well as party leaders Chen Tien and Abdul Rashid Maidin represented the communists, while the Tunku, Tan Cheng Lock, and David Marshall, the chief minister of Singapore, represented the government. Three sessions were held between 2.30p.m. and 8.05p.m. on the first day, and a final session the next morning between 10.50a.m. and 12.48p.m. The two sides discussed the terms of the amnesty, the approaching Malayan independence, and the recognition of the MCP, among other things.

The Tunku explained that two conditions made the amnesty radically different from surrender terms, namely that there would be no prosecution of returnees, and that "surrender terms were made by the Government of Malaya, and the amnesty is made by the representatives of the people". The Tunku argued that it was because the new government was an elected one that an amnesty was now being offered.

The "primary question", as Chin Peng understood it, was the one that the government had expected and had prepared itself to parry, namely the official recognition of the MCP. The Tunku and Marshall managed to hold firm on that score, arguing that the MCP consisted of very few federal citizens, and even if only federal citizens constituted the party, loyalty to the country remained a decisive issue. "Detention" on acceptance of the amnesty, or "investigation", or "inquiry" as the Tunku wished to name it, was another condition that Chin Peng would not agree to.

Chin Peng later wrote that "the other side was seeking ultimately to force all returning CPM members into making political confessions via the process of interrogation". The demand for loyalty to the country would, to him, merely justify the banishment of his comrades "to their perceived countries of origin — either China or India" (Chin 2003, p. 380). He was however prepared "to stop the war immediately" as soon as the elected Malayan and Singaporean governments had control over internal forces. He would not, however, "hand over" MCP weapons even if they were "laid down" unless the MCP was recognized and it was agreed that the returning communists would not be subjected to "restriction of liberty" (CO 1030/30, ff 3-16 — Stockwell 1995, pp. 213–26).

The Baling talks failed to end the Emergency but pushed the Alliance, which was now bound for negotiations in London, into a better position from which to seek an early date for independence. The meeting with the communists provided the regime with more legitimacy and a higher status. The Tunku later noted:

> I don't know whether [Chin Peng] is alive or dead; but the talk with him gave my campaign to end the Emergency a real boost. I went to the people; I spoke on the radio; I used every means possible to tell the people that Chin Peng made it clear that he would not co-exist with me, and that he would set up a Communist government if he won his battle (Tunku 1986, p. 67).

In a seminar held in October 2004 at Singapore's Institute of Southeast Asian Studies (ISEAS), Chin Peng reiterated that his final conclusion was that the Tunku actually made use of the Baling talks to gain further legitimacy in the eyes of the British (ISEAS VCD 7 October 2004). The failure of the talks reportedly left him dejected. Sometime in 1958, the MCP finally decided that the armed units should lie low and not attract attention. A neutral policy towards Thailand was announced, with the claim that the MCP was merely seeking refuge in southern Thailand and had no quarrel with the Thai Government. This strategy had some effect and encouraged certain Thai officials to leave the guerrillas alone (Chin 1995, p. 50). According to former Malaysian

Inspector-General of Police Haniff Omar, during joint border actions by Thai and Malaysian troops at that time, it was a common occurrence for Thai soldiers to inexplicably fire shots into the air. These, he believed, were for the benefit of fugitive guerrillas (Interview 13 September 2005).

The Alliance was now fully armed for the talks in London and a strong optimism was in the air. The next hurdle on the road to *Merdeka* was the attitude of the rulers. Although the nine sultans were unsure about their future role, the Alliance finally managed to convince them to send representatives to London. According to Ismail, the representatives who were chosen were all sympathetic to the Alliance cause except for the Mentri Besar of Perak, Dato Panglima Bukit Gantang. On New Year's Day 1956, two Malayan delegations — one consisting of four Alliance men and the other of four representatives of the sultans — set off for London to talk their way to independence. These included the Tunku, Razak, Ismail and Colonel H.S. Lee, as well as the deputy state secretary of Johor, the chief ministers of Perak and Selangor, and the former chief minister of Kelantan, the legally qualified Nik Kamil, who would provide advice on sultanate treaty matters. These men were accompanied by the secretary-general of the Alliance, T.H. Tan, who acted as secretary for the Alliance group, and Abdul Kadir Samsuddin, who performed similar duties for the representatives of the sultans (Shaw 1976, p. 106). Their cruise ship was the Italian vessel *Asia*.

> We travelled to London in two stages: The first by boat and the second by plane. The whole idea was Tunku's. He had conceived the idea (which worked very well) of throwing the members of the delegation together to mix and work during the whole period of the sea voyage to give them the opportunity of ironing out their differences so that by the end of the voyage they would emerge as one team to face the British government. On

board ship, we met every morning with the Tunku as chairman
and by the time we arrived in Karachi, all of us, including Dato
Panglima Bukit Gantang, were agreed on the lines of discussion
with the British government (Drifting c10).

The eight men thus arrived in London as one single delegation
with common goals to hold talks with the British colonialists.
These lasted from 18 January to 6 February. It was Ismail's first
trip to London, and the Tunku and Razak guided him and other
first-timers in the group around the city.

From the time that we landed in London airport it was obvious
that our mission was going to be a success because a certain
high official of the Colonial Office [Permanent Under-Secretary
Sir John Martin] told us that what we came for would be
handed over to us on a gold platter.

The various parties met at Lancaster House "in an atmosphere of
great cordiality" (Shaw 1976, p. 106). Ismail remembered the
occasion well:

The meeting was conducted in typical fashion. There was a
main meeting called the plenary meeting and in addition there
were the meetings of the various committees. I remember that
in addition to attending the plenary meeting (which all members
of the delegation attended) I attended meetings of the Finance
Committee and the Civil Service Committee. The chairman of
the Finance Committee was Sir Hilton Poynton and he was a
hard nut to crack. At the Civil Service Committee we succeeded
in drafting a scheme of compensation for the expatriate civil
servants in Malaya. The ease with which the Malayan Civil
Service was transferred from the hands of the expatriates is a
tribute to the soundness of the scheme (Drifting c11).

Negotiations for the transfer of power, which included finances,
economic matters and internal security, were quickly concluded.

One further hurdle to clear at that point was the question of British advisers to the sultans. The British wanted them kept until independence was declared, while the Alliance, fearing that these advisers would be used to turn the sultans against the politicians, wished for their immediate removal. The decision seemed to lie with the representatives of the sultans. All except one of them had the authority to vote as they individually wished. Sultan Ibrahim of Johor had however given clear instructions to his man, Dato Seth Said, who was also Ismail's father-in-law, "to urge for the retention of the advisors". To everyone's surprise, Seth decided to disobey his sovereign and instead join the Alliance delegation in asking for the advisers to be recalled immediately (Drifting c11). From that point onwards, the colonial secretary had no reason not to agree to the delegation's request.

Incidentally, Sultan Ibrahim was known as "an autocratic Ruler who would dismiss any civil servant he disliked no matter whether he had the power to or not" (Drifting c11). The Tunku was greatly impressed by Seth's initiative and later appointed him chairman of the Railway Services Commission.

Another difficult issue to handle was whether or not a definite date for independence should be set.

> The British government was reluctant to fix any target date and [...] tie the hands of the independence commission on the constitution which the conference had tenaciously agreed to set up. The members of UMNO in the delegation especially the Tunku, Razak and myself were committed to a target date because at the UMNO General Assembly in Malacca held before the delegation departed for London, a resolution had been passed that Merdeka (Independence) must be achieved by August 31, 1957. After a lengthy discussion, the conference finally agreed to add the words 'if possible' after the words 'August 31, 1957' (Drifting c11).

The issue was in fact deadlocked early in the discussions, and negotiations continued unofficially until agreement was reached on 8 February — incidentally the Tunku's fifty-third birthday — that independence would be granted on 31 August 1957, two years earlier than promised by the Alliance during the elections (Shaw 1976, p. 107). That night, the delegation honoured the Tunku with "a sumptuous dinner" at the Coconut Grove Night Club (Tan 1957).

In the middle of February, the delegates flew home, stopping over in Cairo to meet Egyptian President Gamal Abdel-Nasser. After a night's rest in Singapore, they continued to Malacca where a hero's welcome awaited them. In April, self-government came into being, and the Tunku became chief minister as well as defence minister, Razak became minister of education, Ismail took over the portfolio of commerce and industry, H.S. Lee became finance minister, V.T. Sambanthan became minister for postal services and telecommunications, Suleiman was made minister for the interior, Leong Yew Koh became welfare minister, Abdul Aziz Ishak became agriculture minister, Ong Yoke Lin became health minister and Sardon Jubir was made minister of transport.

Ismail announced in an interview that his two main priorities as minister of commerce and industry were to woo big industry to invest in the country and to improve the economic situation of the Malays (ST 23 March 1956).

The feat of achieving unity for the gaining of independence from the British had now to be parallelled by success in concrete inter-ethnic negotiations on internal matters. The hottest issues were education and language use.

The MCA had recently been actively defending the status of Chinese education, gaining it enough new support to undermine the traditional influence enjoyed by left-wing groups in Chinese schools. The 1952 Education Ordinance called for an integrated system of national schools where only Malay and English would be used, which would replace all the vernacular schools. This was in keeping with the Barnes Report released on 19 September 1951, which meant that contradistinctive recommendations supporting the vernacular schools made in the Fenn-Wu Report submitted in 1951 by a government-appointed committee to study Chinese education were being ignored (Heng 1988, p. 192).

The United Chinese School Teachers Association (UCSTA) had already been formed on 25 August 1951 to resist the Education Ordinance, and was joined on 21 April 1954 by the United Chinese School Committees' Association (UCSCA). In April 1953, Tan Cheng Lock founded the MCA Chinese Education Central Committee (MCACECC) for the same purpose. Under the umbrella of the MCACECC, these bodies held private meetings with the British administration for a repeal of the ordinance, but to no avail. What was gained from this otherwise failed endeavour was the securing of the MCA's reputation as the champion of Chinese rights.

The broad issue of Chinese education also involved the MCA in the Nanyang University project to create tertiary education possibilities within Malaya and Singapore for graduates from Chinese secondary schools. After gaining endorsement from UMNO for the project during the Alliance National Convention of 23 August 1953, a strong sense of solidarity pervaded the MCA (Heng 1988, p. 200).

Immediately after the 1955 Alliance electoral victory, a fifteen-member Education Committee was formed under Abdul Razak to study the future structure of schooling, and the question of the language of instruction in schools. By May 1956, it published what was known as the Razak Report. This then became, on subsequent approval by the Federal Legislative Council, the

Education Ordinance of 1957. In the event, the only opposition came from UMNO councillors — reportedly "mostly from the East Coast" — who were dissatisfied with the fact that Malay was not to be the sole medium of instruction in all schools (CO 1030/ 51, no. 96 — Stockwell III 1995, p. 284).

Lim Chong Eu, a member of the Education Committee, was supportive of the report, and considered it an "inter-weaving of the various immigrant cultures of this country [...] around a strong and dominant theme of the Malay language, our national language, and of Malay culture" (Tan 1997, p. 179). Extreme advocates of Malay nationalism within UMNO, their suspicions aroused further by the fact that the new ordinance was well received by Chinese leaders such as Lim, saw an occasion to attack party moderates.

When the council debated the issue, Ismail gave a vigorous speech in defence of the report, charging that the critics who were trying to suppress the languages of all the people in the country excepting their own, and showing "no considerations for the Chinese and Indians who are already in this country" were in fact taking the imperialist line that they were usually so ready to condemn. It was enough, he argued, that non-Malays accepted the fact that Malaya was a Malay country and that the national language was Malay (Federation of Malaya, *Legislative Council Debates*, op. cit., 16 May 1956; Simandjuntak 1969, p. 201; Stockwell III 1995, p. 285; Tan 1997, p. 179).

Another issue heatedly discussed in the Federal Executive Council concerned security arrangements for Singapore in the latter's negotiations for self-government. The British were willing to grant self-government to the island only if a council consisting of representatives of Singapore, the United Kingdom and the emergent Malayan government was formed to bear responsibility for security matters. Ismail fervently objected to the arrangement, stating that an independent Malaya should not meddle in the internal affairs of another country. On being overruled, he asked for his objection to be duly noted (Drifting c15).

After the major issue of independence had been settled, the internal resilience of the Alliance system was put to the test. Ismail recollected that a strong team of MCA intellectuals held a debate with UMNO on critical issues. Most of these men were new, and "while they sensed that there was trust and confidence which had been built in the Alliance [...] they had not themselves experienced it and their approach at the meetings was at first critical". Ismail felt that all parties soon came to agree that whatever the problem was, the Alliance format would provide an appropriate answer.

> As I saw this spirit emerge and expand during the rest of the conference, I was convinced that whatever happened in the future, this spirit of the Alliance would triumph over all obstacles. As a result of this new consciousness, the solution to many communal problems became possible (Drifting c12).

The major dilemmas that were being faced were those of citizenship, the national language and the special position of the Malays. The following text by Ismail reveals his understanding of Malaya's post-colonial situation (Drifting c12):

Citizenship
Under colonial rule there was a cumulative increase in the population of immigrant races especially those of Chinese origin and to a lesser extent the Indians, the latter brought in mainly to work in the rubber estates owned by the British. No attempt was made to make these immigrants loyal citizens of Malaya. The British were content to see that so long as they obey the laws of the country, they could come and leave as they please. As a result of this policy, when more and more of them settled

in Malaya, the result was an increasing number of aliens in the country who on the whole were richer and more vigorous than the Malays. When the Malays seized political power after the Second World War, their main defence against their more virile and richer neighbours was to deny them the right of citizenship.

The Language Issue

As a result of colonial rule, the only language that could guarantee a livelihood for those entering the government service was English. Otherwise the various races were left to themselves with regard to education. There was a feeble attempt to give the Malays an education in their own language but as this ceased at the primary level and was implemented in a half-hearted manner, it gave no benefit to the Malays. The Chinese were left to themselves and to run their own schools, which were financed through levies that they imposed on themselves, on their rubber production and their businesses. Their education was orientated towards China. As a result only the English educated in the multi-racial population of Malaya enjoyed a common language. The leaders of the Alliance concluded that in an independent Malaya, there should be one language to unify the various races into one nation. The obvious choice was Malay. It was imperative that if the Chinese — the real political problem since the other races were not dominant — were to be persuaded into accepting Malay as the national language they should be granted citizenship as a *quid pro quo*. This was the real basis of the agreement between the three partners, particularly between the Malay and the Chinese.

The Special Position of the Malays

This proved a less intractable problem because the leaders of the Alliance realised the practical necessity of giving the Malays a handicap if they were to compete on equal terms with the other races. The only point of controversy was the duration of the 'special position' — should there be a time limit or should it be permanent? I made a suggestion which was accepted, that the question be left to the Malays themselves, because I felt that as more and more Malays became educated and gained self-confidence, they themselves would do away with this 'special position' because in itself this 'special position' is a slur on the ability of the Malays and only to be tolerated because it is necessary as a temporary measure to ensure their survival in the modern competitive world: a world to which only those in the urban areas had been exposed.

This analysis provides insight into how Ismail perceived the Malayan situation. What is striking is Ismail's belief that the Malays would do the right thing in the long run, as well as his faith in the Alliance as a model of government capable of meeting these challenges taken as a whole.

At the 1956 UMNO elections, Ismail decided as a matter of democratic principle to run against Razak for deputy president. He lost. The Tunku had earlier expressed his wish that Razak, whom he had chosen as deputy before his closest friend Suleiman, should not be challenged. Suleiman was apparently considered overly playful, and had a passion for racehorses that rivalled the Tunku's (Abu Bakar Suleiman, interview 29 March 2006; Tunku 1977, p. 164).

Another hurdle to be cleared on the road to independence was the formation of a Commonwealth commission to help formulate a constitution for the country. Some time before the trip to London, Razak was put in charge of a committee to work out a proposal for how such a commission could be formed, and to have it ready for presentation in London. This was done, and once the British and the Malay sultans accepted the resulting proposal, a commission was indeed appointed. This consisted of Lord Reid as chairman, Sir Ivor Jennings from the United

Kingdom, Sir William McKell from Australia, Justice B. Malik from India and Justice Abdul Hamid from Pakistan. The appointee from Canada withdrew at the last minute for health reasons (Simandjuntak 1969, p. 84).

This was the pivotal Reid Commission set up in March 1956. Lord Reid himself arrived in Malaya in May that year, a month before the other members. After consultations with the Tunku and the high commissioner, a public invitation was announced for all organizations and individuals who wished to do so to submit information and viewpoints to the commission. A total of 131 memoranda were received (Simandjuntak 1969, p. 85).

The commission had its first meeting on 19 June and recorded its intention not to be the cause of any eventual delay in the granting of independence (RC minutes). Its work involved studying submitted documents and interviewing a large variety of groups and individuals. By September 1956, it retired to prepare its report. After basing itself in Rome for four months, it handed over its findings to the British throne and to the sultans. In February 1957, the Reid Commission Report was published, and High Commissioner Donald MacGillivray immediately set up a working committee to prepare a draft formula for the British Government.

The Merdeka Compact that UMNO and the MCA worked out touched on many issues but the most time was devoted to the issues of citizenship, Malay special rights and language. UMNO had been withstanding pressure from the Chinese, especially from Tan Cheng Lock, but finally agreed to adopt the principle of *jus soli* in citizenship questions. This compromise was made in the face of opposition from influential Malay personalities such as Onn Ja'afar and second-level UMNO leaders such as Mohamed Haniffah. Besides pressure from Whitehall, the need to relent for the sake of national stability and the wish to gain concessions on issues of special rights and language helped change UMNO's mind. When the commission released its report, Onn Ja'afar organized what he chose to call the Second Malay Congress to protest the suggested time limit on Malay special rights and the idea that Chinese and Tamil would be given temporary status as official languages (Heng 1988, p. 225).

A constitutional conference was held on 13 May 1957 in London to discuss and amend the recommendations of the Reid Commission. The high commissioner, the secretary of the colonies, and representatives of the Alliance and the rulers were present. The outcome, in short, was that loyalty would dictate the terms of citizenship and the principle of *jus soli* was accepted, while the special position of the Malays was secured through the guardian institution of a paramount ruler — the *Yang di-Pertuan Agong*. No provision was made for a future review of the issue of Malay special rights, despite that being suggested by the commission. The recommendation for a limited use of Chinese and Tamil in the federal legislature was also rejected. Malay was to become the sole national and official language but with English being used as official language for a further ten years beyond independence (Simandjuntak 1969, pp. 84–92; Shaw 1976, pp. 108–11). Since there was insufficient time for general elections to be held before Independence Day, these were postponed to 1959.

With these compromises secured, the struggle for independence was won. The Tunku declared the founding of Malaya at the Selangor Padang in Kuala Lumpur on 31 August 1957, and the Union Jack was lowered over its soil forever.

Chapter 4

POSITIONING MALAYA
IN THE WORLD*

Shortly before Independence Day, the Tunku asked Ismail to become Malaya's first ambassador to the United States of America. He also wished him to double as Malaya's first permanent representative to the United Nations. It was thought important for Malaya to cultivate strong ties with the major power in the world. The United States furthermore represented "modern capitalism" in which Malaya's leaders placed their trust, in contradistinction to the purportedly "old capitalism" that had colonized the region. Ismail agreed to go, but only if it was for a year.

The choice, the Tunku told him, was between Razak and him, and frankly, Razak was badly needed as his deputy. Ismail's friends and relatives were appalled and saw the posting as a silently executed banishment. That thought did not seem to have crossed his own mind, however, and he actually felt satisfaction at being

---

* This chapter is largely based on details taken from Ismail's notes written on issues he encountered as ambassador. He hoped that the Tunku would find them informative and relevant at this early stage of Malayan nation-building. See *Notes by the Ambassador*, 30 December 1957 – 26 August 1958.

offered a position through which he could work at making "our newly independent country [...] known abroad".

> As is usual with me, when I took on the assignment I threw my heart and soul into the job. It was a tough assignment and not made any easier by the lack of prior government preparation. In fact, I had to set up the two missions from scratch (Drifting c13).

Ismail left on 15 July 1957 for the United States to acquire accommodation for the Washington embassy as well as the New York mission. He managed to purchase three buildings in Washington "to conform to our status" and also to secure a lease for an office in New York. Rushing through the chores of the trip, he thought it fortunate that he was now acting as a cabinet minister with the right to negotiate, and could therefore close deals quickly.

He was nevertheless surprised on his return on 21 August to Kuala Lumpur to discover that the cabinet had approved the acquisition of only two buildings. Since the cabinet happened to be meeting the same afternoon that he arrived, Ismail hastily rushed over to the sitting and managed to gain approval for the third building. Ismail would gripe over the fact that certain members of the cabinet had thought his purchases excessively expensive, especially when he was aware of how much higher sums other countries were then spending on their new American embassies.

Strangely, his feelings and thoughts about the Merdeka declaration and celebration on 31 August are not recorded.

As minister plenipotentiary (without portfolio), Ismail left again for the United States on 5 September with his party, which consisted of himself, Ismail bin Mohamed Ali, who was to be economic minister at the embassy, and "four women, nine children and thirty one pieces of luggage". The entourage included

Ismail's second daughter, Badariah, who was making her first inter-continental trip as a mere five-month-old baby. Special food had been prepared for them on the flight. This turned out to be generic curry, as were the specially ordered meals served them at their stopover hotel in Honolulu. Ismail was amused at this, but generally found the trip "partly nerve-racking, partly humorous but never dull".

Interestingly, Ismail Ali, who was three years Ismail's junior, was also one of the many Malayan scholars cut off from all contact with Malaya during the Japanese Occupation. In his case, he was in the middle of his studies in economics at Cambridge on a Queen's Scholarship, and had spent the war years studying law, acting as firewatcher during German raids, working for the British Broadcasting Corporation's Far Eastern Service, and finally teaching the Malay language to military personnel at London University's School of Oriental and African Studies (SOAS). His students were among the men recruited for the British Military Administration (BMA) that controlled Malaya immediately after the colonialists returned to the peninsula. He returned to Malaya in late 1948 (Chung 2002).

In a letter written to Oscar A. Spencer, economic adviser to the Prime Minister's Department in Kuala Lumpur, Ismail confided that his people, with the exception of Ismail Ali, were "inexperienced, and in the case of our UN office in New York, mediocre staff". The only member of the staff trained for the diplomatic service was the first secretary, 27-year-old Lim Taik Choon. Furthermore, Ismail noted that "other countries took at least a whole year to establish an Embassy alone and Nigeria has already had a representative here in Washington preparing for the establishment of an Embassy in anticipation of her independence, which, as far as I can judge, is not even in sight". (Incidentally, Nigeria gained independence on 1 October 1960).

> For the last three months my staff in Washington had to work
> in a building in which the work of renovating was going on at
> the same time, and I and my family had literally to camp with
> hired furniture in our Embassy, while waiting for it to be painted
> and furnished (Letters 18 December 1957).

His family suffered badly from the climate change. With "the dust
and noise of the workmen" renovating the buildings, they
developed skin diseases in the first months. The embassy was, and
is, housed at 2401 Massachusetts Avenue N.W., Washington D.C.

Ismail was worried that the treasury back home might be
objecting in strong terms to the expenses he was incurring,
although "I have done all that is humanly possible under the
circumstances and await patiently what is in store for me." In
those days of trial and error, the few officers stationed under him
in Washington and New York were forced to innovate, and they
devised a simplified code of communication. Interactions with
the foreign office in Kuala Lumpur were painfully slow, leading
them finally to make regular use of the phrase "if we don't hear
from you after such and such a time, we will assume that you
agree with our suggested lines of action". This meant that Ismail
could decide rather freely on matters relating to foreign affairs.

As a rule, Ismail kept an official diary and sent his notes
directly to the Tunku. He felt unsure about the Tunku's interest
in them, however, and said in a letter to the latter that "if you
think it is not useful to you and that you are too busy to read it,
please don't hesitate to say so and I shall stop sending it" (Letters
27 January 1958). Apparently, the Tunku did find them of interest,
since Ismail continued compiling his notes.

Ismail's very first appearance before the United Nations
general assembly was a proud and memorable moment for him.

> Our admission to the United Nations was spectacular. We all
> dressed in the national costume — or at least those of us who

had them. In addition, I had a *kris* tucked into my waist. This
was the first time that a weapon of any kind had been brought
into the General Assembly of the United Nations (Drifting c13).

The straightforward style of politics that Ismail was known for
back home aroused flustered reactions at the United Nations.
Already in his inaugural speech, he argued against the admission
of China into the world body on the grounds that Beijing was
exporting revolution and subversion to Malaya. This aroused the
anger of the Indian representative, the famous nationalist and
non-alignment advocate, V.K. Krishna Menon, who was known
for his strong support of the People's Republic of China. Menon
thought it regrettable that the representative of a new member
should make use of his maiden speech to propose the exclusion
of other nations. Ismail replied that the mere fact of being new
did not mean that Malaya would keep its mouth shut on matters
relating to its foreign affairs policy.

He also antagonized the Indonesian permanent representative,
Ali Sastrowidjojo, when he abstained from voting to include
the issue of West New Guinea on the agenda of the Twelfth
Plenary Session. The Indonesians had apparently been given
reason to expect Malayan support on the matter. However,
Ismail felt that he more than made up for it later on 22 November
when he spoke before the Political Committee. "My speech [...]
was so impassioned, so emotionally in favour of Indonesia that
the Indonesian delegates who heard it cried with emotion"
(Drifting c13).

Ismail thus spent the first sixteen months of Malaya's
independence — September 1957 to January 1959 — in the
United States. It was a trying time for him: "I have never
worked so hard in my life as I did during those years and it took
a lot out of me."

His day lasted eighteen to twenty hours, and included commuting three to four times a week between the two cities. It was also during this time that he evolved from being an inexperienced but enthusiastic international diplomat into a confident and polished expert on foreign affairs. Although he would later blame his early retirement in 1967 on the profound exhaustion he suffered during this period, he believed at the same time that much of what he learned then sharpened his ability to argue Malaysia's case against Indonesia in 1965 at the United Nations.

Zakaria Ali, who was posted to the United Nations at the end of 1958, remembers how things in those days had to be coded and ciphered and then decoded and deciphered, which took a lot of labour and time. The time difference — twelve hours — meant that the New York office would work hard after opening hours to prepare documents for sending to Kuala Lumpur by 9 p.m. New York time. Kuala Lumpur would thus receive them at 9 a.m. local time, and reply by 5 p.m., that is, 5 a.m. New York time, the following morning (Zakaria, interview 12 April 2006).

From the end of 1957 until at least August 1958, Ismail kept proper notes about his experiences in the United States. On 21 January 1958, while attending a farewell dinner for the Australian Ambassador and his wife, Ismail's wife Neno fainted "and was unconscious for half an hour".

Poor woman! She has had a busy day today, having to receive and make calls on three Ambassador's wives with shopping for the Embassy thrown in between. It seems that if my wife has to do onerous official duties as an Ambassador's wife, then she should be entitled too to enjoy the pleasant duties of an Ambassador such as accompanying him on official tours. In fact, this is what I intend to do, unless I receive instructions to the contrary.

Ismail also heard that oil drilling ventures in the Sinai peninsula reported finding reserves "which would surpass the areas in Saudi Arabia". Ismail commented that, if true, this would relieve Egypt's economic plight. He also wondered if this had not been one reason for "Israel's invasion of the Sinai peninsula [on 29 October 1956] and Britain's attack on Egypt over the Suez question [on 5 October 1956]" (Notes 29 January 1958).

On 6 January, Ismail visited the Afghan ambassador. The latter showed great interest in the fate of Singapore. Ismail reported home that he provided the ambassador with "the reasons why we could not take Singapore in". What these reasons were, were not noted down. In a gathering at the New Zealand Embassy the following day, the future of Singapore was again discussed. Ismail reported:

> The Ambassador [from New Zealand] was also interested in the future of Brunei, Sarawak and North Borneo. I said that in the long run there was bound to be a confederation of independent States which were under British colonialism and that if such a confederation materialised, then probably the problems of Singapore would be solved.

Ismail's comment suggests that the idea of forming a greater "Malaysia" was already in wide circulation and that, for him at least, the resolution of "the problems of Singapore" — and that of other British dominions in the region — was merely a matter of time.

On 20 January, Ismail called on the Korean ambassador, and was told by the latter that he "wanted to buy the present Malayan Embassy, but his country could not afford it". This must have pleased Ismail, who had been worried about the money he had spent on the three buildings for his dual mission. Later that day, Ismail visited the Japanese delegation. The Japanese ambassador wondered if his country could be granted most favoured nation treatment by Malaya.

Ismail and his wife attended the Roosevelt Day Dinner on 31 January, and were treated to a presentation by twice unsuccessful Democrat presidential candidate Adlai Ewing Stevenson II, whom Ismail found to be "a beautiful speaker". Since the guests of Mrs Franklin Roosevelt, among whom the couple was included, were seated in alphabetical order, Ismail [that is, Mr Rahman] happily found that he was placed next to the hostess.

An insurance agent called on Ismail on 6 February, and advised him not to inform his insurance doctor about his "rheumatic heart". Ismail was shocked at this and soundly rejected the idea, learning in the process that "one must not be too gullible when dealing with American businessmen".

Beyond the many international matters he had to attend to, Ismail had to deal with certain personnel problems. On 1 February, the office staff petitioned him that their office hours were longer than those at other missions. This irritated Ismail somewhat. Nevertheless, he asked Tunku Ja'afar — Ja'afar ibni Almarhum Tuanku Abdul Rahman, the first secretary and second son of the first Paramount King of Malaya, and who would in 1994 become Malaysia's tenth Paramount King — to investigate the matter. Tunku Ja'afar told him that there was a lack of officers to help him, to which Ismail retorted that Tunku Ja'afar in that case could put in more work himself since he was obviously prepared to carry some of his work home anyway. Friction between the two men would continue over the few months that they worked together. First Secretary Lim Taik Choon was often caught in between, and thought Ismail had a nasty nature. However, although Ismail often lost his temper, he would nevertheless ask for forgiveness afterwards. Tunku Ja'afar, in Lim's opinion, was "a likeable and fun character" to be with. Lim remembers that as a rule, Ismail required that the major American newspapers were made available for him to read at the beginning of each working day, and night meetings were also commonly held at the end of long working days (Interview 13 May 2006).

On 14 February, Ismail had to take his leave from an important meeting of the Afro-Asian bloc to fly back to Washington, and asked that Tunku Ja'afar stay behind so that he could later brief Ismail on the results of the meeting. A recently passed UN resolution on Algeria for a ceasefire was being discussed alongside the French bombing of Tunisian territory and Indonesia's domestic problems. On reaching Washington, Ismail learned that Tunku Ja'afar had already called to inform the office that since he was also leaving early to go to a cocktail party, he had sent a cable to the Ministry of External Affairs reporting on the meeting.

This infuriated Ismail, who found it unthinkable that Tunku Ja'afar would report home on important matters without running them past the permanent representative first. Thereupon, Ismail reported the matter home to "External". As a further shock to Ismail, the *New York Times* carried the story the following morning that the Afro-Asian Group had called on the secretary-general, Dag Hjalmar Hammarskjöld, to express its deep concern over the Algerian situation. This committee had consisted of representatives from Indonesia, Tunisia, Ceylon, Ethiopia and Burma — but not Malaya. The newspaper also reported that the Security Council would meet in three days' time to discuss the Tunisian question. Exasperated, Ismail wrote tersely in his report: "No news from Tunku Ja'afar. I give up trying to 'take this man under my wings'" (Notes 15 February 1958). Apparently, the prime minister had earlier asked Ismail to mentor the young man.

At a dinner on 19 February, Ismail was upset by "an unfortunate incident" that spoiled the event for him. He was given a card on arrival on which was stated the name of the lady he was to escort that evening. Not knowing who she was, Ismail turned to the first person who happened to pass by to enquire. This happened to be the Israeli ambassador. Ismail was almost immediately interrupted by the Syrian *charge d'affaires* and pulled over to "a group of Ambassadors from Arab States". There, the Syrian gentleman proceeded to lecture him in public on "the impropriety of my action in having indulged in social intercourse with the Ambassador of Israel". Ismail's attempts to explain himself were brushed aside, making it necessary for him to send a written memo the following morning to the Syrian gentleman.

During the last week of February, he left with Lim Taik Choon for New Orleans to start a tour of the southern states. They visited the Shell oil refinery outside New Orleans on 22 February and the Kaiser Aluminium Factory the following day. Ismail found them both well organized and "streamlined". On the afternoon of 23 February they were taken to see some horse racing. While the grandstand was "not unlike those one sees in Malaya", the latrines were unique and had signs stating "Whites only".

> I went into one of them, but was not molested. Evidently, 'coloured' in the South means Negroes or those who could be mistaken for Negroes. There were also Negroes among the race-goers but not one of them entered into any of these latrines for Whites only. Either they have a huge urinary bladder or they must have strained themselves, because the weather was cold and no one could possibly go through the afternoon without emptying his bladder.

The next day was spent cruising the Mississippi and watching boats flying numerous national flags anchored along the wharves.

Ismail was amused by the commentator on the cruise referring to his country as "the Malaya States".

Ismail was "pleasantly surprised" the next day when he called on the mayor and was presented with "a certificate and a gold key making me a free citizen of New Orleans". While impressed by how the city had retained traces of its past colonial masters especially the French, he found that the population exhibited the prejudices that "the Southerners have of the negroes".

> These prejudices are difficult to eradicate, because they are based on fear and emotion, totally devoid of reason. For example, one of the taxi drivers who drove us was asked by me why he disliked Negroes. His reply was that he was not obliged to give his reasons. It was enough that he hated them and that they bred like flies.

Ismail and Lim also visited the Naval Air Training School in Pensacola, Florida, where they were shown "superb hospitality" by the admiral in charge, who even organized a cocktail party in their honour. Besides Americans, the school was also training Iranians and Pakistanis.

The pair then flew to Jacksonville where they hired a car to drive up to Melbourne, halfway to Miami: "All along the way we passed scenery which is sub-tropical and made me nostalgic of Malaya". The 500-kilometre trip from Melbourne to Miami that followed was on the other hand "monotonous in its scenery" and they avoided making any break in their journey.

Once back in New York, Ismail decided to catch up on his paperwork. He was agitated when Tunku Ja'afar brought to his attention an enquiry made by the Ministry of External Affairs in October 1957 into security arrangements at the office. Flabbergasted that Tunku Ja'afar had sat on the matter for so long, he went to examine the strong room and was appalled to learn that neither Tunku Ja'afar nor the second secretary were able to work the combination lock. Furthermore, Tunku Ja'afar had already drafted a reply on his own to be sent to the ministry and wanted Ismail to sign it.

> When I read that the External Affairs letter instructed that the reply should be only routed through me, I told him to comply with the instruction. I have ceased to be angry with Tunku Ja'afar, because it would only affect my blood pressure. He seems impervious to correction.

Ismail's responsibilities as ambassador included giving talks to ready audiences. On 4 March, he gave a speech on Malaya's economy, geography and federal constitution to a graduate association at New York University, together with representatives from Japan and Ghana.

On 7 March, Ismail had to get up especially early for the sake of the United Nations Film Unit which was making a film about "A Day in the Life of the Ambassador of the Federation of Malaya". That evening, Ismail, accompanied by Ismail Ali and Tunku Ja'afar, went to the State Department where he officially signed Malaya's entry into the International Bank of Reconstruction and Development (IBRD) and the International Monetary Fund (IMF) (Sodhy 1991, p. 191).

Between 13 and 18 March, Ismail and Ismail Ali went on a tour of the Midwest. They started with a visit to Anderson College, just outside Minneapolis. After being met at the Indianapolis airport by the president of the college and two Malayans — Dr Loh and Dr Ong — they were escorted 72 kilometres to the college by state police cars, which made full use of their sirens all the way, "thereby drawing public attention to us". Ismail noted that the town of Anderson was "the home of General Motors", and "practically all the people other than shopkeepers earn their livelihood at General Motors factories". After a short rest at their hotel, he was rushed off to give a talk at the Lions Club, and was especially amused to learn that "Lions" stood for Liberty Intelligence Our Nation's Salvation.

The questions raised following his speech on "how [Malaya] achieved its Independence, its Constitution, its economy and where it resembles USA", were generally about Malaya's willingness to join the Southeast Asian Treaty Organization (Seato), the Emergency, and the relationship between Malaya and Great Britain in the areas of finance and defence. On the first issue, Ismail referred to the Tunku's statement that Seato would be a question for the population to decide on at the next elections. On the Emergency, he again repeated a statement made by the Tunku hoping that the conflict would end by the first anniversary of Malayan independence. Where Great Britain was concerned, Ismail argued that "we are now a full sovereign nation and whatever ties there are between us and Great Britain are mutually agreed upon on terms of equality without in any way involving any sacrifice of sovereignty on our part".

On 14 March, the duo left the hotel at 7.30a.m. for a reception organized by the Mayor's Committee for a discussion about the United Nations. It was necessary to hold this event at such an early hour because "the members of the committee were working men and had to be at work". After breakfast, Ismail gave the same talk he had given at the Lions Club the night before to several hundred students at Anderson College. Another speech was required of him later at lunch, after which they left for Indianapolis in Dr Ong's car to travel further that evening all the way to Chicago.

That night, they stayed at Chicago's Conrad Hilton, the largest hotel in the world at the time. From there they saw the finer parts of the city bordering Lake Michigan. On the evening of 15 March, Ismail hosted a dinner for the committee members of the Malayan Students Association. The issue that concerned this group, which called itself The Cabinet, was the fact that the Malayan Government had not made any decision on American academic degrees.

> I was told by them that quite a number of Malayans who have American degrees in Engineering and Medicine are anxiously waiting. They wanted to go home and render their services to the country either in Government service or in industry, but they could not do so because their degrees are not recognised; on the other hand, they have been given tempting offers to join American firms, which if they accept would make them American citizens in the long run, and this latter prospect they are not too keen [upon]. They are Malayans and they want to render their services to Independent Malaya.

Ismail sympathized with them, and suggested that Kuala Lumpur discard its colonial policy of recognizing only British degrees. He was generally very impressed by the Malayan students he met: "The thing that moved me most was their loyalty and their pride in our Independence. All this, coming from students, who are all Chinese, augurs well for the future of Malaya."

A visit to Skids Row the next day provided them with a more distressing view of Chicago.

> [Skids Row] is a street infested with incurable drunkards. They spend the whole day either drinking or begging. Then we went to the slums. The buildings here are dilapidated and the rooms are divided into cubicles where the inhabitants sleep covered with newspapers as blankets. The majority of these people are negroes.

The trip continued to Akron where they, as guests of the Rubber Manufacturers Organization, were given an "excellent" tour of the "Akron rubber world". They visited Goodyear's tyre factory, Goodrich Company, which produced rubber goods of various kinds, and the Firestone research laboratory. Two things struck him most after his conversations with executives of these companies. One was that "foreign investment looks on the stability of both the Government of the country and the country itself", and the other was how important "the international economic standing of the country" was to investors.

He also gave a press interview in which he talked about "our effort to streamline our [rubber] industry and to attract foreign capital". He considered American capitalism a "modern capitalism" that would benefit investors as well as domestic labour and the country as a whole.

On 2 April, Ismail attended a conference in New York organized by the Association of Asian Studies (AAS). On the first day of the conference, India's economic development was discussed, and he was treated to a strong criticism of its Second Five Year Plan. Ismail's reactions to this are of interest, given the central role he was to play later both in the corporate world and in the socio-economic planning of Malaysia's future.

> My impression is that India attempted to carry out her Second Five Year Plan using both private and State enterprises and the aim is to create a mixed economy of large and small industries linked to the cottage industries. To achieve this, various agencies were set up. In some cases subsidies were given, in others loans of varying interest rates were given, but in none was there a complete "hand-out". It is interesting to note that the States do not live up to the expectation of the Central Government in raising taxes to finance their share of the Plan. The local politicians, who, although belonging to the same party —

Congress Party —, are looking after their own interests, particularly their popularity with the electorate. This sounds a familiar ring to me.

Ismail went back the next day to listen to Norman Palmer of the University of Maryland speak about "Recent Constitutional Developments in Malaya". Aghast at Palmer's "incoherent and irrelevant speech" filled with views unsupported by any "quotation or a reference to the Constitution", Ismail decided not to stay for the discussion: "It would take another speech from me to correct him." Ismail generously thought that it was probably because Palmer had left Malaya in 1954 that he was "totally ignorant of the most crucial and formative period for Malayan politics — that period between 1954 to 1955".

On 15 April, Ismail had a discussion with the Ambassador of the Netherlands over the telephone. An interesting topic that was mentioned concerned American recognition of Communist China. Ismail opined that such a thing would not be to Malaya's advantage: "So long as Communist China is 'illegal', so long will our efforts to finish off the Emergency be made easier." When quizzed about the fact that Malaya did not recognize Taiwan either, he replied that the neutral position that Malaya had adopted provided her with "a great chance of avoiding ideological conflicts taking place on our soil and also giving the Chinese in Malaya the best chance of being loyal to Malaya".

Ismail was regularly invited to give speeches at dinners and conferences. His audiences would range from "old ladies of means whose pastime is to broaden their knowledge of the world by attending 'talks'" to "men from the Pentagon and officials from the State Department". On 17–18 April, he attended a two-day conference in Milwaukee and spoke on how a newly formed nation such as Malaya viewed American capital, and touched mainly on "our Development Plan and the Federation's attempt

to orientate its economy from a colonial one to that befitting an
independent nation". On that occasion, he was happily
overwhelmed by a presentation on Malayan economic planning
given by H.H. King of Harvard University, who "gave an accurate
description of our Five-Year Development Plan, and his
commentary on it was remarkable for its deep insight into the
problems now confronting Malaya".

Tunku Ja'afar arrived back from leave in Kuala Lumpur on
26 April, and informed Ismail that subject to his agreement, the
prime minister had agreed to his transfer to London. Ismail said
he had no objection. It had already been decided that Mohammad
Sopiee Sheik Ibrahim would succeed him.

The issue of founding a Malayan national bank turns up
every now and then in Ismail's notes, as do rumours of an
impending Malayan application for an American loan to help
finance Malaya's Development Plan. Ismail was repeatedly told
by American businessmen that American capital would become a
major player in Malaya only after the establishment of a national
bank. Various businessmen, including John D. Rockefeller III,
and administrative officials were convinced that nothing would
happen before such an institution had been established. Ismail
accordingly encouraged the Tunku to accept that advice.

Pieces of news that Ismail had on several occasions since
early January been given by U.S. State Department sources
suggested that the U.S. ambassador in Kuala Lumpur was
discussing a loan with the Tunku, that Tan Siew Sin was in an
advanced stage of negotiations for a US$20 million loan, and
that Razak was seeking a US$60 million loan for village
development. On 9 February, when Ismail invited Eric Kocher,
the Director of Southeast Asian Affairs in the American State
Department, to the embassy to discuss the subject of loans, he
learned that the Tunku was planning to visit Washington to

negotiate a loan for village development and that the American embassy in Kuala Lumpur had been told to discourage the Tunku from doing so since the State Department did not think the application would be successful. According to Kocher, "Congress would only agree to give loans on sound economic basis."

On 1 May, Ismail had a conversation with Rockefeller, an "unassuming man" by whom he was "deeply impressed". On being asked whether American capital would widen the gap between the Chinese and the Malays, Ismail replied that "the backwardness of the Malays in the economic sector was due to the past policy of the British Administration to absorb all Malays into Government service". He further noted:

> On the East Coast of Malaya, Malays have been engaged in business for quite a long time and it is more urgent now than ever before that these Malays should learn the "know-how" of modern business, if they were to successfully compete with the others in the economic life of the country. This is where American capital with its modern outlook, which enables investors, labour, and the country to benefit, can play a useful role in helping the Malays. Further, as [Rockefeller] himself had mentioned, British investment in Malaya is not meeting with much competition and as a result has the monopoly in the Federation. For the sake of private enterprise, which really thrives on competition, and for the sake of British investment itself, it is necessary to introduce American capital in order to stimulate competition. Mr Rockefeller agreed with my contention.

Ismail finally heard personally from the Tunku that the government was indeed seeking a huge loan from the Eisenhower administration, and he was also informed that the Tunku feared that a direct request from Malaya's prime minister and external affairs minister would appear somewhat undignified. Should the request be turned down, both Washington and Kuala Lumpur would be placed in an embarrassing position. The Tunku's solution to this dilemma was for Ismail to present Malaya's case verbally to the American secretary of state. Apparently, such a procedure was unprecedented where American protocol was concerned. Similar requests by an ambassador were normally forwarded to the assistant secretary responsible for the region in which his or her country was situated, and not to the secretary of state. The sum Malaya officially requested as of 30 April 1958 was US$19 million, earmarked both for a Klang wharf extension and for a teaching hospital project.

Ismail also learned at this time that the process for creating a national bank had gone into high gear back home. This pleased him greatly, since it accorded with what he had learned about the economics of nation-building.

> Central Bank is one of the attributes of Independence. Until a central bank is established we are not independent financially, and it is idle to talk of attracting foreign capital other than capital from Commonwealth countries. Americans, whom I have met, are chary of doing business unless we are financially independent of UK.

Razak, busy acting as prime minister while the Tunku was away in Tokyo, wrote a long reply to Ismail at this time (Letters 28 May 1958):

> I thank you very much for your note and advice on the question of the establishment of a Central Bank. On receipt of your letter I immediately talked to Spencer and got H.S. Lee to put a paper to the Cabinet. You will by now have seen the Cabinet Paper on the subject and Cabinet has now firmly decided that a Central Bank should be established by the 1st January 1959 — the date you suggested in your letter.

In the event, parliament passed the Central Bank Ordinance of Malaya on 23 October 1958, and Bank Negara was formally established on 26 January the following year.

On Monday 5 May 1958, Ismail arrived at New York airport with Ismail Ali to find that the chromium wheel covers of the official car were missing. He learned that they had disappeared over the weekend after Tunku Ja'afar had left the car at the airport when he went on a trip to St Louis the Friday before. It also turned out that Tunku Ja'afar — now planning his departure — had not been able to attain a release from his house rental contract. He had signed a two-year deal on his luxurious place which, Ismail lamented, was "certainly not suitable for a diplomat". Furthermore, it was situated at an unnecessarily long distance from work. As things looked, his successor, Mohammad Sopiee, would now be forced to take over the contract.

Ismail also noted that Ismail Ali — "who is a senior official and a very capable one" — had had to leave Washington for Kuala Lumpur on two occasions in eight months in order to lead delegations from Malaya to various conferences. He therefore suggested that since the country had not finished with its preparation for attracting American capital anyway, Ismail Ali "should return to Malaya to assume a post worthy of his ability". Razak wrote to inform Ismail that he was dealing with the matter and was looking for a suitable position. According to Lim Taik Choon, the relationship between Ismail and Ismail Ali at this time was characterized by mutual respect — Ismail Ali was famous for his writing skills — and mutual irritation (Lim, interview 13 May 2006).

The two Ismails had much in common, including their love for the fine arts and for literature. With some prodding from Ismail Ali, Ismail became a lifelong member of the Book of the

Month Club. He was also known to have a veritable and eclectic collection of various kinds of music records.

Significantly, the ambassador's residence was bought off the family of Gore Vidal, the famous American novelist, essayist and playwright. Vidal was having great success on Broadway with his play "Visit to a Small Planet" in 1957–58 when the two Ismails came to the United States (Tawfik, interview 21 July 2006; IBDB). During Ismail's term as ambassador, he paid frequent visits to art exhibitions with Neno, and the ambassador's residence would acquire and display works by Malaysian artists such as Yong Mun Seng and Arif. These are now among the more valuable items in the embassy's possession (Tawfik, interview 21 July 2006).

Overburdened with work and dealing endlessly with the uncertainties involved in representing a newly independent country, Ismail finally began to entertain the notion that his posting to Washington and New York was an exile. Razak wrote to reassure Ismail that the Tunku "does not have such a thought in his mind". Apparently, Ismail Ali had informed Razak about Ismail's bad health and suspicions.

On May 13, Ismail lunched at his office in New York with several bankers including the esteemed retired expert on central banks, Thomas H. McKittrick of Chase Manhattan. Ismail was very impressed by McKittrick's knowledge and simplicity: "What a wonderful man to get as first Governor of our Central Bank". Incidentally, Australian W.H. Wilcock would be the one chosen as the transitional first governor of Bank Negara in January 1959 while Ismail Ali would serve as his deputy for two years. After taking over the position in July 1962, however, Ismail Ali would adopt a more nationalistic position and become "increasingly independent of his cautious Australian advisers" (White 2004, p. 70). He would remain bank governor until July

1980. According to Malaysian tycoon Tan Chin Nam, Ismail would later say that corruption in Malaysia could have been curbed if Ismail Ali had returned earlier from his posting in Washington (Tan 2006, p. 208).

Between 21 and 25 May 1958, Ismail and his wife went on a tour of Texas. Dallas airport which had recently been opened, "is the finest I have seen", Ismail said. He was also amazed at the wealth of the Texans, as was evident in the size of their ranches and in the ubiquity of their oil wells. He also had the opportunity to listen to Under-Secretary of State Christian Herter speak in defence of American foreign aid. Ismail, who had "always had an admiration for Herter", felt that "it was good that USA has leaders like him". Incidentally, Herter became secretary of state the following year.

After much difficulty, Ismail finally managed to get an interview with Secretary of State John Foster Dulles. Accompanied by Lim Taik Choon, he went to the State Department at noon on 26 May. In his report sent home the same day, he said that Dulles, infamous for his opposition to communism, "was very sympathetic and deeply appreciated our stand against Communism, [but was] staggered to hear of the amount for which we have applied". On learning that Malaya was requesting a loan of M$455 million, Dulles made the sharp remark that "USA resources were not unlimited". In Malaya's defence, Ismail pointed out in his ten-minute presentation that Malaya was running on a budget deficit of M$150 million and M$160 million for the years 1958 and 1959 respectively. Dulles wondered whether Malaya was aware of the enormous size of the American budget deficit. Ismail retorted that once the central bank was set up and once no resources were needed in a fight against communism, Malaya "would also be able to get along with budgetary deficits [the way] the USA [did]".

Ismail decided to argue by using "the political aspect" of Malaya's continuing fight against its communist guerrillas. He claimed that the communists were conscious of the fact that their armed battle had failed, and were now "resorting to a new tactic, that of pinning down the Government to the present level of expenditure on the Emergency, which is running at the current rate of \$126 million annually, so that it cannot continue to implement its Development Plan", that is, the First Malaya Plan (1956–60). The government's strategy, in turn, was to defeat communism through economic development aided by Western financial support. Ismail told Dulles:

> With elections only a year ahead and if it becomes clear, as it certainly will, that the cost of fighting the Emergency is a major factor preventing the Government from carrying out its Development Plan, then there certainly will be pressure for recognition of the Communist Party, which is all the Communists say they want as a condition for giving up the fight. Further, the Soviet Union, in anticipation of Government difficulties, is not slow to put its finger on the political pulse of the country, for at the last Conference of ECAFE [the United Nations' Economic Commission for Asia and the Far East] at Kuala Lumpur, the Soviet Delegation made feelers of financial help, which was promptly turned down by my Prime Minister. Without the aid of the Government of the United States to rescue the Development Plan, the present Government cannot be certain that it will be returned to power with an effective majority in Parliament at the 1959 elections (Letters 26 March 1958).

To strengthen Malaya's chances for a loan, Ismail provided three reasons why it would be but a once-only affair:

> (1) The Communists in the jungles are all but beaten. If the present Government's policy of attacking on two fronts — the

economic and the military — is pressed forward, the Emergency
as such will end, at the latest in two years' time; (2) further
increases in taxation will then be possible and the Government
will be prepared to raise them if necessary; and (3) the
establishment of a Central Bank will facilitate the expansion of
the floating debt on a sound basis and assist the government
in its long-term operations.

Dulles referred Ismail to Clarence Douglas Dillon, the under-
secretary of state for economic affairs whom Ismail considered
"an extremely able economist", and who had in an earlier meeting
with Ismail given the latter "the impression of quiet efficiency".
Ismail promised the Tunku that he would do his best to convince
Dillon to support Malaya's application. Nevertheless, he appeared
pessimistic about the outcome. At that time, Ismail was on his
way to a three-week World Health Organization (WHO) meeting
in Minneapolis at which he had decided that he would only stay
a week. He told the Tunku:

> I am getting tired and weary with rushing about. I would like
> with your permission to take 3–4 weeks holiday here in America,
> once the loan negotiation is settled (Letters 26 May 1958).

The meeting with Dulles made Ismail miss the first day of Malaya's
attendance at its first WHO meeting in Minneapolis. Ismail rushed
over the following day, and to his great embarrassment found that
the second Malayan delegate to the conference, Dr Mohamed Din,
deputy director of medical services, had not arrived. Thus, for
almost the whole of the two-day commemorative session of WHO's
tenth anniversary, "our seats were vacant and very noticeable,
since we were a new member". Furthermore, that afternoon, he
had no credentials to submit to the other delegates, and thought
that it created "a bad impression for our country, which had just
been admitted as a member". He found it incomprehensible that

his credentials could not have been sent earlier, without them having to be carried by Dr Din.

He met Dr Din on the latter's arrival that evening and was "appalled to hear that he had brought no briefs with him". The following morning, Ismail gave a hurried speech about Malaya's new membership, after which he had to leave. He advised Dr Din to "make an attempt to speak at the forthcoming meetings of the Session, because, firstly as a new member we must make ourselves heard and, secondly, since our contribution is much bigger than other countries, we must at least make our needs clear to other member countries".

He then rushed off to Washington. On 2 June, he was back in New York to discuss with Sopiee the problems he foresaw the latter would have in taking over from Tunku Ja'afar. He also learned from Sopiee that "quite a number of decisions" had been made by Tunku Ja'afar without his approval. This, Ismail informed Sopiee, did not surprise him. The two decided that they must "regularise matters" after Tunku Ja'afar's departure. That evening, a farewell party was given for Tunku Ja'afar and his wife. The following evening, Ismail and his wife hosted a party celebrating the birthday of Malaya's paramount ruler, incidentally Tunku Ja'afar's father. Ismail was again to be disappointed:

> "With the exception of Sopiee, Lim the Second Secretary, and Kumar the Document Officer, all the other members of the staff arrived late. Tunku Ja'afar and his wife excused themselves by saying that they were busy packing as they were leaving the next day. There was no announcer, so that I and my wife had either to pretend to know or to ask the guests their names. It was most embarrassing. The whole party was arranged by one person — Miss Watson, the stenographer".

In contrast to the reception in New York, the royal birthday celebrations held at the embassy in Washington the next evening "was a superb party". The ambassador was very happy with his staff there, which had worked "as a team to make the function a success".

Ismail met Dillon, the American under-secretary of state for economic affairs, on 4 June. Again, Ismail stressed that should any help be granted, it would be "once and for all". There was a real danger, he told the Americans present, that a cutback in development programmes on the eve of the general elections would cost the Alliance an effective majority. A resultant coalition outside of the Alliance would raise demands for a truce with the communists, which would almost certainly mean recognition of the Communist Party. Should things go that far, then the "demand for the acceptance of help from USSR would be irresistible". Dillon informed Ismail that since Malaya faced a "cash crisis, and not a balance of payment or foreign exchange crisis, help from the IMF and the Import and Export Bank is precluded". Government-to-government loans were also not possible. Some kind of help could be arranged, nevertheless, but only after the Americans had analysed the development plan.

On leaving Dillon's office, Ismail continued discussions in the room of Eric Kocher, the director of Southeast Asian affairs in the American State Department. Anthony C. Swezey, also of the State Department, and Lim Taik Choon were also present.

The conclusion reached was that economists at the American Embassy in Kuala Lumpur should be asked to analyse the development plan. Ismail sent a telegram home to advise his colleagues that "besides working on the specific projects already in the plan, Federation should propose to Americans additional specific repeat SPECIFIC projects concerning police and defence, as was done in Burma" (Letters 17 June 1958). He emphasized at least three times in one letter the importance of providing the Americans with "Specific Projects of Security". In reply, Kuala Lumpur asked him to investigate the Burmese case further.

Ismail felt it necessary to keep the British ambassador informed about the loan proceedings at this point. He therefore promised Sir Harold Caccia when the latter came over to the Malayan Embassy on 13 June, to supply him with copies of the relevant documents. These were dispatched to the British the following week.*

In June, Ismail decided to holiday at Cape Cod with his family in their own car for a fortnight. They spent the last two days before the break enjoying New York while Ismail tied up some loose ends. He had noticed that Sopiee was churning out work for him to do "and introducing order and discipline in the office".

Ismail and his wife took the opportunity to go to the theatre with "the Delsons". Robert Delson had been the Indonesian republic's legal adviser in America since 1947, and was actively involved in the Indonesian independence movement. He informed Ismail that a cabinet reshuffle in Indonesia was imminent. On learning about Malaya's loan application, he offered Ismail his services should they be required.

On Saturday 21 June, Ismail and his family left for Cape Cod and returned only on 7 July. The only clear memory that Tawfik Ismail, who was then six years old, has of this family holiday was that they stayed with the Bugbees, a pleasant family who was involved in the rubber trade. Ismail was back at work in Washington on 8 July.

Two days after that, he was in New York. There he signed a sponsorship for an application to include the issue of Algeria on the agenda of the upcoming thirteenth UN General Assembly. He was also asked by the Indian representative to sponsor a joint

---

* Incidentally, Caccia is credited with the famous quotation purportedly made while he was British ambassador in Washington: "If you are to stand up *for* your government you must be able to stand up *to* your government" (*Columbia World of Quotations* 1996).

application to include the question of racial conflict in South Africa. Ismail studied the proposal with Sopiee and eventually agreed to do so, although he felt it necessary to make it clear to the Indians that Malaya was not committing herself to any definite future direction on the subject.

Sopiee had at his own initiative been putting out feelers to see if there was sufficient support for Malaya to be elected a vice president at the UN. Ismail was doubtful when the suggestion was put to him and asked to be given some time to think the matter over. The next day, he informed Sopiee that a vice presidency for Malaya would not be a good idea. He thought it somewhat presumptuous for a new member "to aspire to such a prestige-bearing post". Furthermore, he was unsure about support from the Afro-Asian Group since Malaya's relations with it had been "marked with hesitancy", and this could not have escaped its members whose support would be needed.

Ismail then took a flight back to Washington. This time, instead of the normal one hour, the trip took four hours because of diversions caused by wintry conditions. This happened quite occasionally and Ismail had recently asked for transport insurance for his personnel but had not received any reply.

Soon after that, Ismail managed to arrange an interview with the Burmese ambassador — Burma and Cambodia were major beneficiaries of American aid to Southeast Asia at that time — and learned that Burma's successful request for American aid "concentrated on the expansion of the police force for a definite period, and I believe he mentioned 3 years". A detailed programme of the "amount and type of equipment, the size of the forces, training schemes, etc, was given".

There were indeed signs at this time that popular support for the Alliance government was weakening, causing the Americans some worry. An American policy paper from 28 May 1958 stated:

"This deterioration of the [Malayan] government's political strength, particularly among Chinese and Indian voters supporting neutralist-oriented parties favouring recognition of Communist China and the Malayan Communist Party, could neutralize the progress made in achieving US objectives in Malaya" (Sodhy 1991, p. 189).

In the middle of July, the Security Council was totally engrossed in events happening in the Middle East. American troops had landed in Lebanon and British soldiers had done the same in Jordan. Officially, the Lebanese and Jordanian governments had asked for their assistance in resisting aggression from the newly formed United Arab Republic (UAR) under the Arab pan-nationalist Gamal Abdel-Nasser. The UAR was created by Egypt and Syria in 1957. On being joined by North Yemen in March 1958, it was renamed United Arab States, and lasted only until 1961. Around this highly explosive issue, Ismail jotted down a rare analysis of world politics and some views on big power diplomacy.

It is my belief that America had gone into Lebanon because she was sure that the success of the [republican] revolution in Iraq [on 14 July] would be followed by revolutions in Jordan and in Lebanon, and without the presence of her troops in Lebanon these revolutions would have succeeded. She was convinced that these revolutions were designed, encouraged and supported by the UAR. The British, of course, supported the American action, because she knew that if Jordan and Lebanon went the same way as Iraq, she might as well say good-bye to the Middle East oil.

Without doubt events in the Middle East are manifestations of Arab nationalism, which is personified in Nasser. It has taken a violent form, because peaceful, democratic means of expression [were] denied to it by the support which Western Powers had given to feudalism in the region. It is indeed a sad fact that

Americans, who believe in nationalism, had to fight it in defence of Imperialism and Feudalism.

The question now is how far [...] nationalism, once it has assumed a destructive form, [can] go? Can it be induced to assume a constructive form? As to the first question, I am definite it will spread far and wide, bringing misery and destruction in its path, before finally dying out. As to the second question, I am sure it can, provided America uses her strength and influence against Imperialism and Feudalism, or at the very least refusing to support them and supporting nationalism instead. However, unfortunately, solutions to international problems have to take into account such questions as Alliances and sensitivity of members of the Alliances. The American foreign policy is based on the containment of the Communists, and it was in pursuance of this policy that regional pacts such as NATO and SEATO were formed and the Eisenhower Doctrine was formulated. The premise, on which this policy was based, was that if Communist aggression is halted, two things would happen. Firstly, negotiations on international problems, such as Disarmament and the Middle East questions, could be entered into with the Russians, who would only negotiate if they know that they have been thwarted in their aims by armed resistance. Secondly, ultimately the Russian people would get tired of futile Russian expansionist policy and would start a movement of liberalising the regime and thereby changing Russian policy [towards being] more suited to peaceful co-existence. The motive of [the] American policy of containment is self-preservation. Americans have no imperialistic designs, and of this I am convinced. However, implementation of this policy as manifested in regional pacts, which I have mentioned above, attract strange bedfellows. The British, the Dutch, the French and the Belgians are all colonial powers and they expect the Americans to support them, or at the very least to remain neutral when colonial problems crop up. Therefore, resentment against Americans [is] based on this fact. Many Afro-Asian countries, such as Indonesia [and] the Arab countries, are antagonistic towards Americans, because Americans either remain neutral or move in support of colonial powers or forces which are allied to colonial powers, such as the decadent Arab monarchs and corrupt governments.

Lobbyists were active at the UN that July. Sopiee "was in his element, and what he lacked in experience he made up for it in enthusiasm", noted Ismail, who was watching his new assistant from the sidelines. He saw that his new staff member had taken "great pains [...] to create the impression that he is a loyal civil servant, prepared to submerge his own feelings and views, in order to carry out impartially the official policy and instructions from the Chief of Mission". The tone of suspicion probably stemmed from the known fact that Sopiee was a founder-member of the Malayan Labour Party, and his views were therefore generally more leftist than those publicized by the Tunku's regime that both he and Ismail officially served (Lee 2001, p. 34; Lim 2005, p. 111).

Ismail thought that except for a single occasion, Sopiee succeeded very well in this difficult endeavour to remain neutral. Sopiee once "succumbed" to the temptation of adding an extra paragraph to a press release on the government's guarded stand on the situation in the Middle East. That paragraph was meant to inform Malaya's missions abroad that the prime minister had telephoned the British High Commission and the American Embassy "to express his deep concern at the landing of American and British troops in Lebanon and Jordan respectively". Added to the subsequent press release, this information injected a sharp tone that would not have been there otherwise. When confronted with this by Ismail, Sopiee explained that he mistook the extra paragraph for part of the release. Ismail did not accept this explanation, however. He said instead that if it had come from "a person of lesser intelligence than him, I would have accepted the excuse".

In the event, Ismail warned his government that its "policy of neutralism" was difficult to implement, and required "constant vigilance and fine judgment". There was furthermore always a risk that it could be accused of "neutralism partial to certain countries".

In August, Ismail wrote a private letter to the Tunku where he expressed his worry that Malayans who had not lived in their constituencies for six months prior to the coming general elections might not be eligible to vote, or to contest seats. Partly for this reason and also because he had kept his end of the bargain with the Tunku that he would be Malaya's ambassador to the United States for only a year, he wished to return home by January 1959. Elections were due sometime in July or August that year. January was also a good time for him to leave his post because the United Nations' General Assembly would be ending in the middle of December, and there would be sufficient time for the Tunku to find an appropriate successor as ambassador to the United States. Ismail sought to give some advice to the Tunku on the latter matter.

> One qualification is very essential. A person must be very loyal to the party in power and must be trusted to carry fully the policy of the government, and not a variation of that policy. It is so easy if one is not absolutely loyal to vary a government policy without the government knowing about it until it is too late to repair the damage. I think it is preferable at this stage of the history of our country to have a Malay as our Ambassador to Washington and Permanent Representative to the UN. It is for this reason that, as you know, I fought both tooth and nail

for adequate cost of living and thanks to you and the other
Ministers of the Cabinet the recently approved cost of living is
sufficient for a person without private means to be our country's
Ambassador to Washington.

In the same letter to the Tunku, he mentioned a trip to Vancouver,
Canada, that he and Ismail Ali had made to attend a five-day
seminar held between 28 July and 1 August. This was sponsored
by the Extension Branch of the University of British Columbia.
Ismail found Vancouver "a beautiful city", but thought the
conference somewhat exasperating.

> It was just as well that I went because the representative from
> the University of Malaya was a young English woman whose
> knowledge of Malaya was based on her reading of publications
> in English, which as you know lack insight into the problems
> which faced Malaya before Independence. I was able to give our
> side of the story (Letters, undated).

The young scholar he alluded to was anthropologist Constance
Mary Turnbull, who was at that time attached to the Department
of History at the University of Malaya in Singapore (*UBC Reports*,
May 1958). Her sources, Ismail lamented, "were either the official
files of the former Chief Secretary's Office or the English
newspapers". He proudly stated that "we were able to correct any
misconception Miss Turnbull consciously or unconsciously tried
to tell about the Federation of Malaya."

Another matter that concerned him during his hectic year as
ambassador to Washington was the government's policy
concerning foreign capital. In a discussion with the minister of
commerce and industry, Tan Siew Sin, Ismail sought to achieve a
common stand on the issue since his office often had to deal
with enquiries from potential American investors.

As I understand the position, our general policy at present appears to be that the government welcomes foreign capital for the industrial development of the country and since we believe in private enterprise, we do not seek to impose any control on the type or extent of private capital investment from outside. To attract foreign capital into *new* industries, we have taken legislative measures to confer certain income tax concessions on these new industries on the basis of their pioneer status. Consideration in the granting of these concessions would be based on an order of priority, provided all other things are equal, giving local capital first priority, local capital associated with foreign capital second priority and foreign capital by itself third priority (Letters, undated).

By August, Ismail was feeling very happy with his staff. He wrote to the Tunku complimenting "Cypher Clerk" Miss Khoo for the long hours she put into her work, Sopiee who was "tireless and energy itself", and Ismail Ali for "the ease and the expert manner with which he always wields his pen". Ismail's UN team attempted to get a resolution sponsored at this point and although they failed, the ambassador thought that the publicity "enhanced the prestige of the Delegation".

On 10 September, in a letter to the Tunku, Ismail's concern with all aspects of nation-building was undeniably evident, as was his trademark no-nonsense approach to important state matters.

It has just occurred to me that you and the Cabinet should make a decision to close the Bank of China immediately. From information that I have received here, in Burma and Indonesia, where there are Banks of China, they have been financing political parties, which were prepared to receive their support, in past elections. The same could happen in Malaya. I know

Civil Servants, including the Attorney-General, will advance
reasons why it is difficult to close the bank. However, if you and
the Cabinet decided that it should be done then they must find
a way, otherwise there is no reason for employing them,
especially the Attorney-General (Letters 10 September 1958).

The Tunku replied that they would discuss the Bank of China on
Ismail's return to Malaya. As Ismail had expected, many reasons
were advanced to the Tunku, especially from H.S. Lee, against the
closure of the bank (Letters 22 September 1958).

At the end of 1958, Ismail wrote to the Tunku again about his
decision to return to Malaya and to participate in the 1959
parliamentary elections. Being the first since independence, these
elections were considered vital to the garnering of continued
support for the path the Alliance had chosen for the country.

Ismail was dismayed on receiving news that the Tunku had
decided to make Ismail Ali, who was already director of the
World Bank, *charge-de-affaires* in order to handle the many
duties Ismail had been responsible for. He wrote to inform
Kuala Lumpur that he considered this multiple burden too great
for anyone to bear. Razak wrote back, saying that he agreed
with Ismail on the matter but that there was no real alternative
at the moment, and that "the best arrangement will be for
Ismail [Ali] to be *Charge-de-Affaires* until the elections". Mention
was also made in Razak's letter of some earlier reference that a
worried Ismail had made that Ismail Ali had "a strong prejudice
against expatriate officers". Razak was in agreement with Ismail
concerning the role of expatriates:

They are now our officers and we have to treat them as such.
We disliked British policies but now that we are independent
that question does not arise. We need the services of expatriate
officers for the moment and if they serve us loyally and faithfully

we should not have any prejudice against them (Letters
19 November 1958).

A letter from the Tunku arrived the following week, telling Ismail
that he had been misinformed about Ismail Ali being made
charge-de-affaires. Instead, Nik Ahmad Kamil, who was the serving
high commissioner to London, would succeed Ismail as
ambassador in Washington. Ismail was to be made minister of
external affairs on his return and was to take over certain matters
that had been the responsibility of his brother Suleiman. "Happy
Face Suleiman", according to the Tunku, "is a very sick man but
he is most conscientious about his work, but I feel that unless he
can be relieved of some of the onerous burdens, his health would
suffer" (Letters 24 November 1958).

Zakaria Ali was one of those who joined the Malayan UN
mission around this time. He and his wife Razimah harbour fond
memories of how Ismail's wife Neno, with a tough year of
experience as a diplomat's wife behind her and tutored by an
exacting husband, acted as mentor for the wives of the new staff.

> We were very young then, and were very grateful for the guidance
> and the generosity Neno showed us. I remember she would take
> us shopping. She and her husband would often try to be on
> their own, taking walks into town, etc. In fact, the staff
> affectionately called them "the lovebirds" (Zakaria, interview
> 12 April 2006).

Ismail and his family left New York on 8 January 1959 on the SS
Guilio Cesare bound for Genoa, Italy. From there, they made their
way to Rome for their flight home. Razak promised that proper
accommodation would be waiting for them in Kuala Lumpur
(Letters 19 November 1958). The stay in Italy was the first and
last time that Ismail's family had a holiday of any considerable

length in a foreign country. Ismail and his wife would have three more sons over the next ten years, and the burdens of his political office during the turbulent years of the 1960s and early 1970s made any further adventure of this sort difficult to arrange.

For Ismail personally, the trip was his first direct contact with European civilization, and he experienced a great difference between Italy and the foreign land that he knew best — Australia. While in Rome, he took his son Tawfik along for what the seven-year-old would consider memorable and awe-inspiring visits to the city's many historical sights, all of which helped fire the young boy's lifelong love of history (Tawfik, interview 28 April 2005).

On his return to Kuala Lumpur on 1 February, Ismail was impressed by the progress that had taken place in his absence. He had worried about his political position after being away for such a long time, and was therefore relieved to notice that his "political stock in the party and the country was high". Ismail had also been made Malaya's alternate governor to the International Bank for Reconstruction and Development (IBRD) and the International Monetary Fund (IMF) (Letters 29 November 1958). Malaya had joined the General Agreement on Tariffs and Trade (GATT) as its thirty-seventh signatory on 24 October 1957 (Sodhy 1991, p. 191).

Suleiman had made himself very much at home in Kuala Lumpur by this time, and his family helped Ismail's family settle into their new life in independent Malaya. Tawfik recalls that he would come over to his uncle's house after school everyday because that was then the only place for him to go (Interview 28 April 2005).

On 19 February, Ismail made his first post-independence speech to the Federal Legislative Council, joining in the debate on the Elections (Amendment) Bill. Fresh from his experiences at the United Nations, he joyously declared that Malaya had earned for itself a reputation as a democratic country. "In all democratic countries, freedom of the individual is enjoyed in accordance with law and order. [...] I am sure we all realise that free elections do not mean uncontrolled elections" (*ST* 20 February 1959).

Once Ismail had taken over his new portfolio, the Tunku went on leave to campaign for the coming general elections. As external affairs minister, Ismail immediately decided that Malaya should keep to "an independent line, by which I mean that our stand on international problems should not be influenced by the policies of other countries, big or small" (Drifting c14).

> I learned when I was in the United Nations — where in addition to being a member of the Commonwealth group we belonged also to the Afro-Asian group — that the surest way to get into trouble was not to have a definite policy of our own on foreign issues because then we would be at the mercy of others. Although our policy of moderation in the United Nations did not get the approval of many members of the Afro-Asian group, we were respected because our policy was definite, logical and consistent.

This decision to adhere to strict neutrality was strongly put to the test in Malaya's relations with Indonesia. There was constant pressure from Jakarta for Malayan help in suppressing the West Sumatran rebellion led by Sjafruddin Prawiranegara and his Islamic Masyumi Party (Matsui 2003, p. 17). The huge number of Indonesians domiciled in Malaya made the matter highly volatile, a state of affairs that, according to Ismail, was not helped by the fact that Malaya's ambassador to Indonesia, Senu Abdul Rahman, who later became minister of information and broadcasting, "was a restless type who would have liked to see certain things done which an ordinary ambassador would prefer to leave alone" (Drifting c14). Senu was calling for Malayan intervention in West

Irian, and although Ismail considered Senu "one of my close friends", he could not agree with him on that question.

> I felt that any action we pursued should be done through the United Nations and for us to adopt a unilateral stand would in the long run incur the enmity of Indonesia. It was therefore a common practice for me to throw the letters which I received from our ambassador in Indonesia into the wastepaper basket. [...] Later when Tunku took over the External Affairs Ministry, he was bold enough to take the initiative on West Irian and the result was the foundation of our strained relationship with Indonesia (Drifting c14).

Two Development Loan Fund grants worth US$20 million were allocated to Malaya by the United States in the beginning of 1959, and Ismail's successor as Malayan ambassador, Nik Kamil, signed the agreements on 18 March. About US$10 million were approved for the North Klang Straits deepwater port project, while support for the teaching hospital scheme was disallowed. The remaining US$10 million were granted for the construction of roads and bridges. On 21 April, Ismail, as minister of external affairs, signed an investment guarantee agreement with Washington, which came under the United States' Mutual Security Programme, containing "provisions for the extension of military, economic and technical assistance to other countries" (Sodhy 1991, p. 197).

The elections of 1959 were, as Ismail put it, "a test of whether the Alliance would survive as a party of coalition of the three races in the country — the Malays, Chinese and Indians". The coalition had incidentally been registered as a political party independent of its member parties, becoming more centralized in the process. One of the biggest challenges it faced came from within. This was posed by the MCA's new leader Dr Lim Chong Eu, "a doctor from Penang who had shown up to that time a degree of brilliance in politics" (Drifting c14). Razak had earlier touched on the issue in a letter to Ismail, expressing worries that while UMNO still retained rural support, the MCA was losing its popularity in the towns.

> I do not know what the result of all this will be but if the MCA is to get the support of the good Chinese, the leaders must come down to earth. As I advised Dr Lim Chong Eu, we should not cast the net too wide but should close the ranks. No political leader in this country can expect to get the support of all members of every race but we must always stick to principles and know policies. So long as we are sincere and play a straight game we should be alright (Letters 19 November 1958).

Lim had managed in March 1958 to replace party founder Tan Cheng Lock as party president. This change in leadership reflected a strong desire within the MCA for change in the agreements that the Alliance was based upon, including support for the educational policy and the recognition of Malay rights and privileges.

This shift in strategy by the Alliance's second party exacerbated the dissatisfaction felt by Malay schoolteachers who formed the backbone of UMNO at this point. These wanted Malay to be made the sole medium of instruction in all national schools and were calling attention to the lack of Malay secondary schools. In January 1958, the Federation of Malay Teachers' Organization had gone to the extent of calling for an exodus from UMNO by its members over this matter (Tan 1997, p. 262). Razak told Ismail in a letter that "Tunku had decided to call the teachers up some time and tell them to come down to earth and be more realistic about things", and was hoping that "this will close the issue once and for all" (Letters 28 May 1958).

The Alliance National Council was planning to allocate 30–31 places to the MCA in the general elections, while Lim Chong Eu was pushing for 35, that is, one-third of the parliamentary seats available. Apparently, the MCA's aim was to "safeguard the Chinese against any unfavourable changes to the Constitution given that a two-third majority was required for constitutional amendments" (Tan 1997, p. 262). The status of Chinese education was central to these considerations. Major changes in the demographic constitution of the electorate were also a factor in the political equation. The Chinese electorate, which had amounted to 11.2 per cent back in 1955, had under the new citizenship laws grown to 35.6 per cent by 1959 (Shaw 1976, pp. 118–220).

Lim Chong Eu's explanation of the MCA position given in a private letter to the Tunku dated 24 June was publicly released on 10 July. This upset the prime minister, who experienced the letter's release as a hidden ultimatum, and retaliated by announcing that UMNO was prepared to go ahead without the MCA. On 12 July, the MCA retreated to avoid a crisis and accepted the Tunku's conditions, which were that thirty-one seats would be allocated to the MCA, all MCA candidates would be chosen by the Tunku, and the issue of Chinese education would not be included in the Alliance Election Manifesto (Tan 1997, pp. 264, 266).

The consequences of this failed challenge on the part of the MCA were profound. Lim and a row of major leaders resigned, and MCA members not acceptable to the Tunku were denied the chance of running under the Alliance banner. This further encouraged Chinese voters to seek political leadership outside the Alliance (Andaya and Andaya 1982, pp. 268–69). As a result, the strong ties between the MCA and pressure groups championing Chinese education such as the UCSTA and the UCSCA, were damaged significantly (Tan 1997, p. 286).

In June, just two weeks before elections to state legislative bodies were to take place, widespread fighting between Chinese and Malays broke out on Pangkor Island, off Perak state. Police reinforcements were sent in from the mainland and they managed to avert serious bloodshed. To an extent, this palpable tension caused voters to become more ethnicity-conscious at a crucial period in the country's nation-building process. The eleven state legislature elections held over five weeks nevertheless resulted in the Alliance winning 207 out of 282 seats. Although the party gained almost two-thirds of the contested seats, its share of votes amounted only to a disturbing 55 per cent (Shaw 1976, pp. 118–220). The Pan-Malayan Islamic Party (PMIP) won in the states of Kelantan and Trengganu.

The Federal Legislative Council was dissolved on 27 June to make way for the first fully elected Malayan House of Parliament. Nomination Day on 15 July saw 259 candidates registering to contest the 104 seats: 104 were from the Alliance, 58 from PMIP, 38 from the Socialist Front, 19 from the People's Progressive Party, 9 from Onn Ja'afar's Parti Negara, 2 from the Malayan Party, and 29 were independents (Shaw 1976, p. 122).

The Alliance won 74 of the 104 federal seats, thus achieving a crucial two-thirds majority, although the MCA secured only 19 of the 31 seats it contested for. Voter support for the coalition, however, amounted to no more than 51.7 per cent.

The final push to end the Emergency that the government had started in early 1958 were showing encouraging results and by mid-1959, according to U.S. sources, the military phase of the conflict was coming to a close (Sodhy 1991, p. 196). In May 1959, perhaps because of the improving situation and the waning need for American assistance, the American secretary of commerce, Lewis L. Strauss, refused grant aid — in contradistinction to reimbursable aid — to Malaya. No official reasons were given (Sodhy 1991, p. 189).

Partly due to his participation in the Federal Executive Council in the mid-1950s when the security of Singapore was heatedly discussed, Ismail was appointed in June 1959 as Malaya's representative to the newly self-governing Singapore's Internal Security Council (ISC) (*ST* 9 June 1959). He was personally against the idea — one that was initially broached by Singapore's first chief minister, David Marshall, in Singapore's failed 1956 constitutional conference with the British — that an independent Malaya would be involved in the security structure of another country. The ISC had three members each representing Britain, Singapore and the federation's government. The British were relying on the anti-communist stance of the Tunku to break any deadlock that might occur on security matters between them and the Singaporeans (Loh 1976, p. 21).

When the Tunku was in the Netherlands in 1960, he happened to state that Malaya would sooner or later have to recognize the People's Republic of China. Apparently, because of talks he had held with French President Charles De Gaulle, the Tunku decided to announce on his return to Kuala Lumpur "a sudden change in our policy towards Communist China" in accordance with his statement (Drifting c15; Kuok 1991, pp. 219–20).

Ismail hit the roof. He had not been consulted on the matter, and since the official stand then was that no relationship could be maintained with the Beijing regime as long as it supported the MCP, he was certain that the Tunku's statement would lead to further confusion in an already delicate matter. At the following cabinet meeting, the Tunku tried in vain to explain himself, but

Ismail hurled documents across the table and stormed out. He also threatened to resign, which shocked the Tunku.

> At once I realised my mistake, but when I made the Press statement in America [sic], I had done so on the spur of the moment. I had no chance to warn him previously, nor did I think such a slight departure from policy could cause such an upset. After this explanation, Tun Dr Ismail left the house in a huff. He came again to tender his resignation officially, but I had told my house-boy earlier that if Dr Ismail arrived he was to inform him that I was out. And this he did. After three or four visits, Tun Dr Ismail came no more, so I realised that he cooled down. I was very pleased to see him in the Cabinet again, as if nothing had happened (Tunku 1975, p. 170).

In fact, this event led to a considerable change in Ismail's political career. He was determined to resign, but as stated in his private papers, his brother and some colleagues persuaded him to move to another ministry instead. Philip Kuok said in his autobiography that he rushed off to see Ismail on hearing about his quarrel with the Tunku. Ismail was having a hard time controlling his temper, and persuaded Kuok instead to drive him down to Johor Bahru in his Mercedes diesel car. Kuok advised Ismail to stay away a month and visit his constituency (Kuok 1991, pp. 219–20). Meanwhile, the cabinet arranged for Ismail to lead a commission "to inquire into the position of students in England and Ireland". This was apparently to give him a chance to calm down. At that time, there were about 3,000 Malayan students in Britain and Ireland (*ST* 20 August 1960). Ismail told reporters he would be away for a month, but in the end spent four months altogether in England producing a report of which he was evidently proud, and "which I believe is now used as a bible for the reconstruction of student organisations in the United Kingdom" (Drifting c15).

On his return to Malaya, he took over the Internal Security portfolio created for him, which he considered a "controversial" position "with all the aches but none of the pleasantness of the other ministries". This was the start of another weary period in his political career: "I am sure that this posting, together with my stint as ambassador to the United States, had a lot to do with my failing health" (ibid.).

In July 1960, the twelve-year-long Emergency was officially declared over, although the hunt for remnants of guerrilla forces continued with diminishing returns (Dennis and Grey 1996, pp. 150, 163). Tim Hatton, who was acting Director of Selangor Special Branch in 1960, noted that "the mostly Malayanised civil service, international journalists and the intelligence community in Kuala Lumpur, [in particular] the British and the American representatives, many of whom had arrived recently", believed at this time that the danger from communism had passed. Hatton thought this a grave error, and found it lucky that Ismail, who became minister of internal security in November 1960, and permanent secretary Nik Daud, held the same view he did, which was that jungle warfare was being replaced by subversive activities in urban areas. The two were determined "to counter Communist subversion by explaining in detail to many influential people in Malaya exactly what was happening" (Hatton 2004, p. 241). On 1 August 1960, the controversial Internal Security Act (ISA) came into being to replace the Emergency Regulations Ordinance (Koh 2004, p. 269).

On 1 June 1961, Ismail spoke in parliament to refute claims that the government was stifling the opposition through its threat to "eradicate the cancer of Communism" from the ranks of certain political parties should their leaders fail in that undertaking. He proclaimed on that occasion; "As long as I am Minister, I'll persecute Communists" (*ST* 20 June 1961).

Ismail was also appointed minister of home affairs in February 1962. Besides tough questions on national security, he was now also responsible for housing matters especially squatter conditions and low-cost housing projects. The decisions on internal security that he had to make in his new position caused him no end of worry. When he retired in 1967, he would remark that he was amazed that he had managed to stay appreciated for his services: "I had expected that the last six years which I spent as Minister of the most difficult of portfolios would [have made] me the most hated man in Malaya". The moral dilemma he found himself in is best expressed in his own words:

As Minister of Home Affairs and Internal Security, I had wide powers and also had to deal on security matters with Singapore and Thailand. The most controversial law is the Internal Security Act. Great controversy went on and is still going on about this Act. Its opponents have argued that the Act is inconsistent with democracy, especially those provisions which give power to the police to exercise arbitrary arrest and detention without trial. The students objected to the suitability certificate clause of the Act and since my retirement, this clause has been suspended. I maintained then and I maintain now the view that the Internal Security Act is essential to the security of this country especially when democracy is interpreted the way it is interpreted in this country. To those in opposition to the Government, democracy is interpreted to mean absolute freedom, even the freedom to subvert the nation. When cornered by the argument that democracy in the western sense means freedom in an ordered society and an ordered society is one in which the rule of law prevails, they seek refuge in the slogan that we should not imitate

western democracy one hundred percent. I am convinced that
the Internal Security Act as practised in Malaysia is not contrary
to the fundamentals of democracy. Abuse of the Act can be
prevented by vigilant public opinion via elections, a free press
and above all the parliament (Drifting c15).

As he would repeatedly mention to Chet Singh, his assistant
secretary for political matters, "order comes before law" (Singh,
interview 10 January 2006). Ismail was acutely aware of the risks
involved in the controversial ISA and "did not relish having to
administer it". As a guarantee against abuses and mistakes in the
implementation of the ISA, he demanded of his subordinates a
stringent adherence to due bureaucratic process, and exercised
extreme caution in choosing senior personnel.

To ensure that each case for detention was fully investigated
and the pros and cons well argued before it reached me, I
arranged for it to pass through the hands of several responsible
senior officers of the police and Home Ministry. When it finally
came to me, I went through each case carefully and when in
doubt, I always slept over it. It really took a lot out of me to
approve cases for detention, because some of the people detained
were well known to me. My only consolation is that on my
retirement nobody could accuse me of sending anybody to
detention camp out of malice (Drifting c15).

Chet Singh remembers that working under Ismail between 1962
and 1967 meant that one had to deliver on time whatever was
required. Since the minister pressed himself harder than anyone
else, the staff could not but respond positively to the need for
accountability and integrity in their work: "It was both inspiring
and demanding to work under him, although I do not think at
the same time that any civil servant ever worked under him
without being at the receiving end of his wrath." Apparently,

Ismail deeply feared that Malaysia's development would be undermined not by communism, but by communalism, and by what he termed *"tidak apa-*ism" (nonchalance). He ran a tight outfit, and demanded of his staff that they took the initiative to find out personally the reason for any delay in their dealings with the rest of the state administration before a second reminder was received or dispatched. Second reminders became a rare correspondence at the Home Affairs Ministry after a while (Singh, interview 2 February 2006).

And so it was that between 1959 and 1967, Ismail had to deal with the most sensitive cases affecting Malaya's internal security. Given the tensions of the Cold War period and his overall stature in the government, border issues with Thailand and relations with Singapore also became his responsibility. Where Thailand was concerned, Ismail chose "never to press the Thais for more than what they were willing to agree to". He was convinced that this tactic worked in the long run, and that the proof for this was in the fact that he was the first Malayan minister "to get a Thai minister to sign an agreement giving effective directions to our commanders on the ground to take definite action against the Communist terrorists" (Drifting c15).

A secret police report, probably written in the middle of 1961 and found among Ismail's papers, studied Thailand's southern Muslim provinces and argued that in both Thailand and Malaya, equality was granted to all nationals "irrespectively of racial origin and religion" provided that they accepted the national language and custom. The vital difference was that the Muslim minority in Thailand, unlike the case of the Chinese and Indians in Malaya, was not offered "sound economic opportunities and social benefits" by the central government.

Indeed, their loyalties are diverted from Thailand by the standard of prosperity and impartial administration which is evident in the Federation. The Muslims in South Thailand regard their position as one without hope and see a future devoid of opportunities. In these circumstances, resentment against [the] Thai administration is likely to increase and may lead to a situation where the Thai Muslims will look to the Communists as the champions of their cause (TS–IAR/14/3/1).

Being the busy man that he was, Ismail tried to combine official business with family responsibilities whenever possible. To show moral support for his men out on the field, and to express his belief that the jungles in central Malaya were safe from communist threats, he took his wife Neno and their children Tawfik, Zailah and Badariah on trips during the school holidays up the Pahang River into thick forestation, including parts of the National Park. The children remember that they went on such wonderful adventure tours at least three times (Tawfik, interview 21 July 2006; Zailah, interview 23 April 2005).

Meanwhile in Singapore, Lim Yew Hock's ruling Singapore's People's Alliance (SPA) had been unexpectedly trounced by Lee Kuan Yew's People's Action Party (PAP) in the 30 May 1959 elections. The victors, having secured forty-three of fifty-one seats, decided to release detained communist suspects on 4 June (Lee 1998, pp. 305–10). The British protested, and Ismail "was instructed to raise our objection to the release".

> It was to no avail because Lee Kuan Yew knew that having won the elections by a large majority, he now held the whip in his hand while the British and [we] were not prepared for a showdown. [...]

Ismail, already loaded with work, saw that it was to be his inevitable lot to "carry the burden of representing Malaya on the Singapore Security Council". He made a resolution "to totally involve myself in the work".

> My dealings with Singapore on security problems [were] an
> experience which I would not have liked to miss and also one
> which I would not like to go through again (Drifting c15).

Ismail decided to introduce golf as a part of ISC meetings. Not
only did this make Lee Kuan Yew and Goh Keng Swee good
golfers, he said, the games also "proved productive in our
deliberations on the security of Singapore". They furthermore
provided him with good opportunities for getting to know Lee.
Ismail believed that golf revealed the person's character, and his
analysis of Lee was that he was "very deliberate, and calculates
every move he wants to make". Lee would make others wait for
him, according to Ismail, and would take more time than others
reading the green and pacing the distance between the ball and
the hole: "He does not mind losing to a better player, but he
[will] fight to the last" (Drifting c16).

> As we met more and more often, we began to respect and like
> each other. I never made any attempt to match his brilliance in
> argument and my reply to any specific problem was either a
> simple yes or no and when he pressed me for my reasons I told
> him that he had given the pros and cons so brilliantly that I
> needed only to agree or disagree with his opinion or decision.
> I had never believed that he was a Communist and later on, on
> the verge of my retirement he told me in front of a group of
> people that he studied me closely during the early stages of our
> friendship and only when he was convinced that I did not
> believe he was a Communist did he decide to do business with
> me (Drifting c16).

Ismail was the older man and thought that if the younger Lee
could be "more tolerant and more patient of human failings, he
would do not only himself but Singapore and the whole of South
East Asia much good" (Drifting c16). Lee in turn remembers

Ismail to be "short, slightly tubby and dark for a Malay" who was almost never without his pipe. He also had "curly hair" and wore a "moustache and horn-rimmed glasses".

> I came to like and respect him for his direct and straightforward manner. He knew what his job was [...] and was determined that the Malayan Chinese Communists were not going to win. [...] As I got to know the Malayan ministers better, he was the one I trusted absolutely. He was honest and sincere in his dealings with me, and I believe he reciprocated my friendship and respect for him (Lee 1998, p. 248).

Lee recalls that Ismail was "a restful person to play with, very tranquil".

> He had a sense of humour, and would often chuckle. He was never afraid of being seen with me even when I was unpopular. He didn't care even when pictures of us appeared in the papers. Razak was more cautious, but Ismail never considered me a threat to Malaysia. I found him quite admirable and certainly exceptional. He was not a time-server at all, and did not suffer from any overpowering personal ambition. Golf was to him a kind of refuge away from work, worries and pressure. He played regularly and would concentrate strongly on his game (Interview 7 February 2006).

Despite the mutual respect, the two men would disagree on many issues in the years ahead, when the painful process of regional liberation and nation-building dictated unpredictable and divergent paths.

Chapter 5

THE MAKING AND
PARTITIONING OF MALAYSIA

On 27 May 1961, Prime Minister Tunku Abdul Rahman made the first public reference to the Federation of Malaysia at a Singapore press luncheon, setting off speculation and criticism throughout the region (Memo 23 February 1962). The idea was not new, but where British strategic considerations and local political developments were concerned, the time for it now seemed ripe. The incorporation of Singapore into Malaysia, along with Sabah, Sarawak and Brunei — the last of which eventually chose to stay out — offered the best chance to save the island from a communist takeover (Lam and Tan 1999, pp. 55–56).

The term "Malaysia" had in fact been in use before any talk of independence for such a polity had been advanced. For example, the classic study of the colony by Rupert Emerson from 1937 was titled "Malaysia".* Incidentally, "Malaysia" was also

---

* "Malaysia" belongs to a category that provides us with place names like "Devonshire", "Yorkshire" and "Rhodesia", and would mean "Malay administrative region". "Shire" itself is Middle English and means "official charge; administrative district" (see The American Heritage Dictionary of the English Language).

the name preferred by UMNO when the matter was discussed within the Alliance before independence. In a memorandum to the Reid Commission written on 25 September 1956, the Tunku stated that it was the MCA that wanted the new country to be called "Malaya" (CO 889/6, ff 219-239 — Stockwell 1995, p. 307).

By 3 June 1961, Singapore's PAP had accepted the Tunku's merger proposals (TS–IAR14/1/2). That same week, however, Singapore UMNO, Singapore MCA and the defeated SPA formed an alliance reminiscent of Malaya's successful consociation. This greatly upset the PAP, which was in an unstable state despite its electoral victory. According to B. Simandjuntak, it was this turn of events that precipitated the emergence of the splinter party, the Barisan Sosialis Party (BSP). With Dr Lee Siew Choh as president and Lim Chin Siong as secretary-general, this new grouping came into being on 17 September 1961 (TS–IAR/14/1/3) to become the PAP's most effective opposition (Simandjuntak 1969, p. 117). Within hours, 35 of the 51 branch committees, 19 of the 23 organizing secretaries and "about 70 per cent of the PAP's rank and file" defected. The split cut through the party all the way down to stationery and furniture being ferried away from PAP offices. The ease with which its departing left-wing managed to floor the party left a deep and lasting impression on remaining members (Milne and Mauzy 1990, p. 57).

The PAP was not quite out for the count, however, and soon managed to regroup to campaign strongly for the forming of Malaysia. It also called for a referendum on the merger to be held on 1 September 1962. According to an American Central Intelligence Agency (CIA) report on "Prospects for the Proposed Malaysian Federation", the initiative immediately caused worries that "a series of strikes and disorders" would precede the vote, and might require the intervention of Commonwealth forces.

This in turn could cause postponement of the merger, and, perhaps, the ouster of Lee. In an effort to forestall such incidents, Lee and the Tunku have been urging the British to agree to the preventive arrest of selected BSP leaders before the referendum (CIA 54-59/62).

Helped further by several tactical errors that the Barisan Sosialis made, which included insulting the Tunku and badly misreading the issue of citizenship rights among Singaporeans, the PAP won a 71 per cent slice of the votes in the referendum. Twenty-five per cent of the votes were blank, however, and through a special ordinance were taken to mean that these voters left the matter to the assembly to decide (Milne and Mauzy 1990, p. 58).

In December that year, several Barisan leaders were implicated in an abortive leftist revolt in Brunei. They had made the mistake of helping to recruit volunteers for rebel leader Sheikh Mahmud Azahari, who was purportedly supported by Indonesia. This opened them to charges of subversion (Milne and Mauzy 1990, p. 58; Minchin 1990, p. 126; Selvan 1990, p. 25).

In his memoirs, Ghazali Shafie, who was then permanent secretary in Malaya's Ministry of External Affairs, claimed that the Tunku "had a strong feeling that the *Barisan Sosialis* and the Communists and those opposed to the Malaysia Concept would now mount their best efforts and even actively plot to make as much trouble [as possible] on the eve of the merger". The Tunku then told Ismail to establish a strong liaison with the Singapore Special Branch "to substantiate his hunch" (Ghazali 1998, p. 191). Within the federation, the PMIP put forth a surprising resolution in parliament in May 1962 calling for the Philippines and Indonesia to be included in the Federation of Malaysia plan. This was rejected amidst criticism from various groups, and Ismail accused the party of "daydreaming" (*ST* 3 May 1962).

The Tunku left for Britain for talks on 18 July about the Federation of Malaysia. Razak and Tan Siew Sin accompanied him, while Ismail stayed behind to function as acting prime minister in their absence (*ST* 11 July 1962).

According to a Malayan Special Branch report found among Ismail's papers, Lord Selkirk, the British commissioner for Singapore and commissioner general for Southeast Asia from 1959 to 1963, had earlier assured Lim Chin Siong and other PAP dissidents that no action would be taken against them as long as they did not resort to unconstitutional action. It also expressed considerable alarm over the fact that Lord Selkirk "failed to appreciate that some of these dissidents were Communists or under strong Communist influence. [...] This has tied the hands of the British ever since and is exemplified by their reluctance even to take part in the tripartite professional working committee to consider action to be taken against the Communists in Singapore before merger" (TS–IAR/14/1/2).

The report further informed Ismail that what Singaporean communists feared most was the establishment of a strong central government in Kuala Lumpur "with the authority and the determination to suppress Communism".

> For this reason, if the early capture of the Central Government through complete integration of Singapore is denied them, the Communists must try to reduce the powers which the Central Government now seeks, particularly in respect of Internal Security, in the British North Borneo territories and Singapore. By this reduction the Communists hope to retain freedom of action to advance their influence with the ultimate objective of complete unification of the Malaysian territories under Communist control (TS–IAR/14/1/5-6).

This "freedom of action" presumably included a campaign to undermine "the Singapore Government's ability to neutralize the Communists", further worrying Special Branch that this might in turn lead to Lee Kuan Yew going back on "his promise to take action before merger" (TS–IAR/14/1/11).

The Malayan Special Branch suggested the simultaneous arrest of top and middle-rank leaders, especially Lim Chin Siong, and several cadres, a restriction of movement for other agitators, and a de-registering of organizations known to be a cover for the communists. These actions were to be preceded by concerted mass media efforts exposing communist aims and tactics. Firm action against Chinese communists would presumably also win support for the government in the Borneo territories: "Resolute action when shown to be taken for security reasons alone will have the result of heartening our friends and confounding our enemies and bringing over the uncommitted to our side" (TS–IAR/14/2/1). Ismail led Malaya's delegation to the Seventeenth Session of the United Nations General Assembly and spoke to the plenum on 4 October 1962. He criticized communist China for its "new form of imperialism", naming the occupation of Tibet, subversion in South Vietnam and "encroachment" on Indian territory as examples of Beijing's "very subtle" expansionism (*ST* 5 August 1962).

In mid-December 1962, the Malayan Government carried out a series of arrests. All in all, fifty were detained under the ISA. On 18 December 1962, Ismail addressed the House of Representatives on the issue, quipping that the initiative was done for the good of the Socialist Front, an oppositional coalition formed on Independence Day by the Labour Party, the People's Party, and the Socialist Youth League (Koh 2004, p. ix): "When I die I want it to be written on my epitaph that I saved [the Socialist Front] from being taken over by the Communists" (*ST* 19 December 1962). On 30 January 1963, Ismail publicized an offer to Chin Peng to surrender, but without "special terms". No similar offer was made by Thailand, with whom Malayan border patrols were cooperating (*ST* 31 January 1963). The situation remained tense. Significantly, only three years after the Emergency officially ended did Australian military aid come to an end, when the Second Battalion of the Royal Australian Regiment withdrew on 20 August 1963 (Dennis and Grey 1996, pp. 150, 163).

The Internal Security Council moved against communist elements in Singapore in the early hours of 2 February 1963 in what was called Operation Cold Store. All in all, 133 pro-communists were arrested as subversives, including twenty-four Barisan members and twenty-one leading unionists. Personalities such as Lim Chin Siong, Fong Swee Suan, Dominic Puthucheary and a large section of Barisan Sosialis's executive committee were locked up, decisively crippling the party (*ST* 29 November 1963; Lee 1998, p. 472; Milne and Mauzy 1990, p. 58). Ismail explained that this "most important security operation since the end of the Emergency" was taken "to prevent the Communists from setting up a Communist Cuba in Singapore, and to thwart any attempt by them to stir up violence or disorder in the closing stages of the development of Malaysia" (*ST* 3 February 1963; *ST* 4 February 1963).

While preparations for the founding of the Federation of Malaysia stymied communist ambitions, a serious confrontation with President Sukarno, who professed that the project was a neo-colonial idea designed to steal northern Borneo away from Indonesia, could not be avoided. A referendum was carried out in Sabah and Sarawak to measure popular support for the idea, and to stave Indonesian criticism. The findings could only be announced on 14 September 1963, and showed that a great majority in the two states were positive about the merger. Sukarno rejected this result.

The original plan for Malaysia to be founded on the same date as when Malaya was founded — 31 August — could not be realized, and instead the new federation came into being only on 16 September, which unbeknownst to the Tunku, was incidentally Lee Kuan Yew's fortieth birthday. At Singapore's City Hall, Lee Kuan Yew, with Ismail representing Kuala Lumpur and Duncan Sandys, the secretary of state for Commonwealth relations representing London by his side, declared Singapore part of Malaysia (Lee 1998, p. 504). The ISC was also appropriately dissolved at the same time.

Ismail had reservations about Tunku's generous terms to Sabah and Sarawak, which included forty seats in the federal parliament (Drifting c16). This over-representation of East Malaysia continues to the present day, with the two states having fifty-three out of 219 seats as of 31 December 2003 (Puthucheary and Othman 2006).

Ghafar Baba was a newly elected vice president of UMNO at that time, and later remembered what it was like dealing with Ismail. He once organized a meeting between the minister and some religious leaders.

> Ismail came in, did not shake any hands, went straight to the table, sat down, made his speech and then left. I thought it strange at that time. Why did he behave that way? We needed to gain support. Here we were trying to win votes and he wouldn't even shake hands with people. But today I understand him. To him, people came to listen to his speech. If they wanted to follow him then it was because of what he had to say, not because he had been shaking hands with them. That was the kind of man he was. Some Malays might of course have thought him rather "*sombong*" (haughty).

Similarly, the Tunku had on one occasion told religious leaders wishing to join UMNO that "before you join my party, I want to tell you that I am a gambler, I go horse racing every week, I am also a drinker; I want to let you know this first before you consider joining my party or you might otherwise find out later and run off". It is not known if those religious leaders became UMNO members or not (Ghafar, interview 16 June 2005).

On 21 September, a week after Malaysia came into being, Singapore held its only elections while a part of Malaysia. The contest was strongly fought, and the PAP emerged with thirty-seven of the fifty-one seats. Barisan Sosialis managed to secure only thirteen. What was also significant was that the UMNO-backed Singapore Alliance Party (SAP) also contested in violation of an agreement that UMNO and the PAP would not participate in each other's elections until the new federation had achieved stability. In the event, the SAP failed to secure a single seat, losing even in the Malay constituencies. The PAP was to play tit-for-tat, and fielded candidates against the MCA in the federation's elections of April 1964. It only managed to win a single seat.

Four days after the 1963 elections, the central government cracked down on students in Singapore, arresting twenty from Nanyang University and Chinese middle schools. The reason Ismail gave was that after their failure in the elections, communist elements were planning to regroup and re-organize, and the central government was merely pre-empting this development (*MM* 26 September 1963).

Despite careful planning, things went awry for the new federation almost immediately. Ismail sadly noted:

> However, it was obvious that once Singapore was in Malaysia, the status quo which I hoped would continue was not possible. Personal jealousies and ambitions were so strong and the political

approaches to communal problems were so divergent that either of two things was bound to happen: First, if Singapore continued to be a part of Malaysia, communal clashes of such magnitude as to destroy Malaysia as an identity was bound to occur; second, if Singapore was separated by mutual agreement the chances of cooperation and eventual union of the two countries was a certainty. As it turned out, the latter alternative happened (Drifting c16).

Lee Kuan Yew recalls that he had candid and open conversations on various matters with Ismail "in, between and after parliamentary sessions" during the two years Singapore was part of Malaysia: "Ismail was not one to simulate, if he did not like something he would tell you straight off." Lee once discussed the crucial matter of national language with Ismail:

> I told him that making Malay the national language will not mean the Chinese would be left behind. They will just learn the language, and the Malays will continue to be left behind. He agreed but said the Malays in the kampongs thought that they would gain the advantage that way, and so the government had to proceed (Interview 7 February 2006).

On 14 July 1964, racial riots broke out in the streets of Singapore, leaving twenty-two reported dead and 500 injured. Lee Kuan Yew announced that "all the indications show that there has been organization and planning behind this outbreak" (*ST* 22 July 1964). The Tunku, who was away in Washington at the time, claimed he had evidence that Indonesia was behind the rioting. Further fighting in September claimed thirteen more lives (Fletcher 1969, pp. 43, 57).

The converging of the politics of Singapore and Kuala Lumpur was quickly shown to be unfeasible, and threatened to undermine national security more seriously than the Indonesians could do over Sarawak and Sabah. The Philippines also had claims on northern Borneo, which disposed it to oppose the formation of Malaysia. This led to tripartite summits that failed. When the Tokyo summit held on 20 June 1964 did not lead to any breakthrough, Sukarno initiated coercive methods to destabilize Malaysia.

Indonesian guerrilla incursions and subversion kept tensions high and fuelled a "war of nerves". On 17 August, Jakarta launched its first major attack on Malaysia when thirty to forty heavily armed men landed in Pontian, on the west coast of Johor. The Malaysians easily crushed this operation. Two weeks later, ninety-six infiltrators, mainly Indonesian Air Force paratroopers, were dropped north of Labis, also in western Johor. Aided by New Zealand and Ghurkha soldiers and the British Navy and Air Force, the Malaysians killed forty-seven of these over the following weeks (Muhammad 1978, pp. 20–30).

The Malaysian cabinet decided to declare a state of emergency throughout the country on 3 September, and demanded action by the United Nations "to relieve the tense situation" (*ST* 4 September 1964). The Security Council agreed to a hearing on the matter. Britain, Australia, and the United States gave tacit support to Malaysia to present its case to the world body. According to a recently released document, Canberra directed their high commissioner, Tom Critchley, in Kuala Lumpur that same day to assist the Malaysians both in Malaysia and in New York, and to suggest that Ismail was "the obvious man" to lead the delegation because of his seniority and experience at the United Nations: "The Indonesians are to be expected to put up an effective propaganda showing in the Council and amongst other United Nations members and a convincing presentation of the Malaysian case will be essential" (Dee 2005, pp. 316–17).

Ismail did lead Malaysia's special delegation to the UN, which included the permanent secretary to the Ministry of External Affairs, Ghazali Shafie, and Singapore's Finance Minister Goh Keng Swee.

All in all, the UN Security Council held six meetings between 9 and 17 September to discuss the conflict. Besides the five permanent members of the Security Council, the temporary members at this time included Bolivia, Brazil, Czechoslovakia, Ivory Coast, Morocco and Norway (MEA 1965, p. 1). As fate would have it, the Soviet Union was holding the presidential seat. Indonesia and the Philippines were asked to be present but without being given voting rights.

Ismail had seven years earlier made history as the first man to enter the general assembly armed, in a manner of speaking. He was then bearing a Malay dagger — the *kris* — as part of his full traditional Malay attire. This time around, at the 1144th meeting of the Security Council of the United Nations, he meant to bring with him captured weapons to dramatize the cold fact of Indonesian aggression. The evidence he wished to place on the Security Council table included a Danish-made Madsen mortar, a German-made automatic rifle, an equipment belt with a water bottle and medical packs with instructions for use in Indonesian, an Indonesian air force parachute with the smock and trousers marked with the place name "Bandung", a military helmet of a type not used by Commonwealth forces, and other minor items.

The first secretary at the New York mission at that time, Zakaria Ali, remembers that it was even suggested that Lieutenant Sukitno, the captured Indonesian commando of a raid into Johor, be brought before the council, but the idea was immediately discarded.

Ismail considered it a necessary act of diplomatic courtesy to call on the Russian ambassador, Platon D. Morozov, the evening before the council meeting to inform him of Malaysia's intention to exhibit captured equipment. Morozov said it could be allowed only if the council agreed. After the meeting with the Russian, Ismail told his delegation members and advisers that they had been paying a courtesy call on the Russians and were not asking for permission, and so gave the order to proceed as planned, and without permission from the council (Interview 12 April 2006).

The good relations that the Malaysians had with UN security guards made it possible for the arms to be brought by car into the compound and carried into the building. This was on 9 September. The president of the council was taken aback when Zakaria Ali brought the captured equipment into the chamber. He declared in Russian:

> I must say that in my many years of experience in the United Nations, and if my memory serves me correctly, this is the first time that weapons, whether loaded or not, have been brought to the table where the members of the Security Council are actually sitting. They are not aimed at me so I am not worried, but I do not know how my colleagues on my right feel, as these weapons seem to be aimed directly at them. I would therefore request the representative of Malaysia, unless the Security Council decides otherwise, to have these weapons removed from the table. He has produced them without any kind of authority on my part and in spite of the explanations that I as President of the Security Council gave him yesterday (MEA 1965, p. 6).

Ghazali Shafie remembers Ismail then assuring the assembly that the weapons pointed at them were not loaded, but just as certainly were they loaded "when they were pointed at us". This comment was met by general laughter (Interview 7 September 2005). As was the practice, both Morozov's and Ismail's speeches had to be translated into a series of languages, which meant that the captured arms were kept in full display for a sizeable length of time (Zakaria, interview 12 April 2006).

After the presentation of physical evidence, Ismail moved to the incident of an Indonesian plane flying over Malaysian territory the week before, dropping about thirty heavily armed paratroopers. The Indonesian Foreign Ministry counterclaimed that a C-130 was no doubt in the vicinity but it was in fact heading for Phnom Penh "with a cargo of seventy beautiful Cambodian Dancers who had been in Indonesia for the 17 August Independence Day celebrations". Ismail informed the Council that "a very careful examination has been made of the bodies of those killed and of the persons captured, and this did not reveal any women corresponding to the type alleged to have been carried in the aircraft" (MEA 1965, p. 7). Indonesia's delegate, Dr Sudjarwo Tjondronegoro, countered with arguments against the forming of the federation, which he classified a British "project of neo-colonialism" (MEA 1965, p. 12).

In his speech at the 1145th council meeting the following day, Ismail again put his sense of irony to good use.

> To put the record straight, may I point out that it was made clear beyond all doubt during the meetings in Bangkok and Tokyo that Indonesia insists on maintaining its military presence on Malaysian territory while the discussions or conciliation efforts take place. It is Indonesia's intention that, if a political solution is reached in stages, its troops will be withdrawn in stages: if Indonesia gets half of what it wants, it will withdraw half its troops; and progressively, when it gets all it wants, all its troops will be withdrawn. No self-respecting nation could accept such a principle of negotiation. This is neo-diplomacy, by way of analogy with the word "neo-colonialism" which has been used here. When I was representing my country in the First

Committee and supporting Indonesia on the question of West Irian, I coined the phrase "vestigial colonialism". I said that West Irian should be given back to Indonesia because West Irian was a symbol of vestigial colonialism for the Indonesians. Today the representative of Indonesia used the word "neo-colonialism" in speaking about my country. I use the word "neo-diplomacy" to describe the manner in which Indonesia wants to crush my country" (MEA 1965, p. 30).

In further repelling the argument of the Indonesians — and the Soviet Union — that Malaysia was a neo-colonial creation, Ismail reiterated that his government's main complaint to the UN was "simply and clearly that Indonesia has committed blatant aggression against Malaysia" (MEA, p. 32).

The people of Malaysia today do not need outsiders to champion their struggle against colonialism, because we ourselves rejected colonialism from our land, because the formation of Malaysia itself is a major act of decolonization. The danger that is threatening Malaysia today is not colonialism, but the neo-imperialism of a big neighbour whose avowed policy is to crush Malaysia (MEA, p. 32).

A confidential report sent by the Australian delegation in New York to Canberra, dated 13 September, shows that the Malaysians considered a pending American resolution on the matter acceptable. The British also formulated another that Ismail dismissed as maintaining "the minimum that would be acceptable". The Australians also suspected that "the Malaysians may have already given some other delegations an idea of what they could accept" (Dee 2005, pp. 329–30).

Ismail hardly spoke during the fourth meeting. The fifth meeting on 15 September was shortened after the Norwegians submitted a draft resolution, in order that the members could have time to study that document. This resolution closely resembled the Malaysian draft, and called for all parties to refrain from threats and the use of force, to respect each other's political and territorial integrity, to make every effort to avoid the recurrence of the 2 September incident, and to resume talks (MEA, p. 71). During the sixth and final meeting on 17 September, a vote was taken on the Norwegian draft. Nine voted in favour of it, while two — Czechoslovakia and the Soviet Union — were against it. Seven votes were all that was needed for adoption, but in the event, the Soviet Union's "no" amounted to an effective veto. Despite the veto, and although Indonesia was not placed under any obligation to abide by the terms of the rejected resolution, the moral pressure on it to behave had increased (MEA, pp. 73–86).

The Norwegian draft stopped short of asking for UN observers to ascertain the cessation of armed actions — as the American one had done — nor did it request the secretary general "to keep the situation under review and report to the Council within three months from today", as the British draft had wanted (Dee 2005, pp. 329–30). In his closing statement, Ismail expressed deep disappointment:

> In the final result a draft resolution, which in almost every part of it reflects the central spirit and at every turn incorporates the principles of the Charter in its own actual language, could not obtain passage through the Security Council for obvious reasons. That there could be a negative vote at all in such a situation is a matter of the gravest concern to all the world, particularly to those who, like Malaysia, are small nations which form the majority of the Member States of the United Nations (MEA, p. 85).

Despite the official failure, and given how Cold War super powers were arrayed against each other on the world stage, the result could not have come as a surprise to the Malaysian delegation. The mission did achieve what it set out to do, namely bring its conflict with Indonesia to the full attention of other nations. Ismail also proclaimed that the veto was further evidence that the communists were behind Indonesia's aggression (*ST* 19 September 1964).

Around this time, Vietnam's chairman of joint general staff, General Tran Thien Khiem paid a visit to Ismail. Din Merican, who was assistant secretary at the Ministry of Foreign Affairs, was the link officer. He remembers that Ismail seemed fully prepared for the meeting and had obviously been well briefed on the situation in Vietnam.

> Ismail first listened attentively to the general. He then forthrightly told the visitor that Saigon's problem was partly corruption and partly the fact that the rural population had been alienated. He then explained the rationale of Malaya's Briggs Plan to him (Merican, interview 4 September 2006).

At the Second Conference of Non-Aligned Nations held in Cairo in October later that year, Indonesia refused to sign a declaration apparently because it stressed the principles of peaceful coexistence, respect for territorial integrity and non-interference in the internal affairs of others. This was despite the fact that Malaysia had been disallowed admission for her stand against communism. On failing to stop a UN decision to let Czechoslovakia and Malaysia share a two-year term on the Security Council from 1965, Indonesia pulled out of the world organization and all its bodies excepting the World Health Organization in January that year (Allen 1968, pp. 192–93). Beijing now declared full support for the *Konfrontasi*. Malaysia appealed to the UN for help, tightened its security and asked for more troops and assistance from her allies in the Five Power Defence Pact.

At the end of April 1965, the Tunku went to South Korea for four days and arrived in Tokyo on 1 May to await Sukarno for talks. That same day, Sukarno announced at a massive May Day rally in Jakarta that he would not be going to Tokyo, saying "I am happier to stay with my people" (Keith 2005, p. 69).

On the domestic front, leaders of five opposition parties, including the PAP, the United Democratic Party and the People's Progressive Party (PPP), came together on 9 May 1965 to form the Malaysian Solidarity Convention (MSC) to work for what Lee Kuan Yew now titled "Malaysian Malaysia". Lee's enemies within UMNO saw this as a clever concealment of his plan to remove Malay special privileges. From this point onwards, it became increasingly clear that some radical change in the relationship between Kuala Lumpur and Singapore was needed.

On returning to Kuala Lumpur on 11 May to attend UMNO's annual conference being held three days later, the Tunku found strong resentment being expressed against Lee Kuan Yew for questioning Malay special status. Some members were demanding that Ismail arrest Lee immediately and ban the PAP (Keith 2005, p. 72).

Angry delegates were temporarily placated only after the Tunku assured them that Lee could not possibly convince Malaysian Chinese that they were not already getting a fair deal. On top of that, these voters actually feared Lee's style of politics, he argued. Ismail told the delegates that as long as Lee did not break the law, he would not be locked up. Lee was using democratic weapons, and so UMNO should fight him with the same. He further assured them that Lee was being foolish in thinking that Malaysia could be ruled without the support of the Malays (Keith 2005, p. 72).

This turn of events angered party secretary general Syed Ja'afar Albar. He roused a gathering of Malays on 23 May to raise their voices in calling for the crushing of Lee "so that Dr Ismail can hear the anger of the people" (Keith 2005, p. 127). According to Lee, Ismail "knew where we stood, so he was not out to arrest us".

> We were not trying to undermine the Alliance; we were just exercising our constitutional rights. But I am sure if the Tunku had ordered him to arrest me, or Goh Keng Swee, I am sure he would have done it (Interview 7 February 2006).

Apparently, the authors behind the Separation Agreement were Razak, Ismail and Tan Siew Sin, as well as Singapore's Minister of Finance Goh Keng Swee and Minister of Law Eddie Barker. Observers disagree about whether Goh and Barker had actually forced Lee Kuan Yew to accept the terms by threatening to resign. Nevertheless, secrecy was successfully kept, apparently at the insistence of Singapore, although the Malaysians probably did not want to have it any other way either (Dee 2005, pp. 462, 467, 479, 488–90).

Inter-ethnic tension was running high. On 5 August, Ismail issued a warning to fifty leaders of Chinese guilds and associations planning a rally calling for Chinese to be made an official language. Behind closed doors, Ismail told them that there would be repercussions if such a rally was held and reminded them that the deal made during independence was that citizenship would be granted to non-Malays while English and Malay would be the only official languages until 1967, after which the use of English would be phased out (*ST* 6 August 1965).

On 9 August, when the Tunku presented the amendment to the Constitution of Malaysia and the Malaysia Act to facilitate Singapore's separation from Malaysia, he informed the Dewan Rakyat that tensions had grown to such a state that only two courses of action were open to him:

> Number one is to take repressive measures against the Singapore Government for the behaviour of some of their leaders and number two to sever all connections with the State Government that has ceased to give even a measure of loyalty to the Central Government (Fletcher 1969, p. 91).

What his government was now choosing to do was the second alternative, what he termed "the breakaway" (ibid., p. 95).

Tom Critchley, then Australian high commissioner to Malaysia, noted on 10 August that Lee "did not seek Singapore's partition from Malaysia and that the signature of the partition bill was indeed 'a moment of anguish'" (Dee, p. 466). However, after further discussions with the Tunku, Razak, Ismail and Tan Siew Sin, Critchley altered his view, and wrote back to Canberra on 16 August:

> I find it difficult to believe that the separation was not acceptable to Lee from the outset. At any rate, it seems clear that there was no question of Singapore being forced out of Malaysia (Dee, p. 489).

Critchley's version of events, based on details conveyed to him by major actors and as he reported to Canberra on 16 August, was the following: (1) Tunku made his decision on the separation while in a London hospital on June 29, and told Lim Kim San, Singapore's minister of national development, who happened to be there at the time: "Thus a Singapore Minister knew before Malaysian Ministers". Tunku told Razak on 1 July to discuss matters further with other Malaysian ministers; (2) Goh Keng Swee went to see Razak sometime around 13 July and, as told to Critchley by Tan Siew Sin and Ismail, suggested "disengagement and emphasized Singapore's desire for autonomy in finance". However, Goh quickly agreed with the Malaysian view that "disengagement could be based only on complete separation"; (3) an understanding had been reached between the two sides by 20 July, and Barker was asked to do the legal drafting. Exactly when Malaysian Attorney-General Abdul Kadir bin Yusof was brought in is a matter of some controversy (Dee 2005, pp. 488–90; Critchley, interview 22 March 2005); by the time Tunku returned from London on 5 August, agreement had "to all intents and purposes" been reached; (4) on 7 August, all the major actors met at Tunku's residence, following which Lee Kuan Yew asked for an RMAF jet to take him to Singapore to get the agreement signed by his cabinet that same day (Dee 2005, pp. 488–89).

Things moved fast on the final stretch towards separation, and the need for absolute secrecy for fear of domestic unrest seems to have been met. When Tunku returned to Malaysia on 5 August, he merely announced that he would soon be having talks with Lee Kuan Yew to resolve misunderstandings, and that no major internal and external policy changes were expected. The British, the major sponsor of the Malaysia project, had no apparent forewarning until 8 August that the separation would be realized the following day, and this only after the high commissioner, Lord Head, gate-crashed a party the Tunku was holding that evening. Australia and New Zealand learned about the impending separation from the British. Messages were quickly sent to the Tunku from the leaders of these countries, vainly seeking a postponement of the announcement. Apparently, Sabah and Sarawak were not informed in advance either (Sopiee 1974, pp. 209–11; Dee 2005, p. 468; Allen 1968, p. 207). Australia, being committed to Malaysian defence and having troops stationed in the country, was also greatly upset that they had not been consulted (Dee 2005, pp. 457–59).

Critchley reported to Canberra that the Tunku had informed him that a joint defence council between Malaysia and Singapore would be formed, and that the Tunku regretted not letting the British, the Australians and the New Zealanders know his plans in advance but felt he had no alternative. His reasons for haste, as reported by Critchley, were the following:

> The communal situation had deteriorated and if he had not moved quickly there would have been trouble and 'we would not have been able to continue to fight the Indonesians'. If Singapore had not agreed to an amicable arrangement, the only alternative would have been to send in troops and take over the state (Dee, p. 458).

Goh Keng Swee revealed much later on radio [in August 1997] that at a secret meeting with Razak and Ismail, he had argued that "the only way out was for Singapore to secede", and that knowledge about their decision "must also be kept away from the British" (Kwok 1999, pp. 55–56). Eddie Barker supported Goh's stance, but noted that Razak thought there was nothing the British could do anyway once the leaders of Malaysia and Singapore had made up their minds: "Fortunately for us, Tun Ismail turned to the deputy prime minister and said 'I think Eddie is right'" (Tan 1999, p. 89).

In separate letters to the prime ministers of Britain, Australia and New Zealand, the Tunku provided the explanation that "if my intentions were to become known there would be trouble within the country and so I had to force a measure through as quickly as I could" (Letter to Robert Gordon Menzies, 12 August 1965; Dee, p. 480).

The separation of Singapore from Malaysia became official fact on 9 August 1965, after just two hours of parliamentary debate. The Tunku appealed publicly for the support of the MPs from Sabah and Sarawak and was granted it, and the Separation Bill was passed unanimously.

In an interview, UMNO Secretary General Syed Ja'afar Albar, the man who objected most vehemently to separation, revealed that he was about to enter the chamber to criticize the bill when Ismail stopped him. The minister told him that if he should then speak against the separation, there was a real risk that both Sabah and Sarawak would follow Singapore out of the federation. This appeared convincing enough for Syed Ja'afar to absent himself from the debate and the voting, making it possible for the decision for separation to be unanimously made (Sopiee 1974, p. 212). In noting Syed Ja'afar's absence from the voting, some analysts, such as Patrick Keith, concluded that he stayed away in admittedly highly ineffectual protest (Keith 2005, p. 195). Syed Ja'afar subsequently resigned, although it is not clear if this was to protest the separation or if it was because the only other alternative the Tunku offered him was public dismissal.

Ismail had already sent a letter on 7 August to the commissioner of police in Singapore, John Le Cain, informing him that with effect from 9 August, he was "to take orders from Mr Lee Kuan Yew". The Tunku gave similar instructions to Brigadier S.M. Alsagoff, commander of the Fourth Federal Infantry Brigade based in Singapore (*ST* 9 August 1965).

Alex Josey reported that Ismail in a speech made in Singapore on 6 June had said: "Both the Alliance and the PAP subscribe to the concept of a Malaysian Malaysia, but they differ in their approach to make it a living entity. It is this difference in approach which generates a great deal of heat, and which disturbs the hitherto comparatively tranquil political scene in Malaysia". On that same occasion, Lee Kuan Yew expressed doubts about whether Ismail's liberal understanding of the problem was "sincerely supported by the Alliance" (Josey 1968, pp. 268–69). Lee would later state that "[the] only Malaysian minister who was not prejudiced against Singapore was Deputy Prime Minister Tun

Dr Ismail". After plans for trade cooperation between Malaysia and Singapore initiated after Ismail visited Singapore in April 1971 proved unsuccessful, Lee concluded that "Ismail's lone voice could not prevail against the other UMNO leaders" (Lee 2000, p. 270).

> But he was only number three, and even if he had been number one, I doubt whether he would have been strong enough to control the Ultras and carry out his policy: the gradual reduction of the privileges of the Malays as they progressed until there was a non-communal society with all races on an equal footing (Lee 1998, p. 655).

Ismail's understanding of the troubled relationship between the Alliance and the PAP was that two basic ways of establishing Malaysia were imaginable. While the PAP wanted the immediate imposition of non-communalism, the Alliance way required firstly the creation of harmony between racially organized groups — namely UMNO, the MCA and the MIC — and secondly the ultimate attainment of non-communalism. Reportedly, Ismail thought Lee Kuan Yew's impatience was disrupting Malaysia's racial peace, and what was worse, the latter was instead putting the blame on UMNO (Keith 2005, p. 131). In a letter to *National Geographic* commenting on an article that the magazine was about to publish, Ismail provided his understanding of politics in, and between, Malaysia and Singapore (Letters 22 April 1966):

> When Singapore joined Malaysia the government in Singapore tried to practice in Malaysia what is possible in Singapore but not in Malaysia. For example, the People's Action Party, which is the ruling political party in Singapore, tried to impose straightaway a non-racial political party on the people of Malaysia. It is not surprising that in doing so it stirred communal feelings. In addition to this, the People's Action Party

insinuatingly ridiculed the Yang Di-Pertuan Agong. The approach to National Language differs between the two territories. In Singapore, the approach is through multi-lingualism, i.e. making Chinese, Indian and Malay equal in status whereas in Malaysia the emphasis is on Malay. The other languages, while being allowed to be taught and spoken, are not made official languages in Malaysia. Because of the past colonial policy the Malays are far behind the Chinese in education and in the economic field. It is the policy of the present Alliance Government to redress this imbalance and for this to materialise time and patience are required. Singapore was not willing to be patient and to bide time for this to occur. Because of these difficulties in fundamental approach, the separation of the State of Singapore from Malaysia was inevitable. Singapore and Malaysia are interdependent. Singapore has the finest port in the East and a large portion of her trade depends on Malaysia. At the moment both nations, comparatively speaking, are well off. If they can co-exist for some time, each understanding the other's point of view, the time will come when they will merge again. It is better to wait for this to come because if they do not do so they will sink together instead of coming together.

Chief Justice Suffian had this to say about his old colleague:

He was a realist, aware of the prejudices of every community. He agreed with Mr Lee Kuan Yew's slogan "Malaysia for Malaysians", but he did not agree with the way that slogan was to be translated into reality. He did not agree that it could be done overnight, he knew that the inborn prejudice and resistance of millions have to be worn down patiently, that the millions from every community have to be convinced slowly, that they have to be persuaded steadily in the delicate process of uniting the various races in Malaysia (Suffian 1974, p. 12).

Conspiracy theories have flourished about the "true story" behind the merger and separation, including persistent claims that

Malaysia had been merely a stepping-stone strategy for Singapore to gain independence from Britain, and that the Tunku had been party to it. More grounded hypotheses for the failure of the merger consider the background of Indonesian aggression and the different approaches taken in the federation and in Singapore for defeating communism; the "ideological difference" between Kuala Lumpur's Malay ethno-nationalism and Singapore's "Malaysian Malaysia", as well as the Alliance's "conservatism" and the PAP's "socialism"; conflicting expectations between the Alliance and the PAP on electoral behaviour and ambitions; and the incompatibility of the political styles of the Tunku and Lee Kuan Yew. The fear within the MCA of losing Chinese votes to the PAP and of business competition from Singapore was another factor in the equation that helped to undermine the Tunku's grand plan.

Leading members of the Malaysian Special Branch felt at the time that it was the PAP decision to contest in the 1964 general elections that made Singapore's secession a year or so later "inevitable" (Hatton 2004, p. 271). Lee Kuan Yew maintains that it was in fact the forming of the Malaysian Solidarity Convention (MSC) that changed the power equation radically (Interview 7 February 2006):

> We did join Malaysia, but that did not mean that we had *surrendered* Singapore! If riots were started with a pan-Malay agenda thereafter, you would have had resistance in all the major cities. Now, can you contain that? The Tunku, Razak and Ismail knew they could not. So it was decided that Singapore should get out.

Therefore, according to this reasoning, to stop the MSC in its tracks, Singapore and the PAP had to be jettisoned from the federation. Ismail told pressmen that the main reason for the sudden decision to separate Singapore from Malaysia was to avoid "outside interference" (*ST* 18 August 1965). On 4 September 1965, he was quoted in the *Straits Times* as saying that he considered the separation "a painful but temporary phase" in the history of the Malaysian Federation (*ST* 4 September 1965). He later wrote at the end of his memoirs that "in spite of what was believed, the separation of Singapore from Malaysia was by mutual agreement" (Drifting c16).

Military cooperation between Singapore and Malaysia nevertheless continued uninterruptedly (*ST* 5 September 1965). The seriousness of the security situation was reflected in the fact that Malaysia was holding as many as 500 individuals as "prisoners of war". Ismail acknowledged this in early September when attending the third Commonwealth Conference of Law Ministers and Chief Justices in Canberra. These detainees consisted largely of captured Indonesians and communist sympathizers.

From Canberra, Ismail flew to New York to represent Malaysia again at the United Nations (*ST* 3 September 1965). Singapore was admitted as a member at this UN assembly meeting. Pakistan announced that it was cutting off diplomatic ties with Malaysia because of Malaysian support for four UN resolutions on the Kashmir issue calling for an end to armed conflicts. Ismail told the general assembly that it was Pakistan's "sovereign privilege" to do so, but Malaysia stood by its aim "to put an end to this fratricidal war" (*ST* 7 September 1965). Significantly, Ismail met United States Secretary of State Dean Rusk, but did not arrange any meeting with Soviet Union Foreign Minister Andrei Gromyko (*ST* 28 September 1965). At a press conference held in Singapore on his way home from New York, Ismail called Pakistan's action "very childish" (*ST* 26 September 1965).

While he was away, a Vietnamese delegation visited Kuala Lumpur and awarded several Malaysian leaders with honorary titles. Ismail was made Grand Officer of the National Order of Vietnam (*ST* 7 September 1965).

On 13 December, parliament passed the Societies Bill to replace older ordinances enacted separately for Malaya, Sabah and Sarawak. The government had earlier rejected a move by C.V. Devan Nair (DAP-Bungsar) and Lim Chong Eu (UDP-Tanjong) to refer the bill to a select committee. Ismail acknowledged that the bill did empower the home affairs minister "to declare unlawful any society or branch of a society or class or description of societies which in his opinion is, or is being used, for purposes prejudicial to or incompatible with the interest of the security of the Federation or any part thereof, public order or morality" (*ST* 14 December 1965).

Later that week, the First Malaysia Plan was passed. Ismail spoke up in defence of "the most uncommon" fact — as an opposition MP called it — that Malaysia was spending more on defence and internal security than on education. He said of PMIP member Abu Bakar Hamzah, who raised the issue, that he must be "living in a dream" if he was not aware of the dangers facing the country.

A substantial sum of M$139 million was earmarked for developing housing facilities for the Malaysian Police, especially the Police Field Force and the Federal Reserve Unit. In an attempt to raise the status and increase the independence of the police department, Ismail asked for the title of "*Royal* Malaysian Police" to be given to it. Another measure he undertook to improve the lot of the police was the building of two-room flats for the rank-and-file to replace the one-room flats that they had so far been granted. Because of poor housing, children to policemen who had reached sixteen years of age had had to move out to live with grandparents. These new measures were taken by Ismail to encourage loyalty among policemen (Hanif, interview 13 September 2005; *ST* 21 December 1965).

Members of these organisations have often to be away from
their families and are required to operate in unusual
circumstances. They can be expected to perform their duties
well if they know their families are well accommodated
(*ST* 21 December 1965).

Ismail was in the Philippines over the New Year to attend the
presidential inauguration of Ferdinand Marcos. A.S. Talalla of the
Ministry of Foreign Affairs was in charge of preparations for the
trip, and was also at Subang Airport to welcome Ismail's team
home. To his surprise, Ismail stormed up to him on arrival and
gave him a scolding in front of the crowd of senior officers and
ambassadors gathered on the tarmac: "Do you know you
embarrassed me? The presents were wrongly labelled, and I gave
the cigar box to Mrs Marcos and the tea set to the President!"
(Talalla, interview 30 March 2006).

Ismail was nevertheless full of optimism that Marcos would
soon establish diplomatic ties with Malaysia, and was happy that
the new president was keen on reviving the Association of
Southeast Asia (ASA) founded in 1961 by Malaya, the Philippines
and Thailand (Andaya and Andaya 1982, p. 275).

Allegations of assets mismanagement at Malayan Banking
surfaced in 1966, causing a run on the bank. This led to immediate
government intervention and a *de facto* nationalization of the
institution. As home affairs minister, Ismail took over as its chairman
(White 2004, p. 79). This sudden involvement on his part in the
world of finance and business signalled a new period in his life.
Ismail had by now been in charge of national security for five
harsh years, and was starting to entertain the idea of leaving the
government and going back into private medical practice.

In April 1966, Ismail accepted an invitation from the director
of the South Korean Central Intelligence Service, Kim Hyung-

Plate 1. Abdul Rahman bin Yassin and his wife, together with their nine children. Taken *circa* 1936. *Back row, right to left:* Ismail, Yassin (later secretary-general of UMNO, Esah, Abdullah (later Bar Council Chairman and Senator), Khatijah, Suleiman (later Cabinet Minister and Ambassador). *Front row, right to left:* Fatimah, Zahara binte Abu Bakar, Abdul Rahman bin Yassin, Zubaidah and Rafeah [*Courtesy of Mohd Tawfik bin Tun Dr Ismail*].

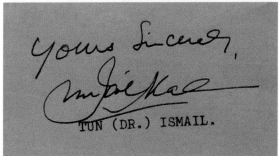

TUN (DR.) ISMAIL.

Plate 2 (*top*). Ismail at Queen's College. He is in the third row, standing in front of the right end of the pillar [*Courtesy of Professor David Runia, Queen's College, Melbourne University*].

Plate 3 (*bottom left*). The signature of Tun Dr Ismail Alhaj bin Datuk Haji Abdul Rahman [*Courtesy of Mohd Tawfik bin Tun Dr Ismail*].

Plate 4. (*bottom right*) Ismail tries horse riding in Tasmania in 1942 during term break [*Courtesy of Professor David Runia, Queen's College, Melbourne University*].

Plate 5. Ismail and Neno pose for photographers on 22 November 1949 after their betrothal was announced. Ismail was then a Johor state councillor. They were married in January the following year [*Courtesy of NSTP*].

Plate 6. Ismail poses with wife and children (*standing from left* – Badariah, Tawfik, Zailah and Tarmizi; *seated from left* – Ismail, Zamakhshari, Ariff and Norashikin), 22 September 1970 [*Courtesy of NSTP*].

Plate 7. Ismail and his wife Neno enjoy a joke together with Tunku Abdul Rahman (*centre*) at the Kuala Lumpur Town Hall, while listening to Radio Malaya's new programme series, "Variety" and "Malayan Musicale", 29 November 1955 [*Courtesy of NSTP*].

Plate 8. Ismail (*in the foreground*), as Minister of Natural Resources, inspects a drainage and irrigation scheme in Johor, 22 September 1955 [*Courtesy of NSTP*].

Plate 9. Ismail's 76-year-old grandmother Che Busun binte Mohamed Salleh (*left*), with Abdul Rahman Yassin (*centre*), and wife, Kamariah binte Ja'afar (aka Ma'Uda, sister of Onn Ja'afar, *right*), June 1956 [*Courtesy of NSTP*].

Plate 10. Ismail waves goodbye as he leaves for the United States to make preparations for his term as Ambassador and United Nations representative, 15 July 1957 [*Courtesy of NSTP*].

Plate 11. Ismail, as Minister Plenipotentiary (without portfolio), takes leave of Tunku Abdul Rahman to fly off to the United States to become Malaya's first Ambassador to Washington as well as Permanent Representative to the United Nations, 5 September 1957 [*Courtesy of NSTP*].

Plate 12. Ismail, Ismail Ali and Tunku Ja'afar at the United Nations listen to opening discussions at the 12th General Assembly, where the Federation of Malaya was admitted as the world body's 82nd member, 17 September 1957 [*Courtesy of NSTP*].

Plate 13. Ismail makes his first call on American Secretary of State John Foster Dulles, 21 September 1957 [*Courtesy of NSTP*].

Plate 14. Ismail and Neno greet Queen Elizabeth II (*centre*) on the English monarch's visit to Washington, D.C. Her husband Prince Philip is behind her, and President Dwight Eisenhower is at far right. Strangely, Ismail did not mention this event in his regular reports to the Tunku, October 1957 [*Courtesy of NSTP*].

Plate 15. Sweden's UN Secretary-General Dag Hammarskjöld arrives at a reception given in his honour by Ismail and Neno at Istana Tetamu in Kuala Lumpur, soon after the couple had returned from New York, and Ismail was made External Affairs Minister, 13 March 1958 [*Courtesy of NSTP*].

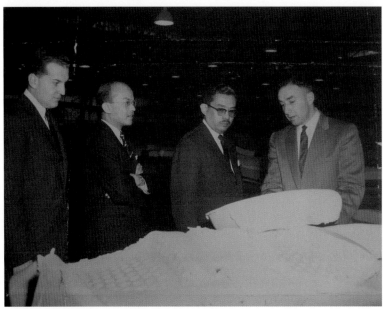

Plate 16. Ismail and Ismail Ali visit the Goodyear Tyre and Rubber Company at Akron, Ohio, March 1958 [*Courtesy of NSTP*].

Plate 17. Abdul Rahman Yassin (*centre*), the first President of the Senate, together with two of his sons, Suleiman (*left*), Minister of the Interior, and Ismail, Minister of External Affairs, 17 September 1959 [*Courtesy of NSTP*].

Plate 18. The Tunku (*left*) enjoys a happy moment with Ghazali Shafie (*centre*), the Permanent Secretary of the Foreign Affairs Ministry, and Ismail, 13 July 1962 [*Courtesy of NSTP*].

Plate 19. Ismail, as Acting Prime Minister, talks to Filipino Vice-President Manuel Pelaez on the first ASA telephone link between Kuala Lumpur and Manila, 31 July 1962 [*Courtesy of NSTP*].

Plate 20. Ismail, then Home Affairs Minister and Minister of Justice, inspects a guard-of-honour mounted by the rank and file of Chong Pang Police Station in Singapore. He is accompanied by Paya Lebar's Acting District Superintendent of Police, Richard Tay, 15 March 1965 [*Courtesy of NSTP*].

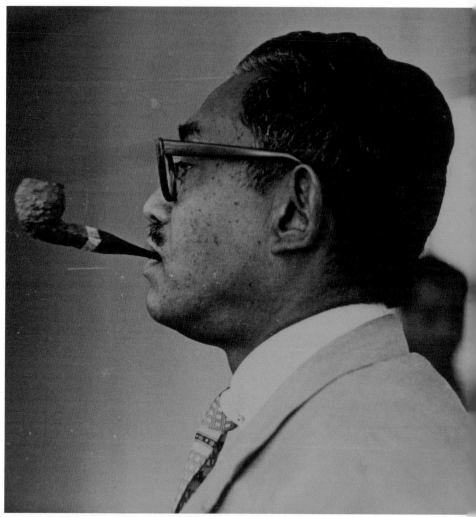

Plate 21. Ismail with his omnipresent pipe, 5 July 1965 [*Courtesy of NSTP*].

Plate 22. The Agong and the Permaisuri Agong (*far right*) attend a Mass Band Parade at Merdeka Stadium marking Malaysia's second anniversary. The Big Three – (*from left to right in middle row*) Ismail, Razak and the Tunku – were also present. Behind them is the Chief of the Armed Forces Staff, Lt General Tunku Osman bin Tunku Mohammad Jewa, 31 August 1965 [*Courtesy of NSTP*].

Plate 23. Ismail returns from Bangkok with a present from Thai Deputy Defence Minister Air Chief Marshall Tan Sri Dawee Chullasapya for Tunku Abdul Rahman. This "Game Winner" golf club was accompanied by a note: "This golf secret weapon is for people who want to win every game, even if it costs a few friends. Wait until your opponent swings to putt and then honk your horn. When this no longer irritates him, change to the bell." 22 August 1966 [*Courtesy of NSTP*].

Plate 24. Ismail arrives in London with Neno in September 1969 for his first medical check-up since returning to the government, and is given a clean bill of health [*Courtesy of NSTP*].

Plate 25. Ismail launches the "gotong royong" clean up at Chow Kit Road in conjunction with National Goodwill Week, 6 September 1970 [*Courtesy of NSTP*].

Plate 26. Ismail (*left*) and Finance Minister Tan Siew Sin (*right*) seeing off Razak as the latter left for London to attend

Plate 27. Ismail plays a round of golf with Lee Kuan Yew. When he became Kuala Lumpur's representative to the Internal Security Council in June 1959, Ismail thought the golf course the best place for him to hold discussions with Singapore's leaders, 23 April 1971 [*Courtesy of NSTP*].

Plate 28. Ismail (*left*), taking a break with Lim Chong Eu (*centre*) and Razak (*right*) at a National Unity Council meeting, 1 July 1971 [*Courtesy of NSTP*].

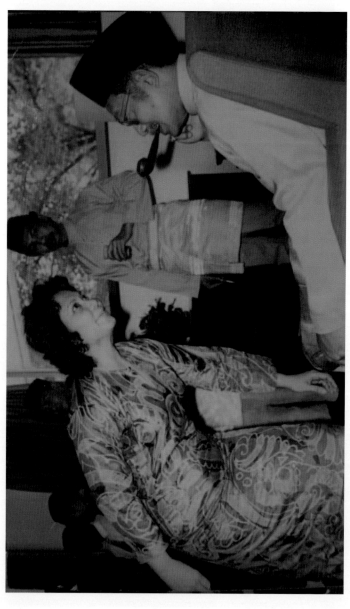

Plate 29. Ismail takes a break during the open house he held for Hari Raya Haji celebrations. His wife Neno comes over to see if he is comfortable. Ismail's private secretary Zawawi Mahmud is in the background, 26 January 1972 [*Courtesy of NSTP*].

Plate 30. Ismail (*right*) is met by Razak (*left*) and other cabinet ministers on his return from a ten-day trip to Indonesia, 15 March 1972. Minister of Works, Posts and Telecommunications V.T. Sambanthan is behind them [*Courtesy of NSTP*].

Plate 31. Ismail is met on arrival in Singapore by the republic's Foreign Affairs Minister Sinnathamby Rajaratnam, 12 April 1972 [*Courtesy of NSTP*].

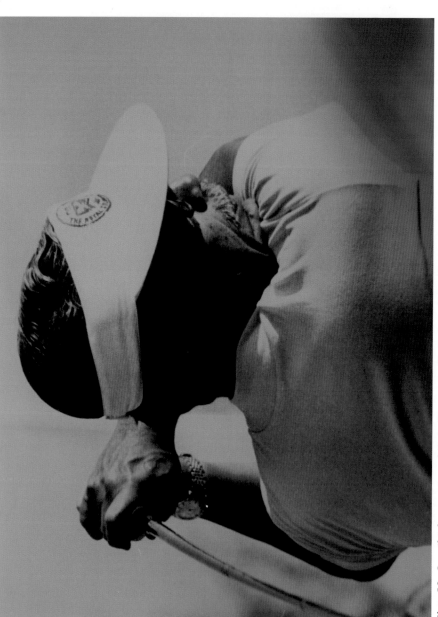

Plate 32. Ismail takes a swing while in Singapore. He had a golf handicap of 15, and was achieving phenomenally good results during the last weeks of his life, 14 April 1972 [*Courtesy of NSTP*].

Plate 33. Finance Minister Tan Siew Sin says farewell to Ismail at the airport, 29 May 1972 [*Courtesy of NSTP*].

Plate 34. Ismail and Neno (*left*) are greeted by Toh Puan Rahah and Razak on arrival at the latter's Hari Raya Puasa Open House, 16 January 1973 [*Courtesy of NSTP*].

Plate 35. Ismail has a chat with students while visiting the University of New England, Armidale, Australia. His eldest son Tawfik, who was a second-year art student there, is standing third from left, 20 March 1973 [*Courtesy of NSTP*].

Plate 36. (*From left*) Ismail, Razak, Pernas chairman Tengku Razaleigh Hamzah, and the Director of the Implementation, Co-ordination and Development Administration Unit of the Prime Minister's Department, Tunku Shahriman Tunku Sulaiman, at the Bumiputera Economic Seminar held at Universiti Malaya, 4 April 1973 [*Courtesy of NSTP*].

Plate 37. Ismail addressing delegates at the opening of UMNO Women and Youth conferences, 29 June 1973. Among those seated are Women chief Aishah Ghani (*second from left*); Youth Chief Harun Idris (*centre*); and UMNO Secretary-General Senu Abdul Rahman (*second from right*) [*Courtesy of NSTP*].

Plate 38. Ismail receives a collection of cheques from Communications Minister Sardon Jubir for the National Heroes Welfare Trust Fund, 21 July 1973 [*Courtesy of NSTP*].

Plate 39. Ismail in his office, 1973 [*Courtesy of NSTP*].

Plate 40. Robert Kuok, who grew up with Ismail in Johor Bahru, and who was one of Ismail's closest friends in the final years of his life [*Courtesy of Robert Kuok*].

Plate 41. The swimming pool in Ismail's garden, where he exercised regularly [*Author's photograph*].

Plate 42. Ismail's final deed as Acting Prime Minister was to officiate at the silver jubilee celebrations of the Peninsular Malaysia Malay Students Foundation (GPMS), 2 August 1973 [*Courtesy of GPMS Treasurer-General Annuar Zaini, here seen at Ismail's left*].

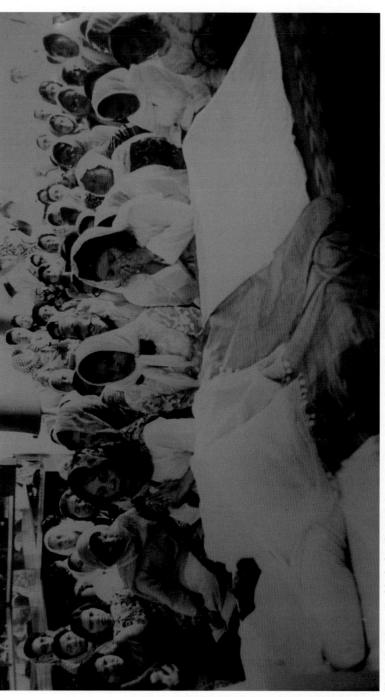

Plate 43. Neno (*in black shawl*), with her two daughters, (*from left to right*) Zailah and Badariah, by her side, prays at their house on Maxwell Road, just before Ismail's remains were moved to the National Mosque, 3 August 1973 [*Courtesy of NSTP*].

Plate 44. A huge crowd turns out for Malaysia's first state funeral, 3 August 1973 [*Courtesy of NSTP*].

Plate 45. The Tunku walks in Ismail's funeral procession, 3 August 1973. He is accompanied by the recently ousted President of the Malaysian Indian Congress V.T. Sambanthan to his right and the Minister of Youth, Culture and Sports Hamzah bin Abu Samad to his left. Deputy Minister of Trade and Industry Musa Hitam is behind the Tunku [*Courtesy of NSTP*].

Plate 46. Malaysians gather to watch Ismail's burial ceremony, 4 August 1973 [*Courtesy of NSTP*]

Plate 47. The army acts on Razak's orders to break through the concrete floor of the Heroes' Mausoleum to prepare Ismail's final resting place, 4 August 1973 [*Courtesy of NSTP*].

Plate 48. Four Catholic nuns were among the many Malaysians of various faiths gathered for Ismail's burial, 4 August 1973 [*Courtesy of NSTP*].

Plate 49. Neno (*standing at right*) with her children at her feet at Ismail's hastily prepared graveside, along with a host of dignitaries. Malaysia's King and Queen are in the middle seated on the floor, (he with *songkok* and she dressed in white), Prime Minister Razak is to their left, and Singapore's Deputy Prime Minister Goh Keng Swee is standing with open suit and tie, at a

Plate 50. Razak calls on Ismail's widow Neno at Maxwell Road after the burial on 4 August 1973. He had returned from Ottawa at around noon that same day. Ismail's eldest son Tawfik, who flew home from Australia the evening before, is in the background [*Courtesy of NSTP*].

Plate 51. On 9 August 1973, a *tahlil* (prayers) session was held at Ismail's house. Those present included *(front row from left)* Minister of Education Hussein Onn, Deputy Minister of Defence Tengku Ahmad Rithauddeen, Inspector-General of Police Abdul Rahman Hashim, Prime Minister Abdul Razak Hussein, and Minister of Communications Sardon Jubir. Besides family members, others who attended were Minister of Primary Industries Taib Mahmud, Minister of Culture, Youth and Sports Hamzah Abdul Samad, and Minister of Agriculture and Fisheries Ghazali Jawi.

The following day, a memorial service was held at the Buddha Jayanti Temple in Kuala Lumpur, sponsored by the MCA and the Buddhist Community of Selangor. Quotations by Ismail were broadcast over radio and television for 40 days after his death.

wook, to visit Seoul. He flew *via* Tokyo, where he had a meeting with Malaysian students. During his eight-day visit to South Korea, he was awarded the Order of Merit (First Class), and reached an agreement that the two governments would "share intelligence on common security" (*ST* 28 March 1966; *ST* 3 April 1966; *ST* 12 April 1966)

Around this time, Ismail brought his son Tawfik along on a two-week trip with Tom Critchley and his wife and his visiting sister-in-law to the islands off eastern Johor, including Pulau Tioman and Pulau Rawa, which were all part of his constituency of Johor Timor. As a rule, Ismail tried to visit his constituency during the school holidays because that was also the best time for him to meet grassroot UMNO leaders, the majority of whom were teachers. That way, he could also take his children along on nature trips during their holidays. As in this particular case, Ismail could also cultivate a personal relationship with important foreign diplomats (Critchley, interview 22 April 2005; Tawfik, interview 21 July 2006).

In May, Ismail was in London to attend the Conference of Law Ministers from the Commonwealth. Fortunately, his long-time physician Dr Stuart C. McPherson was there on holiday at the same time. On being told by Ismail that he had had a mild heart attack in October 1965 while delivering a speech at the United Nations, McPherson took him along to see a heart specialist, a Dr Brigden.

A letter that Ismail received from McPherson soon after informed him that Dr Brigden and a Dr Pappworth thought it most advisable for him to avoid stress. Since "you are more sensitive to personality stresses than most people", McPherson concurred with the view that Ismail should return to being a general practitioner and not continue as a politician. Ismail replied three weeks later that he would consider the matter after further consultation with McPherson on the latter's return to Malaysia (Letters 12 May 1966).

Ismail's fiery temper and readiness to debate were not conducive to his health. Philip Kuok described Ismail as one who "stood up in Parliament prepared to fight anyone with a bluntness that sometimes shocked his own supporters and colleagues, [...] a highly principled man, sometimes immovable and intolerant of another person's irrational views, and easily taking offence in something which he considered to be a matter of principle" (Kuok 1991, pp. 216, 218).

The Tunku had instituted in April that year a new Order of Chivalry, naming it Darjah Yang Mulia Setia Mahkota Malaysia (The Most Esteemed Order of the Crown of Malaysia). Ismail became the first to be given the honour on 8 June, when the Yang Dipertuan Agong conferred its First Class — the Seri Setia Mahkota (SSM, Grand Commander) — on him. This carried the title of "Tun", and the world thereafter addressed Ismail as "Tun Dr Ismail", and his wife as "Toh Puan" (ST 9 June 1966; Abdullah 1986, pp. 96–101).

By 30 September, Ismail had made up his mind to retire. He knew that the resignation of a person in his position was a drawn-out affair, and decided to give the Tunku sufficient advance notice and without being too specific about the exact time. He wrote that day to the Tunku asking to "resign in principle" as minister, based on the prognosis and the advice of his doctors.

> If I were single or only had a wife to support, as when I first joined you years ago in politics to fight for our country's independence, I would have ignored this advice. Now of course, I have five children, all very young and it is unfair to them if I were to ignore the advice. [...] I have worked for so long under

you and as you know have the highest respect, regard and love for you both as a leader and as a friend. It tears my heart to have to write this to you because I know how much support you need in order to lead the Party and the Country (Letters 30 September 1966).

This correspondence speaks against the persistent rumour that Ismail retired in protest against some Tunku policy. The loyalty he was to show the Tunku after the 13 May riots of 1969 further supports the publicly announced reason for Ismail's retirement — ill health. The Tunku read the letter "with great sorrow because I will be losing a very close friend and loyal colleague", and replied on 5 October:

I had before made Suleiman stay on against his own wishes and this I have regretted to this very day. So I feel I would not make the same mistake again. You definitely need this change and I am sure it will do you a lot of good. You will still be in Parliament and in UMNO and the Alliance, so I can always count on you for any help I shall need (Letters 5 October 1966).

Suleiman, Ismail's eldest brother, had been made high commissioner to Australia at his own request. He hoped that a posting to Australia would not be stressful and would not worsen his ill health. But on 7 November 1963 while delivering a speech in Melbourne, he collapsed and died. The Tunku and Suleiman had been close ever since their time together in London, and when the latter's remains were transported back from Australia, the Tunku and his cabinet were in Singapore to receive his body and escort it to Johor Bahru for burial (*ST* 8 November 1963).

Ismail's decision to resign also meant that the Tunku, who had been planning to retire, was obliged to stay on for a while longer (*ST* 25 February 1967). The fact that MCA Secretary General

Khaw Kai Boh was also retiring at the same time fuelled
speculations that the two were leaving over the National Language
Bill that was recently tabled in parliament (*ST* 26 February 1967).
Ismail vehemently denied these rumours, and promised to
stay on if his retirement should lead to any "disturbances"
(*MM* 28 February 1967; *ST* 4 March 1967). His decision to leave
also shocked Finance Minister Tan Siew Sin.

> I was the first person to know about it. He came to see me from
> his doctor's office, immediately after confirmation of the
> diagnosis, and I was badly shaken. Yet he spoke in a calm voice
> and one could not help but admire his tremendous courage,
> because as a doctor, he knew only too well what the diagnosis
> meant. He left the Government soon after, but he made a
> complete recovery (Morais 1981, p. 143).

Some of Ismail's most lasting contributions were in foreign politics.
His strong opposition to communism, his battles against Sukarno
— "the Fuehrer of Jakarta", as Ismail titled him — along with his
distrust of super powers, helped him conceptualize a region free
of power politics. His support for the revival of the ASA as well as
the long campaign he embarked upon later in life to "neutralise"
Southeast Asia, would testify to this. He told the Foreign
Correspondents' Association of Southeast Asia on 23 June 1966
in Johor Bahru that Malaysia hoped for "the early realisation of
the widest participation possible". This optimism was driven by
the agreement reached between Indonesia and Malaysia on
28 May to end their three-year-old confrontation, and by the
normalisation of ties between the Philippines and Malaysia
(*ST* 4 June 1966).

> We look forward to a regional association embracing Thailand,
> Burma, Indonesia, Singapore, Malaysia, Philippines, Cambodia,

Laos and Vietnam. [...] We have no choice. We, the nations and peoples of South-East Asia, whatever our ethnic, cultural or religious backgrounds might be, must pull together and create, with hand and brain, a new perspective and a new framework. And we must do it ourselves. We must create a deep, collective awareness that we cannot survive for long as independent peoples — as Burmese, Thais, Indonesians, Laotians, Vietnamese, Malaysians, Cambodians, Singaporeans and Filipinos — unless we also think and act as South-East Asians (*ST* 24 June 1966).

Interestingly, when speaking to a group of college officials the following month, U.S. President Lyndon B. Johnson quoted the above words, together with an expression used earlier by Singapore Foreign Minister S. Rajaratnam on the need to build "a world civilisation in the Pacific through co-operation and peaceful competition" (*ST* 15 July 1966). In the event, the ASA was transformed on 8 August 1967 through the Bangkok Declaration into the Association of Southeast Asian Nations (Asean) comprising Indonesia, Malaysia, the Philippines, Singapore and Thailand (Solidum 2003, p. 22).

On 31 January 1967, Ismail wrote to Lee Moke Sang at the Malaysian High Commission in the United Kingdom to say that he would soon be coming to London for a heart check-up. He also told Lee about the house he had bought at Maxwell Road, Kuala Lumpur, incidentally from the lawyer P.G. Lim. The house was built as a present for Lim by her father (Lim, interview 14 May 2006).

The cost of the house has exhausted all the savings that I have had but it gives me satisfaction that I have managed to buy it out of my own savings without asking any favour from anybody. It also gives me satisfaction that on resigning from the Cabinet I have not used my influence or asked for any favour from any quarter to secure land at [a] special price either from the government or private individuals (Letters 31 January 1967).

Ismail's last day as minister was 14 March 1967, after which he went on leave — more specifically to London for a check-up — before beginning his new life. His departure from the top of the power pyramid amounted to a major change in Malaysian politics (*ST* 24 February 1967). On that occasion, the editorial of the major English newspaper, *Straits Times*, proclaimed "it is difficult to think of a ministry he has not headed, a political role he has not played, a central event he has not influenced" (*ST* 25 February 1967).

Student leader Annuar Zaini described the effect of Ismail's retirement on many young Malays at that time in the following terms: "We had not had enough of him, you see. For us, it was as if someone we were in love with was leaving the stage before we had had time to really enjoy his presence" (Interview 20 April 2006).

The president of the oppositional PPP, D.R. Seenivasagam, who had often been at parliamentary loggerheads with Ismail, called him "no doubt a hard man, but his greatest attribute is his frankness and honest belief in his actions. In dealing with him as a Minister, one knows exactly where one stands" (*ST* 25 February 1967). Ismail was the longest serving minister in the cabinet when he retired.

In an informal chat with a large group of Malaysian students in the United Kingdom early in 1967, Ismail optimistically described the National Language Bill as "the last barrier in the Alliance government's race for a united Malaysia" (*SM* 26 March 1967). On that trip, his doctor in London found that his heart condition had deteriorated somewhat and ordered him to avoid strenuous office work. He was ordered to have half-yearly check-ups in Kuala Lumpur, and should further signs of deterioration appear, he was to rush to London for surgery (*ST* 4 April 1967). Ismail also took the opportunity to make an official visit to Brussels, before coming back to Kuala Lumpur *via* London to stand in for what he thought was the final time as acting prime minister. The Tunku would be visiting Ceylon and Razak was going to Australia (*ST* 12 March 1967; 16 March 1967).

On 12 April, the anti-graft cabinet committee that Ismail had led finally tabled a motion for the setting up of the Anti-Corruption Agency (ACA). The suggestion was that the ACA would initially be placed under the inspector-general of police and the home affairs minister for a few years before being detached to become an independent body (*ST* 13 April 1967).

On 29 April, which was a cloudy day, a body of 100 variously uniformed policemen and 200 vehicles honoured Ismail and his family with a huge colourful farewell parade at the Police Depot in Kuala Lumpur. In an impressive show of respect, all the top brass from all police districts throughout both East and West Malaysia were present (*ST* 30 March 1967).

Ismail retired officially at the end of May, and was immediately thereafter appointed on the recommendation of Robert Kuok, as chairman of the board of directors of Malayan Sugar Refinery. He was also elected to the board of directors of Guthrie Corporation.

Many on the international stage would miss Ismail's brand of politics. Australian High Commissioner Tom Critchley's general understanding of "level-headed" Ismail and his role in the Malaysian leadership was that of "a catalyst" who would always cut to the chase, and who would often be responsible for making things happen (Dee 2005, p. 479; Critchley, interview 22 April 2005). Lee Kuan Yew mused: "Within the leadership of Malaysia, he was a source of moderation and common sense, a stable man not given to extremes, always very firm in his views, and who would not go with wild theories" (Interview 7 February 2006). He wrote Ismail a note to wish him well:

> It is a great privilege to have known you and it is more than a perfunctory courtesy which prompted me to send this note of my esteem and good wishes. You will always be one of my good friends and I would wish you to know that if there is anything I can do to be of service to you please do not hesitate to let me know (Letters 30 May 1967).

It was around the time of Ismail's retirement, after Philip Kuok and his wife Eileen Cheah had moved to The Hague, where Philip became Malaysia's ambassador, that Ismail "transferred his friendship" to Robert Kuok and Joyce Cheah. Another couple close to Ismail and Neno at that time was Sammy Senn and his wife. Senn was attached to Nestle Malaysia and would later become its chairman, and also chairman of the International Chamber of Commerce. According to Robert Kuok, Ismail's closest Malay friends at that time were his old colleague from New York, Bank Negara president Ismail Ali, and his wife Maimunah Latif.

Kuok supposed that the nature of Ismail's work was what caused him to be careful about whom he chose as his close friends: "Doc was a stickler for fair play and correctness, and asking him to use his political power to help you was tantamount to asking to be put in jail! Every Malay colleague feared him because of this, including Mahathir" (Interview 10 February 2006).

Lee Kuan Yew recalls that Ismail and his wife were always friendly to him and his wife: "One characteristic about Ismail was shown in the fact that while other ministers were keen to talk about their exploits with women, they would at the same time joke about Ismail's fidelity to his wife. Ismail did not display his piety, it was a private business for him" (Interview 7 February 2006).

Several of Ismail's children remember how a Chinese peasant woman once came to their house in a truck filled with vegetables as gifts for the minister. She was hoping that Ismail would help secure the release of her son who had recently been detained. Ismail told her to take her gifts away or get thrown into jail as well (Interviews 23 April 2005). This unwillingness to compromise on Ismail's part left a strong impression on his colleagues, relatives and friends. Kuok recalls:

> He was like that all his life, clean as a whistle. Lived within his means. I would pick up bills. That he could accept, but we never went to him for anything. From 1966 till his death, I was perhaps his closest friend, because of the relationship through Eileen, and my wife Joyce. We would talk seamlessly. There was no feeling of race or religion, although I am agnostic and he was a Muslim. He liked good drinks, but always in moderation. I never saw him even on the verge on being tipsy. He was always in control of himself. You would say, in Confucian terms, that he was a man who led a very correct life, a man of the highest integrity. Money, favours, political hypocrisy or deceit, all those were anathema to him (Interview 10 February 2006).

Ismail recognized corruption as a great ill but understood that for Malaysians of all races, going into the government "is one of the easiest ways to make money; and they know very well that some of them will be thrown out in the five-yearly elections [...] so they accept bribes and become corrupt". He discussed the matter with Philip Kuok:

> I only wish that people will one day establish themselves in the professions and the business world, and then enter politics like

the British politicians. [...] My message to the youth [...] is that they should not go into politics until they are financially or professionally secure (Kuok 1981, pp. 217–18).

Tan Siew Sin tried to persuade the Kuok brothers to become ministers around this time, but both refused. Robert Kuok remembers: "My mother was against it. Doc also wished me to stay out of politics, which he thought a dirty business, by the way — 'Your growth is unstoppable now, Robert, keep to it'" (Interview 10 February 2006).

Abdullah Ali, a second cousin and close friend of Ismail, and who was later high commissioner to London, remembers that Ismail was one of those who believed very early in Robert Kuok's business acumen and encouraged the latter in his undertakings when he was minister of commerce and industry back in the late 1950s (Interview 8 September 2005).

The Tunku's cabinet decided to present Ismail with a bonus of M$61,500 for "Cabinet services" on his retirement. On 19 January 1968, Dr Tan Chee Khoon, member of parliament for the Labour Party, took the government to task over the matter, calling it "a wanton waste of public funds", and that Ismail, on retiring, was not exactly a pauper. Finance Minister Tan Siew Sin, a man otherwise known for being stringent with national spending, defended the government's decision. "[Tun Dr Ismail] had to retire purely because of ill health. As such, we felt that it was only fair that he should receive payment of the basis of $1^{1}/_{2}$ months' salary to every year of service" (ST 20 January 1968).

On 23 January 1968, Ismail, by then a backbencher, proposed his three-point plan for Southeast Asian security. The fundamentals were that the region must undergo political neutralization, guaranteed by all the big powers including communist China, non-aggression treaties must be signed between the countries in the region, and a declaration of peaceful co-existence should be made by the various Southeast Asian countries that they would not interfere in each other's internal affairs (*MM* 24 January 1968). This line of reasoning, born of the troubles Malaysia had had to face since the 1950s often with Ismail in the frontline, together with the worries small countries tended to have in light of the Cold War, came to exert a strong and lasting influence on Malaysian foreign policies and on the architecture of regionalism in Southeast Asia. The vice chairman of the Labour Party, Lim Kean Siew, commended the proposal the following day, asking the government to immediately form a "small, select and proficient" committee to examine the country's defence problems in light of the withdrawal of British troops from Malaysian soil by the end of 1971 (*ST* 25 January 1968).

Ismail's retirement was far from tranquil in the beginning. The danger posed by his heart condition was surpassed by the recurrence of neck cancer. By the middle of June 1968, Ismail was back in London for radiotherapy — "fighting for his life", as he later told Philip Kuok — against lumpy growths behind his ear that he had noticed in mid-May (Letters 19 October 1968). For three months he stayed on his own. His wife who was then in a stage of late pregnancy, could not accompany him. Philip and Eileen Kuok sometimes travelled across from the continent to visit him.

The growth was malignant and it was sad to see Tun Ismail living alone without his family, and having to be taken to the clinic every few days. Lee Mok[e] Sang described the scene to me, and how [Ismail] had to sit there among the crowds of people, most of them terminally ill, waiting his turn for the radium treatment. Not surprisingly, he suffered intense depression. I would fly to London with my wife every weekend to be with him. When we met, he was cheerful enough; but I could see that the treatment was getting him down (Kuok 1991, p. 220).

Lee Moke Sang, who was an important member of the Malayan Labour Party (Lee 2001, p. 34), was an officer at the Malaysian High Commission's Labour Department. According to Ismail's daughter Zailah, members of the Malaysian Embassy had been told not to go out of their way for Ismail — now a private person — during his stay in London. Lee nevertheless went against instructions and was at hand to meet Ismail and care for him (Zailah, interview 23 April 2005).

A.S. Talalla ("Bertie") was first secretary in London at the time, and he occasionally visited the Kensington area flat where Ismail was staying for a chat and to bring him the day's newspapers. Ismail was feeling miserable, and on learning that Talalla occasionally went for concerts in the city, asked to accompany him: "You buy the tickets and I'll buy dinner". Talalla also remembers that Ismail was "bemused" by how he had become nobody once he was out of office. Ismail gave the young man "the useful advice" not to expect anything from the civil service on retirement so as not to be disappointed, and to treat anything unexpected coming his way as a bonus (Interview 31 March 2006).

The sudden change in social and political standing was something that Ismail had a hard time adjusting to during his short retirement, and on one occasion when he attended an event at Radio Television Malaysia in Kuala Lumpur and found that no place had been reserved for him, he turned around in anger and left without a word (Zailah, interview 23 April 2005).

Musa Hitam recalls how much more light-hearted Ismail became during his retirement, and how he was happy driving his own sports car and wearing colourful and youthful clothes (Interview 26 October 2005). According to Abdullah Ali, Ismail would dress up fashionably, probably according to flashy British designs of the time (Interview 8 September 2005). Though no longer a leader of the country, Ismail's interest in Malaysia's nation-building process did not wane. On 19 October 1968, he wrote to Philip Kuok about the country's state of affairs. The MCA had managed to set up the Tunku Abdul Rahman College, and this was countered from the Malay side by a demand for a national university using Malay as the medium of instruction. Such an institution — Universiti Kebangsaan Malaysia — was in fact founded in 1971 at Bangi, Selangor.

> I remember advising Siew Sin after the first election after Independence that we should dissolve the parties which now constitute the Alliance and form a single multi-racial party. Now of course, the golden moment has passed and we have to make the best of the present set-up of the Alliance and trust that the leaders will continue to get the support of the moderates in the constituent parties which make up the Alliance (Letters 19 October 1968).

Where the economy was concerned, he wrote in the same letter that Malaysia could not keep up with Singapore "because we vacillate and procrastinate in our decisions". A sense of pessimism ran through this correspondence.

> We have become prisoners of the committee system so much so that the sub-committees of the committees, the members of which are government officials, actually hold the real power. So when you mentioned to me in your last letter that sometimes you get frustrated in your work it was no surprise to me because I experienced it for almost fourteen years. [...] I must say that

my one year's experience in business has shown me a new light in the relationship between business and government.

Ismail's nephew, Abu Bakar bin Suleiman, who became a doctor and who inherited his uncle's medical books from Queen's College, remembers Ismail advising him to leave the Ministry of Health in order to avoid the debilitating bureaucracy (Interview 29 March 2006).

After his resignation, Ismail accepted various positions in business corporations. He succeeded his father as chairman of the board of directors of Malayan Banking, became chairman of Guthrie Ropel and of Food Specialities (M), was made director of Cathay Organization, Cathay Theatres and Cathay Film Distributors, and was chosen head of Sports Pool (M) (*Sunday Times* 3 December 1967; *ST* 4 December 1967). He was installed as the first president of the Malaysian–American Society (*MM* 24 January 1968), and also joined the board of directors of British Petroleum (Malaysia) (*ST* 2 April 1968). According to Abdullah Ali, it was Ismail who coined the term "Ropel", possibly from the words Rubber and Oil Palm Estates Limited (Interview, 8 September 2005).

On 5 May 1968, Ismail, who was already head of Johor UMNO, was elected to lead Johor Alliance as well. By August, the Alliance as a whole started preparing for the general elections due the following year. UMNO's secretary-general and Education Minister Khir Johari was put in charge of the whole exercise, while Minister of Information and Broadcasting Senu Abdul Rahman was responsible for "publicity and liaison". Ismail was officially chosen to lead "election strategy" (*MM* 24 August 1968).

A letter to Philip Kuok in Europe written a year into his retirement, showed Ismail in a contemplative mood:

Here in Malaysia many changes have occurred. On the political front, education continued to be a controversial subject. The setting up of the Tunku Abdul Rahman College by the MCA and the Malay reaction to this by demanding a National University using Malay as the medium of instruction, and the changes which were made by the Ministry of Education in implementing this policy — all these caused a certain amount of uncertainty among parents in Malaysia and bring again into focus the ever-present racial problem in the country (Letter 19 October 1968).

On 31 December 1968, Ismail's father Abdul Rahman Yassin, the first president of the Senate, retired at the age of 78, just after another of his sons, Abdullah Abdul Rahman, became Johor senator (*ST* 23 October 1968; *MM* 28 October 1968).

Sometime in 1967–68, Robert Kuok started to consider founding a local shipping company to compete with established firms from developed countries. By late 1968, the idea had come far enough for him to seek approval from top ministers in the cabinet. This he did in one single hectic day, and so managed to establish the Malaysian International Shipping Corporation (MISC). Finance Minister Tan Siew Sin announced this venture publicly on 7 December. The company had a start-up capital of M$20 million and the directors were Robert Kuok, Ismail, G.K. Rama Iyer who was the under-secretary (special duties) in the Prime Minister's Department, and Frank Wen King Tsao, who was chairman of the Textile Corporation of Malaya (*Sunday Times* 8 December 1968). Ismail in turn "induced" Leslie Eu Peng Meng, the son of his old friend, the Olympiad Eu Eng Hock, to give up his shipping post in Bangkok and return to Malaysia to help out (Kuok, interview 10 February 2006; Rama Iyer, interview 11 April 2006; Eu, interview 9 September 2005). MISC is today a subsidiary of Malaysia's petroleum company, Petronas, and controls one of the largest tanker fleets in the world.

Ismail and Neno spent the Christmas weekend that year together with the Tunku and about seventy other guests on a three-day cruise from Port Swettenham to Pulau Langkawi, where the Sultan of Kedah inaugurated the Langkawi Golf and Country Club that was affiliated to the Subang golf course (*ST* 23 December 1968). Incidentally, the Tunku and Ismail were then the president and the vice president respectively of the Subang National Golf Club.

Sports Pool, which acted as agent for the British football betting houses Littlewoods and Vernons, of which Ismail was a director, had its licence revoked at the end of November 1968 — exactly one year and fifteen days after it started operations in Malaysia. A government spokesman said the company had only been allowed on a trial basis, and in any case the directors themselves had decided to end operations. Ismail explained that part of the reason was that the company was making losses (*ST* 19 November 1968). In March 1969, Ismail also relinquished his position as president of the Malaysian–American Society (*ST* 20 March 1969).

Ismail was by now feeling comfortable with his new life. However, he complained about "residual effects" from his latest fight against cancer — "having a dry mouth, which restricts my enjoyment of food and also prevents me from making long speeches" (Letters 15 April 1969). His wife remembers that they spoke about "the things that husbands and wives would have normal conversations about", and Ismail, who was otherwise never strict with her, would caution her only about expenditure outside of normal household costs (Zailah, interview 23 March 2005). As yet, Ismail had not decided to stand again for nomination to represent his constituency of Johor Timor. He had, however, made up his mind that "even if I stand for election, and win, I shall not accept appointment as a Minister". "This is because, when I was critically ill in London I made a pledge to myself and to God that after I recovered from my illness I would not again become a Minister."

In April 1969, when the electoral campaign was in full swing, Ismail made plans to attend Guthrie Corporation's Group Planting Conference in London scheduled for 21–23 May (Letters 15 April 1969). He was quite certain that his political commitments would be over and done with by then. This was not to be.

Malaysian politics wanted him back. This time, it would be for good.

PART TWO

Remaking Malaysia

Chapter 6

FORCED FROM RETIREMENT

In mid-March 1969, Education Minister Khir Johari, who was director of election operations for the Alliance, presented the manifesto for the upcoming general elections to a committee of which Ismail was a member. The rather uncontroversial themes chosen were "higher standard of living for all" and "national unity" (*MM* 11 March 1969). Ismail subsequently campaigned in Johor for the 10 May general elections, calling for a strong and united government led by one party, and warning against the possibility of a coalition government, using Indonesia as a bad example to follow. When campaigning in aid of Chinese Alliance candidates running for the parliamentary seat of Muar Pantai and the state seat of Bandar Maharani, Ismail called for the Democratic Action Party (DAP) to be driven "back to Singapore so that it will not create confusion in the minds of Malaysians", and said that the opposition party's slogan of "Malaysian Malaysia" was a Singaporean invention.

He did extremely well in his constituency of Johor Timor, winning 9,639 votes against his PMIP opponent's 2,419 (*ST* 12 May 1969). The Alliance Party, however, suffered a string of setbacks, and given the rising tension that followed wildly jubilant demonstrations in Kuala Lumpur organized by the opposition, a request was made by Razak to Ismail for the latter to return to his former post of Home Affairs Minister. Serious trouble was in the air. Ismail realized that the government faced a potential crisis, and was therefore willing to grant Razak his request on condition that the Tunku agreed to it.

He wrote a letter at 5p.m. — less than two hours before actual rioting broke out — to Eric Griffiths-Jones, the chairman of Guthrie Corporation, suggesting that the latter should not expect him to come to London the coming week. Ismail informed him that the Alliance's majority had been badly reduced: "Tun Razak had strongly pleaded that I join the government. I told him to ask the Tunku and if he wants me I have no alternative but to accept. Tunku very likely to ask me." (Letters 13 May 1969).

Razak obviously trusted Ismail, and the latter's retirement at a relatively early age for health reasons was evidence that he did not harbour any high political ambitions of his own.

The 1969 electoral campaigns were unique in that there was an absence of any outstanding national security issue (Milne and Mauzy 1978, p. 161), and touchy issues of racial relations, language and special rights dominated the debate. The elections campaign in 1955 had been about national independence, while that in 1959 centred on communist designs and the Alliance consolidating its position as representative of the three major races. The 1964 elections were in turn preoccupied with Indonesian aggression and tensions between Singapore's PAP and the Alliance (Andaya and Andaya 1982, pp. 261–80).

Domestic matters were coming to a head, and the 1969 elections results continued to chart the steady loss of support that the Alliance had experienced since 1955. Its share of the popular vote fell this time from around 58 per cent to 48 per cent, and with the loss of twenty-three parliamentary seats to the opposition, it no longer held the two-thirds majority it had always relied on to secure constitutional reforms. The winners were the PMIP, the DAP and the Gerakan Rakyat Malaysia Party (Malaysian People's Movement). The MCA, the Alliance's second largest component party, suffered the heaviest losses (Owen 2005, pp. 417–18). This latter fact helped alter the power configuration of Malaysian politics forever.

The major English daily *Straits Times* reported on the morning of May 13 that UMNO campaign leaders had met for a three-hour meeting a day earlier and in light of the MCA's poor showing, were pushing for a cabinet that would reflect UMNO's increased relative strength within the Alliance (now fifty-one parliamentary seats to the MCA's thirteen). The Tunku had earlier said that he would announce his cabinet by 13 May. The group wanted Ismail recalled to his old position "to strengthen" the cabinet, a request that seemed to have been immediately forwarded to Ismail by Razak. The group was also asking for the controversial Syed Nasir Ismail, formerly director of Dewan Bahasa & Pustaka, to become education minister, and for Ghafar Baba to be promoted from minister without portfolio to minister for commerce and industry. It was further suggested that Education Minister Khir Johari should take over the finance portfolio held throughout the 1960s by MCA leader Tan Siew Sin. Tan was to be moved over to the defence portfolio that had been held by Razak, who would then concentrate on rural development besides being deputy prime minister (*ST* 13 May 1969).

Many were assuming that a DAP-Gerakan coalition would replace the Alliance in the vital state of Selangor (Gagliano 1971, p. 16). Clarification came only in the afternoon of 13 May, when the Gerakan publicly stated that it would remain "neutral" in the Selangor State Assembly, thus allowing the Alliance to form a minority government. At 2.00 p.m. that day, the president of the badly trounced MCA, Tan Siew Sin, after heavy criticism from UMNO members, announced after an emergency meeting of the party's Central Working Committee that the MCA, in accepting the election results, would no longer participate in the Alliance government, although it would nevertheless continue supporting it in parliament (Gagliano 1971, p. 17).

Ismail heard about this turn of events from his wife, who heard it from Tan Siew Sin's wife whom she had accidentally run into on the streets (Tawfik, interview 28 April 2005). He was horrified. According to Tan, Ismail "came straight to my house to urge me to re-consider our position". Ismail wanted at least Tan to stay in the government (Morais 1981, p. 143). He warned Tan of the further polarization that would follow an MCA withdrawal, that it would play into the hands of both Malay and Chinese extremists, and that it would end in heavy bloodshed. It was, however, already too late, for the news had been officially announced (von Vorys 1976, p. 325).

Others, such as Mahathir Mohamad who lost his parliamentary seat to a PMIP candidate, were at this time advocating that the MCA be excluded from the government. Interestingly, Ghafar Baba admitted that it was he who suggested to fellow Malaccan Tan Siew Sin to pull the MCA out of the government "to shock disloyal Chinese voters to their senses". He had not really expected the older man to go along with the idea (Ghafar, interview 16 June 2005).

In a letter to Guthrie's Eric Griffith-Jones in London written on 3 June, Ismail extrapolated that the MCA's decision was "one of the factors that triggered off the rioting".

> I tried by pleading, by exhorting and by threat to impress on Tun Tan Siew Sin the irresponsibility and the childishness of the decision taken by the MCA, but in vain (Letter 3 June 1969).

Another letter to Philip Kuok provided further details about the series of events taking place that fateful day:

> I did my best to convince Tun Tan Siew Sin that this decision of the MCA was irresponsible, it was childish and that it was letting down those Malays and Chinese who have elected the 12 successful MCA candidates and I warned him that this decision if not revoked would contribute to rioting and chaos in the country. I spent one and a half hours with Catherine [Siew Sin's wife] trying to persuade her to persuade Siew Sin to revoke the decision but all my effort was in vain. So it was with this tension, with this irresponsible decision by the MCA that the riot started (Letters 4 June 1969).

Racial clashes broke out on the evening of 13 May even before Ismail had decided to return. He identified panic within the Alliance as one of the immediate causes for the outbreak of violence. Another was the series of triumphalistic demonstrations in Kuala Lumpur carried out by the opposition (Letters 3 June 1969). These had increased throughout the three days following the Saturday elections, as it became increasingly certain that the opposition had scored a significant victory. At dusk on Tuesday, inter-communal killings took place in Kuala Lumpur.

An assembly of UMNO supporters from throughout Selangor had gathered to participate in a massive counter-demonstration led by the state's Mentri Besar Harun Idris. It was to start at 7.30p.m. from his residence near Kampung Bahru in the middle of the city. Many came early and armed, purportedly for their own safety, since the parade was to wind through Chinese areas. The commonly accepted story is that word then arrived that Chinese and Indians in Setapak had attacked a group of Malays who were on their way to take part in the march (Gagliano 1971, pp. 17–18). Daud Ahmad, who had worked with the secrets registry at the Home Affairs Ministry since early 1967, questions this long accepted version of how the riots were sparked off. He was living in Kampung Bahru, and was among those gathered outside Harun's house on Jalan Raja Muda that fateful evening. He knew of no news arriving from Setapak about any fighting:

> Anyway, the timing would not have been correct, according to the reports I later looked through. What happened on the spot was that a car passed by, with a group of Chinese, shouting vulgarities and insults at the Malays gathered there. This car managed to drive off unmolested. Immediately following that, a couple of Chinese came along on motorcycles, and unfortunately for them, the rage of the crowd was released on them, although they themselves had not hurled any insults at the crowd (Interview 28 June 2005).

In any case, by 6.45p.m., violence had erupted. By 8.00p.m., a curfew was declared, as police and military reinforcements rushed into the city. All in all, 2,000 military and 3,600 police were deployed (Gagliano 1971, pp. 18–19). The rioting nevertheless spread throughout the night, throughout the next day, and throughout the country.

Ismail's eldest daughter Zailah watched the riots on TV on the 8 o'clock evening news and informed her father, "who remained calm, but took out his pistol, put it into his pocket, and went out with my mother to dinner at his friend Sammy Senn's place at nearby Kenny Hills" (Interview 23 March 2005).

On the morning of 14 May, Zailah answered the phone. It was a call from Razak. She passed the call to her father. Soon, an escort of armed policemen arrived and her father left with them. She recalls Ismail telling her later that he was going to rejoin the government. The 16-year-old asked what difference that would make to their lives, and he replied: "There will be no more long holidays, and we will have to cut back on a lot of things" (Interview 23 March 2005).

Tunku Abdul Rahman had been recuperating from a gruelling campaign that had lasted ninety days. He rushed back to Kuala Lumpur to arrange a meeting with top aides such as Razak and Tan Siew Sin. Ismail and Hussein Onn, although not in the cabinet, were also summoned along with General Ibrahim Ismail, and the inspector general of police.

> There was panic and near pandemonium among the ministers and officials, since they were not prepared for such an event. However, Doc Ismail managed to keep calm. Tun Razak wanted to get into an official car and face the mob, but was dissuaded from doing so. Doc Ismail told him bluntly, "You will be torn to pieces". The Tunku was inclined towards declaring martial law, but General Ibrahim said he would not advise that course of action. "If you do that," he said, "I cannot [provide any] guarantee [that I will] be able to hold back the members of the Armed Forces and officers who might take over control of the Government (Kuok 1991, p. 222).

According to Karl von Vorys, the leader whom Ismail warned — with the words "They will kill you" — against going to the rioting areas might have been Tan Siew Sin and not Razak (von Vorys 1976, p. 341). The person who stopped the Tunku from considering handing over power to the military was reported by others to have been Ismail, who warned the prime minister, "once you do that you won't get it back" (*The Star* 2 August 2004).

A state of emergency was declared on Thursday 15 May, and parliament was suspended. The National Operations Council (NOC) was formed the following day, with Razak as director of operations. This body was modelled on the organization of the same name which operated during the Emergency (Ong 2005,

p. 207). The reasons the 66-year-old Tunku was to give later for
not taking on the NOC directorship himself and for giving it to
the 47-year-old Razak instead, were the latter's experience with
security issues and the Tunku's bad health. The prime minister
was then suffering from glaucoma and other ailments (Gagliano
1971, p. 20).

According to Robert Kuok, after the Tunku had failed to calm
the public, Ismail decided to appear on TV. Ismail asked Kuok to
fly in from Singapore in order to take a quick look at a speech
that he had written and was to deliver live on television. The idea
was to assure Malaysians that things were under control. Kuok
remembers the occasion thus:

> I was left alone in his study for just a few minutes to look
> through the speech. Afterwards I asked him: "Doc, who suffered
> most? The Malays or the Chinese?" He hesitated but a second
> and then said: "Of course the Chinese". I then said: "But your
> statement will strike terror into their hearts even more, Doc".
> He replied: "That was never my intention. What do I need
> to do?" I then suggested that he remove a phrase here and
> a sentence there. He agreed to all the changes (Interview
> 10 February 2006).

Ismail then went on the air and declared: "Democracy is dead in
this country. It died at the hands of the opposition parties who
triggered off the events leading to this violence" (*ST* 19 May
1969). No doubt, democracy in Malaysia was dead for the moment,
and what it would resurrect as — if at all — was as yet far from
clear. Ismail saw it as his duty to bring it back to life. He later told
pressmen that "a powerful government is one that is not afraid to
practise democracy" (*UM* 18 July 1969).

As Chief Justice Suffian Hashim was to say at the first Tun Dr
Ismail Oration held by the Academy of Medicine in Malaysia in

Kuala Lumpur on 6 September 1974, "...when the Tun said that democracy was dead every one knew that it was only his method of telling the people that unless the Government and the people together made every effort to meet the challenge of the times, democracy would remain forever dead for Malaysia and would never revive" (Suffian 1974, p. 7). Although Suffian and Ismail were old friends, the two had had little private contact after one became a judge and the other a minister. The two considered it inappropriate, and wished to avoid any clash of interests (Tawfik, interview 21 July 2006).

Musa Hitam witnessed Ismail on television and recalls how "a sense of relief came over us; the sheer force of the man's reputation for fairness was *magic*" (Interview 26 October 2005). Chet Singh, who was then with the Penang Development Board, remembers feeling "comforted" on hearing the announcement that Ismail was returning as Home Affairs Minister (Interview 2 February 2006).

The general understanding then was that the Tunku had lost authority within the party and among the Malays, and was in no position to manage the crisis at hand. This notion was entertained even within the foreign community. A report written on 16 May to London by the British high commissioner expressed strong anxiety over the situation because "the Tunku had shown himself to be personally unsure over the situation and taken no grip over the situation" (MOD: DS 11/12 6/5/1/9). No doubt there were others who would have been willing to assist the leadership, but unlike them, Ismail was broadly considered "a man of formidable reputation for integrity and talent in all communities", with views "more cautious and more sophisticated than those of his younger colleagues" (von Vorys 1976, pp. 309–10).

The NOC held its first meeting on 19 May (*ST* 20 May 1969). Hanif Omar, who was officer in charge of the Police Department in Ipoh, was assigned to the NOC as chief of police staff. He remembers that the first thing Ismail wanted him to do was to arrest Harun Idris, and "for murder". A few others agreed immediately, but Hanif suggested that an investigation be carried out first since he had heard contradicting versions about what transpired on the evening of 13 May, including one about the violence actually starting in Gombak in the north of Kuala Lumpur, and not outside Harun's residence. Apparently, Harun had almost fainted when he realized that racial violence had broken out in front of his home (Hanif, interview 13 September 2005). Ismail agreed to this suggestion and the result of the subsequent investigation was released five months later in the official NOC report — *The May 13 Tragedy*. Harun was not arrested.

The significance of the absence of the Tunku from the NOC was not lost on most observers. A claim was made in the beginning that "no major decisions were made by the Council without the Prime Minister's consent" (von Vorys 1976, p. 345). As Philip Kuok was to see the situation years later, "Tun Razak could virtually [have become] a dictator at that time, but he never used his power in that direction. Next to him was Doc Ismail" (Kuok 1991, p. 223). Noordin Sopiee, in an obituary written on the occasion of Razak's death, somewhat dramatically noted that "The Tun probably worked harder than any dictator in history to get rid of his dictatorial powers and to work himself out of a job" (*NST* 15 January 1976). Wahab Majid, one of the few who had recently founded Bernama News Agency (on 20 May 1968), was press secretary to Ismail after the latter's return to the Ministry of Home Affairs. He remembers that Razak did toy with the idea of "benevolent dictatorship", but was in effect discouraged from having such thoughts by Ismail's incessant push to restore parliament as soon as possible (Interview 6 July 2005).

The NOC consisted of six Malays and two non-Malays, and was headed by Razak as director of operations, with General Ibrahim Ismail as the chief executive officer (CEO). The other members were Ismail (minister of home affairs), Hamzah bin Abu Samah (minister of information and broadcasting), Ghazali Shafie (permanent secretary, ministry of external affairs), Abdul Kadir Shamsuddin (director of public services), General Tunku Osman Jewa (chief of staff of the armed forces), Tan Siew Sin (MCA president) and V.T. Sambanthan (MIC president).

The daily meetings of the NOC were without much debate, while the "military and police members provided estimates of the situation and at times defined their needs". Ismail's stand "was regularly sought, and all, even the Deputy Prime Minister, deferred to his opinion" (von Vorys 1976, p. 346). Abdul Rahman Hamidon, who was the first NOC secretary, was impressed by the mutual respect that was evident between Razak and Ismail. He recalls how he would be sent by Razak to consult Ismail on most matters and how Razak made it clear to those working under him that such was to be the *modus operandi* (A.R. Hamidon, interview 9 September 2005). Abdullah Badawi, who would later become prime minister, succeeded Abdul Rahman Hamidon as NOC secretary. He remembers that Razak chaired most of the meetings and Ismail would act as his unofficial deputy. Razak would always look to Ismail for a cue whenever a new matter was introduced, and if Ismail should follow a reasoning that was not in agreement with what Razak had initially said, the meeting would become longer and Razak would try to accommodate Ismail's opinion. The two were never seen to disagree in public (Abdullah Badawi, interview 14 May 2006). True to his reputation, Ismail was as demanding of his new staff as he had been of his old, and would not accept any excuse for documents not being in place or being prepared (Abdullah Badawi, interview 14 May 2006). According to General Ibrahim, Ismail would not stand for any beating around the bush either (Ibrahim, interview 23 March 2005).

Abdullah remembers that when his own father, Ahmad Badawi bin Abdullah Ibrahim, then assemblyman for Kepala Batas, heard on the radio that Ismail had returned to join the NOC, he banged the kitchen table and exclaimed: "Now the team is complete!" Abdullah conscientiously compiled the notes he took at NOC meetings and bound them together "like an encyclopaedia" (Abdullah Badawi, interview 14 May 2006). These are until today still classified as confidential documents.

As violence continued throughout 14 May, a 24-hour curfew was imposed on the whole of the West Coast, south of Perlis and north of Johor. Among the first things the NOC did were to suspend the elections that were still being held in Sabah and Sarawak, and to stop the publication of all Malaysian newspapers.

By the end of that first week, things had calmed down enough for the curfew to be lifted in most areas. Over 15,000 refugees were by then encamped throughout the capital at stadiums and auditoriums. Razak announced that fifteen newspapers would be allowed to resume publication under NOC control, press curfew passes were revoked indefinitely, and news about the crisis would thereafter come only from the official Information Co-ordinating Centre (Gagliano 1971, pp. 21–22).

There were worries that the government was taking too hard a line in trying to get things under control. A report sent on 16 May from the British Kuala Lumpur High Commission to the British Ministry of Defence stated that "the Tunku and his government seem to throw overboard multiracialism and is flagrantly directed towards Malay supremacy with no effort being made to reassure the Chinese or to work with them" (MOD: DS 11/12 6/5/1/9).

This understanding seemed justified. When an emergency cabinet was announced on 20 May, offers of cooperation from the opposition were rejected (Gagliano 1971, p. 23). The MCA had agreed to be included, however, and Razak told the press that there had never been any intention on his part to form an all-Malay cabinet. He explained that the relationship between this cabinet and the NOC would be similar to that between the cabinet and the council of the same name that existed during the communist emergency. "[The NOC] will not be superior to the cabinet, but the director of operations will have powers far above the ministers" (*ST* 17 May 1969).

In the panic of the first week, a request was made to the British for army equipment. Although military assistance was not mentioned, the British found themselves in an awkward position. Though willing to help the Malaysian Government maintain law and order, there was apprehension that they might get dragged into domestic affairs should the communist threat increase (FCO 24/484).

By the end of May, official figures showed that the riots had left 177 dead, 340 injured, 136 houses burnt and 119 vehicles damaged. Singapore suffered some street violence, but the situation there had quickly been brought under control (Gagliano 1971, pp. 22, 24). In the following months, official casualty figures did not go up by much. By 31 July, 196 had been killed and 439 injured, 180 by firearms, while 9,143 had been arrested and charged in court (NOC 1969).

In a letter to Philip Kuok in Holland, Ismail admitted that he had hesitated in rejoining the government. He also provided details about how he viewed the process that led to the riots:

> I had just recovered from my recent illness and further I was
> just enjoying my new life, preparing for my future and also the

future of my children. [...] In the elections, it was obvious that the opposition parties were adamant to bring down the Alliance by every possible means they could think of. Finally they decided to play on communal politics. They therefore decided that the PMIP should play the extreme Malay nationalism type of politics, and the non-Malay parties like the DAP and the Gerakan would play the Chinese type of communal politics. [...] Since the Alliance's policy is based on a compromise, it could not therefore please all the Malays or all the Chinese but could only please the moderate Malays and the understanding Chinese (Letters 4 June 1969).

According to Ismail, this tactic of polarization was what tore asunder the fabric of cooperation built up by the Alliance since 1955.

On 12 June, Eric Griffith-Jones wrote Ismail a letter from London to plead for his understanding that the former could serve Malaysia best by remaining as objective as possible in counteracting the bad publicity that was being given Malaysia. The points that he was going to make to the international press, he told Ismail, would include the following (Letters 12 June 1969):

(1) "the Malay police behaved splendidly and with exemplary impartiality between the races." However, he added as a private message to Ismail that "the Army are reported by the same sources to have been responsible for excessive force against Chinese — it does seem on the best information that I have that the Malay Regiment rather lost its head". This supported the point, he added, that trained police strength, and not the army, was needed to quell violent disturbances and rioting;

(2) "the essential services such as water, electricity, telecommunications and medical services continued to operate throughout with little or no interruption";

(3) "the trouble was confined virtually exclusively to the Kuala Lumpur area and neither faction has attempted reprisals elsewhere";

(4) "instances have been reported of Malays giving shelter to Chinese, and vice versa", and :

(5) "the Malays who reacted to the Opposition's 'victory' celebrations were Selangor Malays reacting to the loss by the Alliance of an overall majority in the Selangor state elections".

Philip Kuok wrote to Ismail on 18 June: "We have all learnt a severe lesson. You and I have always feared that this might one day happen, a fear that had always been kept deep down in our hearts" (Letters 18 June 1969). In his autobiography, Kuok remembered Ismail proudly telling him that Johor Bahru, their hometown, was the only large multi-racial urban centre "where there was calm and complete peace during the aftermath of the May 13 riots" (Kuok 1991, p. 67).

The NOC decided that to secure lasting law and order, certain amendments to the original constitution were needed. To achieve this legally, parliament had to be resumed, and to guarantee acceptance of those amendments, a two-thirds Alliance majority had to be secured. Polling in East Malaysia had also started on 10 May, and was to have taken a few weeks to complete. This had to be suspended when emergency rule was declared, and was resumed only on 6–27 June in Sabah and on 6 June–4 July in Sarawak. Both the Tunku and Razak felt unsure about what the electoral results in East Malaysia would be, and according to Ong Kee Hui, the founder chairman of the Sarawak United People's Party (SUPP), it was Ismail who was "prepared to resume the elections under certain specified considerations to which he had given serious thought". A ban was needed to stop the opposition from raising issues "sensitive to the Malays such as their special rights and position, the national language, religion, and the position of the sultans". Such conditions could be imposed by the NOC under emergency laws (Ong 2005, p. 207).

Ismail also realized the importance of allowing the continuation of balloting in East Malaysia. It would in effect amount to a temporary restoration of democracy in Malaysia. He announced publicly:

> If the Alliance fails to get the two-thirds majority necessary for approving amendments to the Constitution, then we will have to negotiate with the opposition about support in our wish to isolate in the Constitution the several contentious communal problems. If they do not agree, then I do not see how we can recall Parliament. The blame for this will rest on the opposition. If on the other hand the Alliance gets the two-thirds majority, then the blame for any delay in returning to parliamentary democracy will rest with us (*ST* 6 May 1970).

As things turned out, the results gave the Alliance and its allies altogether 96 seats in the 144-member parliament — precisely a two-third majority. In the states of Perak and Selangor, induced and negotiated defections from the opposition secured a majority for the Alliance. One Gerakan federal parliamentarian also defected.

By the skin of its teeth, therefore, and through a string of strategic manoeuvres, the regime managed to facilitate the country's "return to normalcy". In the event, the Father of Malaysia — Tunku Abdul Rahman — was left with little choice but to retire. It was argued that the "reality" of Malaysian politics was such that for the country to retain democratic practices and to remain multi-racial, the status of the Malay language, the special rights of the native peoples, the status of the sultans, and citizenship rights for immigrant peoples had to be put beyond public debate, as had the status of Islam as the state religion.

The Tunku's spontaneous reaction to the break-out of violence had been to blame "Communist terrorists". This he did already on the morning of 14 May in a national broadcast. Despite vigorous objections from Ismail and others, he then decided to write a book to tell his side of the story (*May 13: Before and After*). The British High Commission in Kuala Lumpur reported to London that Ismail had said "the communists had not been prepared at the time of the riots either to cause them or to exploit them" (FCO 24/486). In fact, he claimed that they were "as much surprised as we were" (*ST* 21 June 1969). Six weeks later, Ismail phrased his understanding of the riots as follows:

> The disturbances on the 13th of May were the results of an explosive situation, built up during 5 weeks of electioneering, during which sensitive communal issues were raised and unfortunately succeeded only to inflame the electorate. The explosion itself, was, therefore, spontaneous and had caught all of us by surprise (*Siaran Akhbar* Pen.7/69/67).

He sought to differentiate the reasons for the violence of 13 May from those that caused the violence to continue. In July, he proclaimed as acting director of operations that in contrast to the outbreak of violence on 13 May, "current isolated incidents, such as those which occurred on 28th of June, were the results of premeditated acts of violence and arson by undesirable elements of our society" He added that these acts were without any "mitigating circumstances and they are therefore the more to be condemned and will be vigorously stamped out" (*Siaran Akhbar* Pen.7/69/67).

Given this reasoning, it was not surprising that the NOC aimed for as quick a return to "normalcy" as possible, and that the initial measures taken were aimed more at preserving order than anything else: "There was no search for new political formulas" (Gagliano 1971, p. 24).

The most prominent persons arrested immediately after the riots included V. David of the Gerakan and Lim Kit Siang of the DAP. The latter would remain detained for two years. There were 251 persons detained under the ISA before 13 May, but by July, the official figure had risen to 368 (von Vorys 1976, p. 347).

Groups that suffered public blame from the national leadership in the weeks following the riots included "opposition parties", "communist terrorists", "secret societies" and "anti-national and subversive" elements. As researcher Felix Gagliano then noted, these terms tended to mean "Chinese" to most Malaysians (Gagliano 1971, p. 23).

According to lawyer Dominic Puthucheary who had strong ties with Chinese-educated left-wingers, opinions about the fairness of the ISA arrests naturally differed. Generally though, English-educated left-wingers considered Ismail to be "the most reasonable person" in the regime. "But naturally, his decisions were based on the reports of his subordinates, and these could have weaknesses" (D. Puthucheary, interview 6 September 2006).

British documents reveal that the Australians had sent an officer to Kelantan at this time to study the PMIP. He reported that PMIP leaders at this time were quite comfortable with the Tunku and Razak but "were concerned about Tun Ismail", and were willing to accept emergency rule for six months before challenging it. Apparently, Ismail was eyeing them in return, and his concern was for a "Malay backlash" in the northern states of Kedah and Kelantan. PMIP leaders were, however, conscious of the fact that if any trouble should break out in those areas, the NOC would not hesitate to use it as reason enough to detain them (FOC 24/486 and 489).

In the months following 13 May, Ismail adopted an un-compromising stand against all he considered to be endangering the return to social normalcy, be they rumour-mongers, perpetrators of violence, government servants or Malay ethno-nationalists within his own ruling party. As Maurice Baker, Singapore's High Commissioner to Malaysia, remembers: "Ismail was a very decisive and strict man. He would arrest anyone who made trouble irrespective of race — Chinese, Indian or Malay — and send them off to Pulau Jerejak. I believe this uncompromising attitude helped to stop the spread of violence during those critical weeks" (Interview 9 June 2005). General Ibrahim also believes it was Ismail's reputation for being uncompromising and tough that helped to restore order (Interview 23 March 2005). Tengku Ahmad Rithauddeen, who was an under-secretary in the Ministry of Defence and who later became defence minister, remembers Ismail declaring that he would arrest even his own mother if she did anything illegal (Interview 4 September 2006).

Ismail launched thirty-three raids against "secret society thugs", and arrested over 2,000 for "rehabilitation" on Pulau Jerejak, an island off Penang that he had turned into a detention camp. While the police patrolled Chinese areas, the military were placed in Malay areas. After the initial disturbances, the Malay Regiment was moved into Kampung Bahru to replace the Sarawak Rangers, who were made up mainly of Ibans (von Vorys 1976, p. 348). However, in an interview given much later, General Ibrahim Ismail does not recall the Sarawak Rangers ever being involved (Interview 23 March 2005).

Abdul Rahman Hamidon claims that despite the crisis, things never got so out of hand that the civil administration needed to hand matters over to the military. The different branches of the police force functioned well and remained in control of law and order (A.R. Hamidon, interview 9 September 2005).

In the atmosphere of distrust following the inter-racial riots, fear and the lack of information made many susceptible to rumours. Ismail identified rumour-mongers as the major culprits in keeping violence alive. On the evening of 4 June, Ismail gave a speech over radio and television, stating that rumours then going around were claiming that fresh disturbances would occur on 6 and 7 June.

> The Government is determined to kill rumour-mongering and to this end has decided to take drastic measures. Persons who indulge in rumour-mongering, whether maliciously or otherwise, will be arrested and detained. These persons are to be regarded as enemies of society who deserve no mercy (*Siaran Akhbar* PEN.6/69/44).

In truth, rumours thrive when reliable news is not forthcoming from official and other central sources. The NOC's Information Co-ordinating Centre (ICC), which before cooperating with the Ministry of Home Affairs had been called the Police Control Centre, was blamed for its "infrequent bulletins [...] couched in repetitious generalities" (von Vorys 1976, p. 359; Gagliano 1971, p. 27). In the meantime, the NOC also warned the public against "Communist elements who are making attempts to exploit the present situation". It issued orders to heads of department "to streamline their Ministries and Departments". Only a week after these orders were given, Ismail, as acting director of operations, was already gravely concerned over delays on this matter. He wanted quick changes within the governmental institutions, "especially Ministries and Departments having direct dealings with the public". Disciplinary regulations were strongly imposed, and he warned the public service that "he would not hesitate to take action against them under the emergency power given to him" (*Siaran Akhbar* PEN.6/69/263).

Renewed disturbances in Kuala Lumpur on 28 June — when curfew-free hours was extended by an hour to 1.00 a.m. — left 6 people dead and 17 injured, and 24 houses burned down.

Forty-seven additional arrests were subsequently made. The official number of arrests between 13 May and 5 July reached 8,114 persons, comprising "all the major racial groups of this country" (*Siaran Akhbar* PEN. 7/69/67).

> Of this number, 4,192 have been charged in court, 675 released on bail while 1,552 were unconditionally released. The rest, comprising almost entirely of gangsters, subversives, secret society elements and those carrying offensive weapons are being detained (*Siaran Akhbar* PEN. 7/69/67).

Figures from the end of May showed that 5,750 were arrested over the first three weeks of the crisis (Gagliano 1971, p. 22). Detentions over the following five weeks thus amounted to 2,364. Judging from this decrease, things were successively calming down.

There was widespread worry at this time in various quarters of society that the opposition was not being sufficiently consulted. On 25 July, for example, Syed Hussein Alatas, Tan Chee Khoon and V. Veerappen, of the Gerakan, wrote a note to the Tunku, carbon-copied to Ismail, that "the Government should start on dialogue with the opposition parties so as to get their support as well" (Letters 25 July 1969). Incidentally, that same month, the NOC took new initiatives to secure mass support. Goodwill committees were set up throughout the land under a National Goodwill Committee (NGC) led by Tunku Abdul Rahman, to which the leaders of opposition parties were recruited (Gagliano 1971, p. 25; Comber 1983, p. 79). This body was not so much a part of NOC strategy as it was the result of "spontaneous movements to restore some kind of friendly inter-communal relations after the riots" (Milne and Mauzy 1978, p. 89). The Department of National Unity (DNU) was also created that same month under Ghazali Shafie to formulate a national ideology and devise new socio-economic programmes.

Meanwhile, the struggle between Malay ethno-nationalists (the "ultras") and "moderates" had expanded. The Tunku and all that his regime had come to stand for over the preceding thirteen years were being challenged by younger UMNO members, some of whom went so far as to seek a one-party rule that would exclude non-Malays from holding government posts (Comber 1983, p. 77). Attempts were made to brand the Tunku "pro-Chinese" and to blame his regime for failing to safeguard Malay rights. Rumours were rife that the Tunku had been forced aside by Razak, and that Razak was in league with the "ultras". These were strongly denied both by the Tunku and Razak (Gagliano 1971, p. 27). On 12 July, Mahathir Mohamad was expelled from UMNO for his open opposition to the Tunku, and soon after, Tunku-critic Musa Hitam, who had earlier been "smuggled in by Razak as the lowest ranking in the whole Cabinet", was sent on "study leave" to Sussex University in England to put him out of the way of the Tunku's wrath (Gagliano 1971, pp. 27–29; Milne and Mauzy 1978, p. 173; Musa, interview 26 October 2005). Razak told the young man not to worry and to bide his time and to "learn as you go along". On a visit to London during his time in Sussex, Musa Hitam ran into Ismail at the High Commission. He remembers that Ismail turned to the high commissioner and said: "Look after this boy, we need him" (Musa, interview 26 October 2005).

According to Tengku Razaleigh Hamzah, it was Ismail who had wanted Mahathir expelled, and who was later instrumental in stopping two attempts to re-admit him into UMNO (Razaleigh, interview 28 June 2005). On 15 July, Ismail banned offending documents criticizing the Tunku. He was strongly concerned that law and order were breaking down, and was adamant that there would be "no coups in the country and no coups in the party" (von Vorys 1976, p. 377). Later, in a television broadcast, he said:

I must warn the extremists and others as well, that if the anti-Tengku campaigns or activities are carried out in such a manner or to such an extent as to cause undue fear or alarm among members of any community, or if they are likely to lead to violence or to any breach of security or public order, I will not hesitate to exercise my powers under the law against those responsible for such activities (*ST* 13 August 1969).

He had taken the "ultras" to task on 2 August on Television Malaysia, accusing them of believing in "the wild and fantastic theory of absolute dominion by one race over the other communities regardless of the Constitution". He admitted that "polarization has taken place in Malaysian politics and the extreme racialists among the ruling party are making a desperate bid to topple the present leadership" (*Siaran Akhbar* PEN.8/69/22). According to J.R. Bass, this speech by Ismail came at a strategic time and "represented to non-Malays a thankful sign that the Alliance pendulum had reached the furthest extension of its pro-Malay swing" (Bass 1973, p. 633). Ismail also declared that there was no split in the UMNO leadership. The Tunku's "basic policy regarding the creation of a united Malaysian nation based on a multi-racial society" remained the same. This policy, he said, "does not interfere with the special position of the Malays, and others similarly placed as the Malays, and at the same time it safeguards the rights of the other races". Nevertheless, he did admit that, "in the past the implementation of this provision had left much to be desired".

Without this special provision, the Malays at this stage cannot hope to hold their own against other communities in normal competition. This is a fact that cannot be denied. I am confident that with the passage of time, the Malays will be quite capable of meeting the non-Malays in normal competition, without the special position (*Siaran Akhbar* PEN.8/69/22).

He issued a warning to "extremists and others", who were purportedly "in the minority" against continuing the smear campaign against the Tunku (*Siaran Akhbar* PEN.8/69/22).

That same day — 2 August 1969 — large segments of the military made a public pledge of allegiance to the Tunku (Gagliano 1971, p. 29; Comber 1983, p. 78).

Musa Hitam, who was by then a directly chosen member of UMNO's executive council, recalls a meeting where most of the top men of the party were present, and where he took the opportunity to present his ideas about Malay education. Ismail, whose silence often commanded as much respect as his speeches, suddenly cleared his throat to speak. Musa remembers the following:

> Ismail spoke in Malay, which is very significant: "Adakah ini bemakna bahawa Che' Musa kata Pemuda UMNO itu *pressure group?*" (Does this mean that Mr Musa is saying that UMNO Youth is a pressure group?). Complete silence. You could hear a pin drop. So I took a deep breath and said that that was true from a political-scientific perspective, but we represent the young so we have to voice the views of the young. After a while, he replied in English: "You've got a point there". You could hear sighs of relief in the room. There was always an element of fear when one dealt with him, but commanding fear alone does not make a great leader. This man was both feared and much respected, and that was for the fairness of his views. That was why he was a great leader (Musa, interview 26 October 2005).

Calls for the Tunku's resignation continued to be heard throughout August, and a thousand-strong student demonstration at Universiti Malaya had to be tear-gassed by the riot police. On 2 September, a week before Ismail left for London for heart treatment, the NOC banned any demonstration or utterance calling for the resignation of the Tunku. That same day, seven students called on Ismail to demand the release of four arrested students. The busy minister had them shown to his room, but soon threatened to end the interview if they did not reword their demand as an appeal instead. This they did, and the four were released the following day "on humanitarian grounds" and, Ismail stated, in consideration of the anxiety their parents had had to suffer (*MM* 4 September 1969; *ST* 3 September 1969).

A student who participated in demonstrations at Universiti Malaya at this time and who still wishes to remain anonymous, recalls that the students knew that they could demonstrate quite safely on campus grounds but that the police had orders from the ministry to stop any march beyond the gates. According to him, a demonstration led by Anwar Ibrahim, who later became deputy prime minister, once felt overly bold and decided to leave the compound.

> Once we were outside the safety of the campus, a Black Maria started moving towards us. We continued walking and chanting until the police van drove close to us and turned so that its back doors faced us. Suddenly, these banged open and out stepped none other than Tun Dr Ismail himself, with pipe and all! We bolted back into the campus, all of us, except for Anwar, who was way in front. He probably did not see that no one was left behind him. The van took him away (anonymous, interview 9 September 2005).

The Tunku perceived Ismail's return to politics as "Dr Ismail's last and final act of kindness to me".

> [Ismail] had already retired from Government service to be the head of the Guthrie Group of Companies, in which post he was earning a salary three times that of a Minister. [...] When he saw what was happening, and realising the attempts being made by

young UMNO extremists to embarrass me, and to oust me, to be more correct, he came and asked that he be taken back into the Cabinet. When he returned, he used his own dynamic personality and strength to the full to rout these elements. [...] On his own initiative, he went on the Radio declaring that "anyone who had any design on the personal safety and dignity of Tunku Abdul Rahman would be arrested". That broadcast had a great effect on the extremists, who quietened down (Tunku 1977, p. 171).

Maurice Baker, Singapore's High Commissioner to Kuala Lumpur between 1969 and 1971, was a very close friend of Razak and through him, of Ismail as well. He recollects:

Ismail loved the Tunku, he really loved the Tunku, for his human weakness and for his greatness. Razak too said Tunku was his political father. In the end, they tried to keep him on as long as possible. Some said that Razak was impatient to become the prime minister, but this was not true, not true at all (Interview 26 October 2005).

Musa Hitam suggested later that the tension could perhaps be analysed as one between "leftists" and "rightists", where Razak himself, along with Mahathir and Musa Hitam, were the leftists, while the Tunku and his followers, such as Khir Johari, were the rightists. Ismail, Musa added, could not be easily placed along this spectrum, mainly because as home affairs minister, he tried his best to remain apolitical and to be the unrelenting chief executor of the laws of the country, and making many politicians uncomfortable in the process (Interview 26 October 2005).

Ismail's adherence to rules was common knowledge both among those who worked under him and those who had official dealings with him. He was known to have refused an audience to a cousin who had turned up unannounced at his office, and had instead asked this relative to wait in line (Tawfik, interview 28 April 2005). Ghafar Baba recalled that a chief minister from Malacca once came for an appointment, and brought along two or three of his own acquaintances. Ismail told him off, saying that he had made an appointment only to see him, and not the others. He then eased the tension by saying that as luck would have it, he had enough coffee in the office to serve them. On another occasion, an UMNO leader from Penang came fifteen minutes late for a meeting with Ismail and was told: "What kind of loose leadership do you provide in Penang? No wonder you lost." This gentleman later confided to Ghafar that he hoped he never had to meet Ismail ever again (Ghafar, interview 16 October 2005).

Aishah Ghani, formerly head of UMNO's women's wing, remembers Ismail as a firm man whom she found "approachable", and who never opposed proposals put forward by the party's women (Interview 7 July 2005). Many others, however, did not consider Ismail that easily approachable. Abdullah Badawi remembers how on one occasion, Syed Nasir Ismail and Syed Ja'afar Albar had been granted a meeting with Ismail. Despite rushing desperately, they arrived late. Ismail waited in his heavily air-conditioned office, and as soon as the appointed time was up, he started to leave the office. He happened to run into the two men in the corridor outside his office, but Ismail did not so much as look at them and continued to walk past them without breaking his stride. The two stood by sweaty and alarmed, and did not venture to stop the minister as he whisked by (Interview 14 May 2006). Once, a group of foreign ambassadors came ten minutes late for their appointment, and Ismail refused to see them (Noordin Omar, interview 6 September 2005).

According to Noordin Omar, Ismail's young *aide-de-camp*, the minister would usually be dressed and ready for evening functions

ten minutes before it was time to depart. Then, exactly on the
dot, he would leave the house, and members of his entourage
would all be ready as well.

> Tun Ismail may have looked very stern but he was always
> generous, as was Toh Puan. No other Cabinet Minister could
> conceivably allow his lower-ranking staff the full use of his
> private pool the way Ismail did (Noordin, interview 6 September
> 2005).

Hanif Omar recalls that although Ismail was a gentle person
capable of great warmth, he could quickly "blow his top" when
faced with incompetence. This kept his staff on their toes. Gopal,
Ismail's capable but jumpy private secretary, would nervously
make sure he had with him a pen and all the files that might be
required whenever he was suddenly called into the Minister's
office (Hanif, interview 13 September 2005).

Press Secretary Wahab Majid remembers that Ismail did not
mind if officers argued with him, and interestingly does not
consider Ismail to have been unreasonably bad-tempered. Ismail's
relationship with both the local and foreign press was normally
good. Wahab, with whom Ismail would discuss his speeches and
press releases beforehand, credits this to the substantiality of his
ideas (Interview 6 July 2005).

In a "personal & confidential" letter to Razak, Ismail provided
an optimistic view of how he hoped to remain fit, and which
incidentally explains the regular early evening swims that he
took in his pool at home (Letters 29 July 1969). Apparently, the
idea of regular swims had come from Indian Prime Minister
Jawaharlal Nehru, who kept the same exercise routine:

> I have tried so far to keep myself physically fit by rigorous
> exercise because I believe in the theory that the human body

is endowed with [the] wonderful power of compensation. Rigorous exercise would make my heart muscle strong enough to counteract any deterioration as a result of a leak in the valves of the heart, a disease from which I am suffering (Letters 29 September 1969).

Nehru's influence on Ismail extended beyond devotion to physical exercise. Ismail was deeply impressed by the close relationship that Nehru had with his daughter Indira, and by how the two corresponded while Nehru was in prison in the early 1930s. Ismail wished for a similar close relationship with his eldest daughter Zailah, and would discuss things freely with her, and encouraged her to do the same with him. This contributed to the fact that Zailah always felt that she could talk about anything with her father. Ismail had realized already when Tawfik was a boy that he was a history buff, and subsequently managed to present his son with a copy of Nehru's *Glimpses of World History*, which is a collection of the 196 letters written by the imprisoned Nehru to the 13-year-old Indira.

Ismail's regular swims may have been inspired by Nehru, but his early experiences in Australia in the 1940s had already convinced him that physical exercise was important not only to the individual, but to society at large. Soon after he was married, he encouraged his wife Neno to play golf and badminton. She attributes her lifelong good health to the exercise routines she was prodded by her husband to develop during the 1950s. Over the years, she organized badminton teams among the wives of the elite, and the civil servants (Tawfik, interview 21 July 2006; Zailah, interview 23 March 2005).

In a letter to Dr Donald Cordner, an old classmate from Melbourne and a fellow doctor, in which Ismail apologized for missing their twenty-fifth anniversary of graduation, he stated that he had had two serious illnesses and was now struggling with a third. In 1960, he had suffered from sub-acute bacterial endocarditis. In 1967, he had cancer of the naso-pharynx, and had a check-up in London for aortic and mitral stenosis (Letters 18 August 1969). He learned from his ear, nose and throat specialist that "my main trouble in the future would still be my heart condition" (Letters 29 July 1969). Heart surgery for him was considered a necessary measure should a later diagnosis reveal signs of deterioration.

Things had stabilized reassuringly throughout the country by 12 August — exactly three months after rioting first broke out — and inter-racial fighting appeared restricted to a few cases of arson and "minor cases of assault". An intensification of border checks following a press report that arms and ammunition were being smuggled into Malaysia to communist insurgents did not turn up any evidence to support the claim (*Siaran Akhbar* PEN.8/69/305).

The open confrontation over the Tunku's position seemed over, and Ismail took the opportunity to ask to be allowed to travel to England for a medical check-up and for probable treatment: "Now that the situation in the country is much brighter, I seek permission to go to London with my wife. I am asking her to come along in case I have to receive treatment" (Letters 12 August 1969). The three-month period he endured in mid-1967 when alone in London prompted him to bring his wife along this time.

Ismail and Neno left for London on 9 September. His English doctors gave him a clean bill of health, and a further piece of good news was that no sign of a recurrence of neck cancer was visible. This meant that no decision on a heart operation had yet to be made for at least two more years (Drifting 30 March 1970). That was the medical prognosis then. As fate would have it, his heart already started to deteriorate the following month, and plans were swiftly made for a heart operation in early 1970.

Ismail held talks with Malaysian students while in London. His niece, Wan Arfah binti Tan Sri Wan Hamzah, was then a student there. She remembers that Ismail was asked why, despite being the man who had saved Malaysia, he was still not the prime minister. He said: "My health does not allow it". In answer to the question why he was not fully nationalizing education when that was the obvious long-term solution to national disunity, he again bluntly replied: "My health does not allow it" (Interview 29 March 2006).

He dismissed the simple explanation forwarded by the students that the 13 May events were caused by economic grievances: "I told them that if it was purely an economic factor, people would not have killed one another. It was something deeper than that" (*Siaran Akhbar* Pen.10/69/59). What he might have meant by this can be gleaned from his speech made two months earlier on 2 August on national television and radio.

> [The Malays] must be the judges to determine whether or not the special position is no longer necessary for their survival. Any other course would certainly provoke internal disorder — perhaps of a much bigger dimension than the disturbances of May the 13th (*Siaran Akhbar* PEN.8/69/22).

Ismail was at the same time conscious of the pitfalls of preferential treatment such as that later summarized under the New Economic Policy (NEP). He tried to contribute towards avoiding some of these by imposing a twenty-year time limit on the policy. Ghazali Shafie, who was directly involved in the project, also thought a time-limit was required because if things did not change substantially within twenty years, then some change of strategy would be called for in any case. There would be no point in continuing in the same failed direction (Ghazali, interview 7 September 2005).

The situation required new perspectives, and the Razak-Ismail administration looked around for help. One of those whose ideas were sought was James Puthucheary (1923–2000). Puthucheary, who was an NCC member, authored the book *Ownership and Control in the Malayan Economy* while imprisoned in Singapore between 1956 and 1959. This work was at that time practically the only thorough analysis of the political economy of Malaya written by a Malayan, and came to be highly regarded in leftist intellectual circles. The thrust of his argument was that state intervention through public corporations was required if the imbalances resulting from the colonial economic structure and their lasting effects on inter-ethnic relations were to be rectified (Puthucheary 1998, pp. 30–31).

Razak, following the advice of Ismail and others, sought Puthucheary's advice, and at least one meeting was held between top leaders and Puthucheary, where the lawyer presented his arguments on how the socio-economic situation of Malaysia could be reformed (D. Puthucheary, interview 4 September 2006). It is difficult to dismiss the claim that Puthucheary's ideas exerted a strong influence on the formulation of the NEP. The consciousness of the colonial heritage on the socio-economic structure of Malaysia is undeniable in the affirmative action programme, as is the type of government intervention suggested by Puthucheary in his book.

> The theory that investment by the government should be complementary to private investment and that inter-government loans can only be supplementary to supplies of private foreign capital has to be reversed. Both local and foreign private capital has to be complementary to governmental investments of domestic and foreign capital.

The old theory must be reversed not because of any doctrine or feeling that state economic activity is virtuous and private capital evil; but because private capital, domestic or foreign, is unable and unwilling to make those investments which will bring about the development that Malaya urgently needs (Puthucheary 1960, p. xxii).

The NEP did change the class structure of the Malay population and to that extent it did succeed. However, later politicians have not recognized the time limit, and Malaysia remains unique today as a democracy that practises widespread preferential treatment in favour of the electorally dominant ethnic group.

In presenting his views on Malay special privileges, Ismail had a propensity to use a golf metaphor. He told Philip Kuok that "this handicap will enable them to be good players, as in golf, and in time the handicap will be removed. The Malays must not think of these privileges as permanent: for then, they will not put their efforts to the tasks. In fact, it is an insult for Malays to be getting these privileges" (Kuok 1991, p. 217). Ismail had used the same metaphor in his broadcast on 2 August.

The special privilege or position accorded to the Malays under the Constitution is mainly intended to enable them — to borrow an expression from the game of golf — "to have a handicap", which would place them in a position for a fair competition with better players. Therefore, like a golfer, it should not be the aim of the Malays to perpetuate this handicap but to strive to improve their game, and thereby reducing, and finally removing, their handicap completely (*Siaran Akhbar* PEN. 8/69/22).

On his way back from London, Ismail stopped over in Copenhagen as a guest of the Danish Government. A Danish daily ran an interview with him on 3 October, and considered a visit by the Malaysian minister of home affairs a clear indication that "the situation in his country has improved". Ismail explained to the Danish that "we want to create a United Malaysia of Malays, Chinese, Indians, etc., just as the United States is a fusion of many different elements". Among the lessons learnt from 13 May, he said, was the one that "we cannot yet practice democracy in the manner of Denmark or England".

> Belgium is an example of how difficult it is to get different groups to co-operate. Our politicians will have to promise not to misuse the racial issues. We intend to retain democratic principles and to return to the parliamentarian form of government (*Berlingske Tidende* 1969, as translated from Danish by the Malaysian Embassy at The Hague).

This echoed a statement he had earlier made in Kuala Lumpur that "it is not necessary that we should adopt wholesale Western style democracy" (*ST* 21 June 1969).

Chapter 7

A LACK OF TIME

Razak announced the formation of the National Consultative Council (NCC) in January 1970, with himself as the chairman. Its function was to involve representatives of various social groups — "political parties, the professions, religious groups, the press, the public services, trade union and minority groups" — in discussing the riots and "finding permanent solutions to our racial problems" (*ST* 13 January 1970). Where the NOC was the *de facto* government, the NCC — six of whose members were also with the NOC — was to function as the country's "parliament". The DAP, however, declined representation after a request that their detained secretary-general Lim Kit Siang be accepted as a member was rejected (Milne and Mauzy 1978, p. 90).

The NCC started with a membership of sixty-three men, but after complaints about the complete lack of women membership in it, lawyer P.G. Lim of the Labour Party, who later became ambassador to the United States and also to Yugoslavia, and Aishah Ghani, who was later head of UMNO Wanita, were included, swelling the NCC to sixty-five members (Lim 2005, pp. 113–14). It was within this body — freed from observers and pressmen — that consensus on various issues was sought.

Questions such as the removal of "sensitive issues" from public debate, the careful formulation of the *Rukunegara* — Articles of Faith of the State — and the construction of the New Economic Policy were cogently discussed within the NCC. However, only summaries of the proceedings were ever recorded. These are still classified as top secret documents.

Sometime at the end of 1969, Razak and Ismail — and three medical personnel who were subsequently sworn to secrecy — learned that Razak, the *de facto* prime minister, was suffering from leukaemia. Ismail took the Kuok brothers into his confidence. Robert Kuok recalls: "Doc told me that Razak was dying already in early 1970, when I was often in Kuala Lumpur. Sometime after Doc passed away, my brother Philip confided in me that Razak was critically ill, which I already knew" (Interview 10 February 2006).

Tengku Razaleigh Hamzah, head of the national oil company Petronas, was informed by Razak a week before the prime minister passed away in London in January 1976, that Razak used the pretext of having tea and discussing political matters to visit Ismail at his home at 22 Maxwell Road in order to be examined in secret by his doctors in a building situated behind the garage. This building had in effect been turned into a clinic for his sake (Razaleigh, interview 28 June 2005).

To make matters even worse for Ismail, in early February 1970, before leaving for London for treatment, he discovered definite signs that his neck cancer had recurred. He had happened to touch a lump behind his ear while shaving, and asked his wife to describe it fully to him from behind. He then drove to the hospital, where the growth was confirmed to be cancerous. It was decided then "that no time must be lost and that I should straightaway fly to London" (Drifting 30 March 1970; Kuok, interview 10 February 2006).

Pressure was steadily building up within Ismail's family for him to slow down. His father, Abdul Rahman Yassin, sent him a letter — written correspondence between father and son having been a life-long tradition — asking him "seriously to resign your present post as soon as possible". The father was of the view that Ismail had broken his vow to his family that he would leave politics, "and you must now repent". He even expressed the hope that Ismail "had a will made in case anything happens to you".

> No one is indispensable in this world. You have made enough sacrifices. Do not overdo it! You are now fifty.* Serve your God rather than the ungrateful cowards who flatter you and only make you carry on the donkey's burden! (Letters 20 February 1970).

Of course, Abdul Rahman Yassin was not privy to the fact that Razak, the *de facto* prime minister, was dying, and that Ismail, being his deputy, could see no option but to continue in his position. At that point in time, Ismail was as indispensable as any deputy prime minister could be. One regret his family said Ismail had was his failure to return to Johor Bahru to make peace with his father before the old man passed away in May 1970.

Robert Kuok remembers that Ismail had on one occasion had a face-to-face quarrel with Abdul Rahman Yassin — "it was the grandmother of quarrels". Ismail's father tried to stop him from going for a heart operation, feeling that Ismail would not survive it.

> The chances of survival for a valve operation in those days were 50–50, and the longer one waited the worse one's chances became, and soon Doc could no longer go for any such operation. I could sense it in his behaviour that he had resigned himself to it (Kuok, interview 10 February 2006).

---

* Ismail was in fact fifty-five years old then.

As things turned out, Ismail's trip to London for throat cancer treatment had to be postponed for a month because of vital matters of state.

> I was in the middle of launching an important legislature programme on anti-corruption measures and I was determined that should there be any blame, or what was worse, any demonstrations taking place, I must be in Malaysia to face it (Drifting 30 March 1970).

This vital piece of legislature was Emergency (Essential Powers) Ordinance No. 22. In passing it on 23 February, Parliament equipped the ACA under its director Harun Hashim with the authority to freeze or forfeit "ill-gotten" assets of public officials and politicians without having to confer with the home affairs minister. Ismail had secured the support of both the Tunku and Razak before he pushed for this ordinance, which was meant to "cover loopholes" in the Prevention of Corruption Act of 1961. The older legislature was useful only when bribery involved direct payments by members of the public to officials and politicians.

Ismail provided two reasons why the new ordinance was needed. Firstly, the country was ruled by the NOC, and without a functioning parliament in place, "corrupt practices" tended not to be revealed. Secondly, it had not been the practice in Malaysia, as was the case in many other democracies, where "those caught doing unconstitutional acts" would resign. The new law now treated such individuals as criminals instead. A "corrupt practice" was defined as "any act done by members of the Administration, as defined in the Federal Constitution, MPs or State Assemblymen or public servants, whereby they have used their public position for pecuniary or other advantages" (ST 24 February 1970). As a consequence of this ordinance, the chief ministers of both Perak and Trengganu were removed from office for corruption offences in the following months.

On 24 February, Ismail played host to Japan's Crown Prince Akihito, who was visiting the Police Training School in Kuala Lumpur. Japan had been giving various forms of support to the Malaysian police, such as judo lessons and the use of training facilities in Tokyo (*MM* 25 February 1970).

The second issue of *Balai Muhibbah*, the official publication of the NGC that hit newsstands at the end of February, carried an interview with Ismail, where he announced that amendments to be made to the Elections Ordinance would forbid candidates from discussing issues of race, national language and Malay rights. The ban applied to private meetings as well as public rallies, as well as to parliament itself (*Sunday Times* 1 March 1970).

Ismail optimistically told reporters at Subang Airport on 2 March, "we are on the way to a Malaysian Malaysia, but we have a long way to go" (*ST* 3 March 1970). His flight was unfortunately cancelled, and he could not leave until 8 March, which meant that he missed two appointments with his London doctors (*MM* 4 March 1970; *ST* 10 March 1970). Ismail used the delay as an opportunity to attend a three-day meeting of the NCC. A statement released on 4 March showed that Ismail talked to NCC members about "the necessity of providing safeguards in the Constitution to ensure that Parliamentary democracy would not place the country in any danger like the one that occurred on May 13 last year" (*ST* 5 March 1970).

Ismail and his wife were away from the country for nine weeks altogether, which allowed him time to meditate over his situation and "reflect on the future of my country" (Drifting 30 March 1970). His treatment involved daily visits to the doctor (*ST* 25 March 1970), but his heart operation had to be postponed because of his cancer treatment. Robert Kuok remembers Ismail telling him later that he suffered from depression during treatment to the extent that even suicide crossed his mind more than once: "All my taste buds were gone. All I ate tasted like sawdust. I couldn't face life anymore." Apparently, that was one of the reasons why he later switched to drinking champagne, especially Dom Perignon, because he could at least sense the bubbles (Interview 10 February 2006).

In his absence, Ismail was awarded the Republic of Indonesia Medal Second Class when President Suharto visited Malaysia in April. On the way home in May, Ismail and Neno stopped over in Holland for two days to visit Philip and Eileen Kuok. Wahab Majid, who was Ismail's constant travelling companion, remembers that the Kuoks were always very warm hosts, and had a fine wine cellar in their residence. Ismail greatly appreciated Philip's collection of reds and whites, and heartily encouraged Wahab to have a taste because "wine is not really that alcoholic" (Wahab, interview 6 July 2006).

They arrived home on 19 May (*ST* 16 May 1970). The first anniversary of 13 May had recently passed without incidents, something many saw as a very encouraging sign for the country (*ST* 15 May 1970). Five days later, on 24 May, news arrived from Johor Bahru that Ismail's father had passed away that morning of a heart attack at eighty-two years of age. Ismail and Neno flew down immediately for the funeral.

The tiresome job of explaining the riots to the general public had by now become Ismail's responsibility. He had to suggest how the situation would be remedied and work out how confidence in the parliamentary system could be rebuilt. Along with other Malay leaders, he was convinced that certain constitutional restrictions, given the stage in the nation-building process that Malaysia was in, had to be put into place. There were nevertheless doubts in his mind. In a fiery speech to the NCC made earlier that year, Ismail explained his understanding of preferential treatment, and his dislike of the term "Bumiputra".

> I regard the Special Position of the Malays as a handicap given to the Malays with the consent of all the other races who have become citizens of this country so as to enable the Malays to compete on equal footing for equal opportunities in this country. That and that alone is the only aim of the Special Position of the Malays. But unfortunately the Malays themselves have tended to give the impression consciously or unconsciously that the Special Position of the Malays is a sign that the Malays are placed superior to the other races in the country. The biggest mistake that the Malays made of course was to coin the term "Bumiputra" because this term tended to convey an entirely different meaning to what was intended for the Special Position of the Malays. By coining "Bumiputra" the non-Malays suspected the Malays of wanting to classify themselves as first-class citizens while they were relegated to second-class (Letters 23 February 1970).

On that occasion, he also appealed to the opposition to support the government's proposals for constitutional changes. He focused on three provisions made in the constitution, which were "the result of compromises reached between the various races of the country". The question of citizenship had by and large been solved in that spirit — two and a half million who were not eligible for citizenship in 1957 had since then become citizens of the state — but that of language had not been. The ten-year period for the implementation of Malay as the national language had passed, and differing interpretations of the future status of English and other languages had caused "suspicion and distrust between the races". The third problem involved the special position of the Malays, and the countervailing interpretations it had engendered.

Ghafar Baba recalled an occasion when Ismail's fear of widespread vulgarization of Malay special rights was proven justified. In those days, Ghafar said, younger party members would challenge each other to get the stern doctor to smile.

> An UMNO man complained at a meeting that despite Malay rights, the Malaysian contingent preparing for the Munich Olympics was made up mainly of Chinese. "Where are Malay rights there?" he asked. No one knew what to say, and it fell on Ismail to answer: "Special rights are only in the field of economics, not in sports," he ventured. "Do you mean to say we should use strings to make Malays good at high jump?" At that he burst out laughing. That was one of the few times I saw him laugh so heartily (Interview 16 October 2005).

On 24 August, Ismail wrote Philip Kuok, who was then in the middle of a transfer from The Hague to Bonn, to say that he would be going to London and New York in October. The letter also sought to keep Kuok informed of developments back home.

> Tunku will make an important announcement on matters of which, I am sure, you already know. I do not expect any trouble after that announcement. On the whole things are going very smoothly here and a few weeks ago I visited Singapore to have a chat with Lee Kuan Yew about closer relationship between the two countries. I suggested in the first instance that closer relationship should be established between the Ministers and the Permanent Secretaries and later on to percolate to other levels. Unfortunately, as you may have read in the Foreign Affairs Despatch, the Singapore Police at the lower level created an incident in which three Malaysians, one Chinese, one Indian

and one Malay, were detained and had their hair cut short. This prompted Lee Kuan Yew unfortunately to postpone his goodwill visit to Kuala Lumpur to have talks with the Tunku (Letters 24 August 1970).

According to Maurice Baker, Singapore's high commissioner to Kuala Lumpur at that time, Lee Kuan Yew's decision to stay away upset Ismail greatly since the latter believed that the Singaporean leader's presence would have helped ease the situation. Student demonstrations broke out and Razak had to issue a stern warning on the spot to student leaders that they would be in deep trouble should anything happen to Baker, who had appeared on university grounds in a diplomat's car (Baker, interview 9 June 2005).

The relationship between the two sides was otherwise surprisingly relaxed because of skilful diplomacy and mutual understanding among the leaders. Baker recalls for example that Goh Keng Swee, Singapore's finance minister then, was especially fond of Ismail (Baker, interview 9 June 2006):

> Tan Siew Sin, Ismail, Goh Keng Swee and I were discussing something one day, and Siew Sin was upset that my number two had penetrated the MCA and was able to reveal some plans to the Singapore government. Siew Sin informed the gathering that Singapore had a spy in the MCA. Ismail then told him: "You know, Siew Sin, the job of a foreign diplomat is to get information for his government so that it can prepare itself for eventualities. That is the job of a diplomat, don't you know that?" Ismail knew the diplomatic mission well, Siew Sin didn't.

On National Day 1970, the DNU publicly presented the *Rukunegara*, which proclaimed five principles: (1) Islam is the official religion of the federation, but other religions and beliefs may be practised in peace and harmony without discrimination against any citizen on the ground of religion; (2) Loyalty to the *Agong* (the paramount ruler) and to the country; (3) The upholding of the constitution, including such provisions as those regarding the sultans, the position of Islam, the position of Malays and other natives; and the legitimate interests of other communities; (4) Equality before the law and the guarantee of fundamental liberties for all citizens; and (5) Conduct by individuals and groups must not be arrogant or offend the sensitivities of any group, and no citizen should question the loyalty of another citizen on the ground that he belongs to a particular community (*Rukunegara* 1971).

The Tunku also announced that day that he was retiring. On 21 September, the sultan of Kedah took over as paramount ruler, and so it was arranged for him to accept the resignation of the Tunku, who was incidentally his uncle, the following day, and at the same time appoint Razak as his successor. Razak took charge of the defence and foreign affairs portfolios as well, and appointed Ismail as his deputy. He also requested his brother-in-law, Hussein Onn, to leave his law practice and take over the politically strategic Education Ministry. Tan Siew Sin was placed in his old position as finance minister, and Ghazali Shafie left the civil service and became minister with special functions in place of Khaw Kai Boh. Ghazali's job was to study race relations while being in charge of the DNU as well as the newly formed General Planning Unit (GPU), a watchdog body placed directly under the Prime Minister's Office (*ST* 24 September 1970).

The partnership between Razak and Ismail continued to work extraordinarily well. A.S. Talalla, who was then principal assistant secretary at the Ministry of Foreign Affairs, could not recall any instance when Razak went against suggestions made by Ismail: "Whenever he was told that Dr Ismail had expressed a view on a certain matter, Razak would go along with it without exception; Until today, I think of that administration as the Razak–Ismail

Administration" (Talalla, interview 30 March 2006). Maurice Baker echoes the same sentiment:

> Razak was very troubled by the situation at the time. You see, he was a good man for long-term planning and so forth, but when immediate action was required, he was known to hesitate and to think twice. Tun Ismail, on the other hand, was one who would act as soon as his mind was made up. He would just act. That was the difference between them, but the combination was perfect (Interview 9 June 2005).

The CEO of the NOC, General Ibrahim Ismail said the thought of intervention following the riots never entered the head of the military command because "we were never brought up that way, and our trust in Razak and Ismail, who made a superb team, was very strong" (Interview 23 April 2005).

Observers commonly state that Malaysia, along with Singapore, is unique in having a military that has always remained loyal to the government. As researcher Felix V. Gagliano noted, as long as the British defence forces (removed in 1971) shielded the country, no large standing army was needed, and "the tradition of civilian supremacy was strongly reinforced" (Gagliano 1971, p. 41). General Ibrahim claimed that "the tradition of civil loyalty was, and is, very strong in the army, largely thanks to the British system of training. It lives on today through the ranks" (Interview 23 April 2005). As a sign of the times, General Ibrahim himself underwent training in New Delhi together with future Prime Minister Hussein Onn in the Johor Military Forces just before the war, and both served in the British Indian Army after the Japanese invasion (Ibrahim 1984, pp. 11–18).

Some scholars caution against putting too great an emphasis on the causal status of the tradition of civilian supremacy since "there have been too many instances in other parts of the world where British-trained armies have participated in overthrowing civilian governments" (Zakaria and Crouch 1985, p. 126).

As further noted by observers, intensive contacts with the military apparatus of neighbouring countries such as Indonesia and Thailand, where the role of the military had been much more central, meant that the Malaysian military had not been unaware of its capacity to seize political power. However, in the Malaysian case, the police force had always been more important than the military. The regrettable history of military intervention in countries throughout the region also provided bad examples to avoid.

Another possible reason for the loyalty of the military at that particular time was the fact that the then Chief of Armed Forces, General Tunku Osman Jewa, who was also a member of the NOC, was the nephew of Tunku Abdul Rahman. Such close "familial connections" among leading households in Malay society acted as a stabilizing factor in the country's politics (FCO: 24/486; Zakaria and Crouch 1985, pp. 119–21).

Nevertheless, fear that a military coup might actually take place was very real in some quarters. Britain's Foreign and Commonwealth Office was strongly concerned that the situation would affect British and Australian nationals in Malaysia and also spill into Singapore. However, They were told by their people in Kuala Lumpur on 4 June:

> No one is seeking to use the Armed Forces deliberately to repress the Chinese section of the community. The Government [is] seeking to build up and equip their security forces in order to improve what is at present a fragile law and order situation in the towns and might become a dangerous security problem in the country as a whole (FCO 24/486).

A newly retired defence adviser to the British High Commission in Kuala Lumpur briefed top British officers in early October that "the only conceivable coup" would be one that was aiming "to overthrow a government which was not governing with Malay interests in mind [and as long as] the government is dominated by Malays and makes only unavoidable concessions to protect their interests the army will support it" (FCO 24/486).

On 2 October, Ismail freed several political detainees including DAP Secretary-General Lim Kit Siang. The party's president, Dr Chen Man Hin, publicly praised him for keeping the promise he had made to Socialist International when he was last in London: "We respect him and we always knew he was a man of principles" (ST 3 October 1970).

Ismail flew off on 4 October to attend the United Nations' Twenty-fifth Commemorative Session in New York, stopping over in London for medical checks "for a throat ailment", advising the British Foreign Office at the same time that he did not wish to have discussions during his week-long stay there. He asked instead for a meeting with the British premier in New York the following week.

Besides putting aside considerable time to study British prisons and to visit slum clearance areas after resting from his medical check-ups, Ismail also received a courtesy call on 6 October from Lee Kuan Yew, who was also en route to New York. It was significantly the first meeting that the Singaporean leader had had with a top member of Malaysia's post-13 May cabinet (ST 6 October 1970; ST 7 October 1970). Ismail also kept an appointment with about 300 Malaysian students, and advised them to define their role in the nation-building process and "not to make the mistake of trying to apply Western standards of democracy in Malaysia" (ST 11 October 1970).

He then flew to New York and stayed at the Waldorf Astoria. On 15 October, while leaving the hotel to attend the UN session, Ismail was "pushed and shoved" by American security guards overzealous in protecting other delegates who were considered "security risks". He considered it a "misuse of power" and prompted Malaysia's representative to the United Nations, Zakaria Ali, to make an official protest to the Americans (*ST* 4 November 1970).

In his speech to the United Nations that day, Ismail called for the neutralization "not only of the Indo-China area but also of the entire region of Southeast Asia, guaranteed by the three super powers, the People's Republic of China, the Soviet Union and the United States"(*ST* 16 October 1970).

British reports on informal talks held later at the Waldorf Astoria between Ismail and Prime Minister Edward Heath show that the British were by then starting to take the Malaysian stance on neutrality seriously (FCO 24/824; *ST* 24 October 1970). The two leaders discussed security issues covering Chinese support for the neutralisation policy and for Communist guerrillas in Malaysia, and the improvement of relations with the Thais, "in contrast to what Tun Razak had been saying". Ismail thought it unrealistic to expect China to stop supporting the communists in Malaysia, but was optimistic that the insurgents could be contained. He believed that sustained economic growth would decisively nullify the attraction that communism held for the poor (CO 1027/563). Ismail also informed Heath that Malaysia stood firmly against any resumption of arms sales by Britain to the South African apartheid regime (FOC 24/1187; *ST* 24 October 1970).

Before leaving New York for Kuala Lumpur *via* London, Ismail gave speeches to several important American foreign relations bodies, arguing that economic ties between Malaysia and the United States could and should be much better (*ST* 29 October 1970).

Back home, and as was the tradition, Ismail held an open house for the public on the occasion of Hari Raya Puasa. That year, the Muslim holy day fell on Sunday, 30 November.

In December, Ismail informed Philip Kuok in a letter that "Parliament will reconvene on the 22 February, and I am now busy supervising all the legislations of 'sensitive issues', because Tun Razak has delegated completely these problems to me" (Letters 11 December 1970). The family would first be spending their Christmas holidays and New Year in Penang, staying at the Kuok residence in Bukit Mertajam. After that, Ismail planned to visit the detention centre on Pulau Jerejak as the start of a three-week long tour of West Coast states, ending in Johor (*ST* 22 December 1970). Press secretary Wahab Majid remembers with fondness that he was often invited along on Ismail's holidays, and as further proof of Ismail's generosity, he and his family had an open invitation to make use of Ismail's private swimming pool (Wahab, interview 6 July 2005).

Razak and Ismail published separate New Year messages to the nation on 1 January 1971. Both chose to remind Malaysians of the importance of security and of "sound economic development". Ismail wanted his countrymen to "strive forward together to build a truly united Malaysian nation from the diverse elements of our multi-racial society" (*ST* 1 January 1971). Just before leaving Penang, Ismail announced that he would talk to the prime minister about the acquisition of Minden Barracks as the site for the new Universiti Sains Malaysia (USM) (*MM* 2 January 1971). Apparently, he thought it better for Penang, whose economy was highly dependent on tourism at that time, that the first thing tourists saw when arriving by plane was a university campus and not an army camp (Tawfik, interview 28 April 2005).

Edward Heath paid a short visit to Malaysia en route to a Commonwealth meeting on 12–13 January, and called on Ismail at his house at Maxwell Road. While there, he took a dip in the swimming pool (*ST* 14 January 1971). Canadian Prime Minister Pierre Trudeau had also used the pool when he visited Malaysia the year before. Trudeau had not wished to miss his daily swimming routine, and since security arrangements were most easily made at Ismail's house, he was welcomed there for morning swims (Abdullah Ali, interview 8 September 2005).

The story that runs in Ismail's family is that this pool came into being after Neno had fretted over rumours that there was a grave in the garden of their newly bought house. Ismail had the spot dug up to calm her, and after that thought it better to build a pool there than to close up the hole. Over the next forty years, Neno went into that pool only once.

Quite often, Ismail would have movies shown at the weekend on a mounted big screen beside the pool. Indeed, a Filipino fashion show was once held there as well (in September 1971) as an official event. Interesting, in planning for such occasions, Ismail would often consult the Chinese calendar, which he considered scientifically charted knowledge (Tawfik, interview 28 April 2005). Regular guests at these home parties included Ismail Ali, "his great friend" from the Washington days (Wahab, interview 6 July 2005).

The day following Heath's visit, Ismail and Neno left for a four-day trip to Johor (*ST* 14 January 1971).

Preparations were underway for UMNO's general assembly that was to be held on 22–24 January. This was the first since the May riots, and it would also be the last that the Tunku would preside over (*ST* 22 January 1971). Significant changes in the party's middle-rank leadership were expected, which would reflect the result of the conflicts between the different factions.

UMNO's central executive committee announced major institutional changes on 13 January to streamline the party apparatus. Six bureaux were formed — politics, finance, economics, education, social and religion. Ismail was put in charge of the finance bureau, which would include sub-committees on party finance and fiscal policy (*ST* 14 January 1971). The party's conviction that the Alliance had to be reformed was already made clear on 7 December the year before when Razak, on taking over as chairman of the Alliance, immediately announced the forming of a committee to reorganize the party and re-examine the relationship between the party and the government. Ismail was put in charge of this body (*ST* 7 December 1970).

Ismail moved earnestly about this new task of reforming the Alliance. On 15 January, one week before the UMNO general assembly, the MCA and the MIC were given a rude jolt when Ismail stated during a closed-door session attended by 200 Alliance officials at Istana Bukit Setulang, the residence of the Johor Mentri Besar, that the two parties were *hidup segan, mati tak mahu* [shy to live and afraid to die], and that it might be better, if that situation continued, for UMNO to break ties with them. This derision was generally understood as a ploy to make them more proactive (Tan and Yong 1971, p. 98; *ST* 16 January 1971; *ST* 18 January 1971).

According to Ismail's press secretary Wahab Majid, what the newspapers played up was somewhat taken out of context, and leaked information had been blown out of proportion (Interview 6 June 2005). On 18 January, Ismail issued a statement to say that his view of the MCA and the MIC was in relation to how the two parties had failed to perform in the 1969 general elections, and strove to explain and re-activate the common Alliance stand on

Malay rights and the Malay language in the face of attacks by the opposition (*ST* 19 January 1971). It was effectively a post-mortem by him on the poor electoral showing by the Alliance, but announced dramatically to serve as a lesson for the future.

The speech was significantly made merely a month before parliament was to resume. As a transcription of it shows, Ismail criticized the Alliance partners for their unwillingness to change and was in fact telling them to restructure their party apparatus as UMNO was doing, and for the Alliance as such to stop being "superficial" and acting only for the sake of elections. The parties, he said, had to consider the fact that they were dealing with a new generation of voters who were more educated and more critical.

Ismail provided a scathing analysis of the weaknesses of the Alliance. The coalition rode on the euphoria of Independence in the 1959 elections, he said, while in the 1964 elections, the confrontation with Indonesia united the people despite the government not always succeeding in its domestic policies: "Luckily for the Alliance, Confrontation gave the electorate no other choice but us." By 1969, however, new oppositional parties had been established and they made full use of the weaknesses that the Alliance had always had. Ismail, bent on revitalizing the Alliance, did not think it sufficient that the coalition had an efficient machinery or financial resources. What was needed was widespread understanding of what the Alliance was about: "We cannot expect the electorate to understand our policy if party members themselves do not understand it."

When under attack on the issues of national language and Malay special rights, many within the coalition had "faltered" and "felt besieged because they were weak in their understanding of the issue". Ismail argued that UMNO had had to remedy its partners' lack of understanding and commitment to the political structure that the Alliance had built.

Thus in the 1969 elections the sensitive issues of National Language and Special Rights handicapped the Alliance generally and caused the bloodshed of May 13th. We therefore enshrined the issues in the Constitution as subjects that cannot be raised in any form by the Opposition. Thus the weakness of our partners is protected. In future the MIC and the MCA cannot turn to UMNO and say they face difficulties with these issues because from now on they will not be troubled by such issues. In the future, we require an agreement on the implementation of policy and less time should be spent in explaining to each other the issues already accepted as part of the Alliance policy. In the future we should concentrate on the proper implementation of the National Language and the protection of the Special Rights of the Malays and defend the citizenship of the non-Malays.

These three issues should be the basis of frank and sincere discussion among the three partners of the Alliance in order that we can achieve a respectable victory in the next general elections. But if we fall back on the old ways and speak without candour and sincerity and "sweep the problems under the carpet" I think the Alliance will lose even more seats in the next general elections. If we do not achieve such an understanding then we may as well dissolve the marriage rather than continue with a relationship where we are all shy to live and afraid to die (Letters and Speeches).

While the MIC chose not to rise in any obvious way to the challenge, the reaction from the Chinese was all the more ambitious and came to include the formation of the Chinese Unity Movement and the Perak Task Force, both aimed at increasing Chinese unity. Both failed badly, and the MCA continued to lose its special position in the governing constellation.

Although the MCA had survived many obituaries, the internal rifts, combined with the new Alliance coalition-building strategy,

seemed to relegate the MCA to the position of a rump party
(Milne and Mauzy 1978, p. 177).

The political changes that followed the May riots were thus
profound, and the official understanding of the causes for the
violence became the backbone for Malaysia's domestic policy.
Racial violence was to be avoided at all costs in the future. This
"never again" mentality has in time thoroughly permeated
Malaysian political discourse.

In his speech to the Alliance members, Ismail also argued
against the principle that the government must rise above the
party. Thirteen years had already passed since Independence, and
he considered it time to blame the practice by some leaders of
distancing themselves from the party for the weaknesses the
party now had (Letters and Speeches; *ST* 30 January 1971).

> We must instil in our minds that in a democracy, government
> and party cannot be separated because this government is an
> Alliance government and not a DAP government or a Gerakan
> government. Thus if we are the government we must strengthen
> our links with the party. [...] Because we are the government we
> use this Residence [of the Johor Mentri Besar] and these cars to
> entertain and meet with party members and let us not be cowed
> by the Opposition criticising us for alleged misuse of government
> property. Our answer to them is, we are the government. This is
> a political party and this is democracy.

Apparently, what concerned him was commitment to party goals
and the maintenance of contact with party members. He was
calling on Alliance members to show more conviction about the
correctness of what they claimed to be aiming for. In that speech,
Ismail also provided some insight into what he thought of the
relationship between the government and its civil servants.

> Our responsibility is to administer the government efficiently.
> If we run it efficiently we can fulfil the promises we made to the
> people. If it is not run efficiently and we quarrel with the civil
> service, there is no common respect and when we face the next
> elections without fulfilling our promises and if we suffer losses
> it will be our loss and not the civil servant's loss. We are the
> government and they are the staff of that government and will
> continue to be so no matter who runs the government.

Where financial matters were concerned, things seemed turned around in his mind, and the line between government and party could not be crossed. For example, after Ismail was put in charge of a committee in 1971 to construct a building to house UMNO's headquarters, he made it a point of principle that the land that was to be used must absolutely not be government property. The money had to be raised from among UMNO supporters. In the event, Tengku Razaleigh Hamzah, who had just prior to the occasion paid a deposit for a piece of land on Maxwell Road, was pushed to transfer it to the party for the project (Razaleigh, interview 28 May 2005).

In the UMNO elections that year, Tunku critics, despite counter-attacks by his supporters, managed to win clear victories. The support they enjoyed was wider than had been expected, and all the three new vice presidents were associated with this group. Harun Idris became president of UMNO Youth, and Musa Hitam was elected his deputy. Khir Johari, an incumbent and Tunku loyalist, lost his post. Both Razak and Ismail were unchallenged as president and deputy president respectively (*ST* 22 January 1971; *ST* 25 January 1971). Tunku critic Mahathir Mohamad was not a party member at this time, and could not run for office. Later at the Silver Jubilee General Assembly in May, amendments to the UMNO constitution for stricter party discipline were passed, giving Razak solid control over the party (Milne and Mauzy 1978, p. 174).

Ismail continued to have misgivings about the youth wing being overly critical of the mother party. Abdullah Badawi and Tengku Razaleigh remember an occasion when Ismail took Harun to task for trying to form a party within a party, and dared the youth leader to challenge the party leadership openly (Abdullah, interview 14 May 2006; Razaleigh, interview 28 June 2005). Abdul Rahman Hamidon remembers that Ismail was the only man that Harun Idris showed respect for (Interview 9 September 2005).

Tengku Razaleigh, who was later finance minister, remembers Ismail as "a real Malaysian" and "a pillar of strength" during that period:

> The Chinese did not have much confidence in Razak, but they did in Ismail. Razak was always associated with Malay and rural affairs, *et cetera*. Ismail was a principled man — and was seen that way by the different races. He was the Rock of Gibraltar. Once he decided on something, you could be sure that he had gone through the relevant details and studied them. What is confidence unless it is based on the people's belief in the leader? (Interview 28 June 2005).

After the UMNO general assembly, Ismail and his wife left on 26 January for their pilgrimage to Mecca, together with their good friend and old Washington colleague, Bank Negara chairman Ismail Ali. In Jeddah, he spoke to journalists and called for the Muslim world to achieve "economic solidarity". The "question of the hour", he added, was "the liberation of Palestine and the Holy City" (*ST* 4 December 1970; *MM* 29 January 1971).

Chapter 8

NAILING THINGS INTO PLACE

On 23 February 1971, parliamentary rule was finally reinstated in Malaysia. To make way for this, the NOC became the National Security Council, while the NCC and the NGC were suffused into the National Unity Council. The latter's task was to advise the prime minister on the issues that were being banned from public debate, and to conduct research into race relations (Comber 1983, p. 83). The first exercise of the new parliament was to debate the Constitutional (Amendment) Bill, and for seven days, MPs had their say on this vital document (*ST* 24 January 1971). On 3 March, the lower house passed this main pillar for Malaysia's political restructuring with a vote of 125 to 17. The opposition was split, with all parties except for the DAP and the PPP supporting it. What the bill did was to place certain issues considered dangerously sensitive beyond political challenge. These concerned citizenship, the national language and the use of other languages, the special position of the Malays, legitimate interests of non-Malays, and the sovereignty of the sultans (*ST* 4 March 1971).

Ismail argued that the passing of the bill itself did not guarantee political peace in the future. How much longer democracy would live depended, he said, "on how the Opposition political parties behave and [on] the response from the public". He made a pledge in parliament that day on behalf of the Alliance:

> We shall not take advantage of any loopholes in the Bill, nor conjure up other sensitive issues which will cause racial strife; We shall see to it that Alliance members scrupulously interpret the spirit and letter of the Bill; We shall see to it that those who do not are severely punished; We shall see to it that the provisions of the sensitive issues are truly implemented in letter and spirit (*ST* 4 March 1971).

In winding up the debate, Ismail challenged those still opposed to the bill to resign if it was passed, since they had claimed they would not sit in a house that "cut its own tongue". When no one immediately took up the challenge, Ismail continued his attack: "Now that I know they are not willing to sacrifice for their conscience I know how to deal with them" (*ST* 4 March 1971).

While the *Rukunegara* was formulated to provide moral direction, the Second Malaysia Plan (1971–75) was implemented to herald the twenty-year-long NEP. The latter's goals were two-pronged: (1) Eradicating poverty by raising income levels and increasing employment opportunities for all Malaysians, irrespective of race; and (2) Accelerating the process of restructuring Malaysian society to correct economic imbalance, so as to reduce and eventually eliminate the identification of race with economic function. These would, "in turn, be undertaken in the context of rapid structural change and expansion of the economy so as to ensure that no particular group experiences any loss or feels any sense of deprivation in the process" (*Mid-Term Review* 1973, p. 1).

It appeared that the battles within UMNO had ended in a compromise. As Ismail wrote when warning against radical reforms in the field of education:

Malay aspirations could not be implemented 100 per cent in the country, as it would give rise to racial clashes. If the Malays insisted that their aspirations be carried out fully, then Malaysia would become a *desert* for the poor non-Malays who would have to defend themselves (*Utusan Melayu* 8 August 1970).

Razak aide Abdul Rahman Hamidon gathered that Ismail was convinced that in order for the NEP to work, the whole economy had to expand. This meant that unemployment had to be minimized, foreign investors encouraged, and the civil service made efficient (A.R. Hamidon, interview 9 September 2005).

On 10 March, Ismail led a delegation to the Fourth Meeting of ASEAN Foreign Ministers in Manila. He told newsmen before leaving that in accordance with Malaysia's neutrality policy, any country in the region could join ASEAN as long as its principles were adhered to. The neutrality policy, he explained, was a Malaysian project to prevent small countries in the region from being used as pawns by big powers (*MM* 12 March 1971; *ST* 14 March 1971).

Differences in economic interests after Singapore and Malaysia went separate ways became more pronounced with the years. The common airline — Malaysia-Singapore Airlines (MSA) — jointly owned since 1966 after the two countries separated, soon fell victim to divergent dynamics. Each country held a share of 42.79 per cent each in the airline, with Brunei owning the rest (*ST* 11 March 1971).

Singapore had become dissatisfied with how Malaysia's domestic flight services were developing, and wished instead to invest in international traffic. Tension increased over the idea that Singapore, in wishing to call its new airline *Mercury Singapore Airlines*, was unfairly trying to retain the initials MSA. An announcement by Malaysian Finance Minister Tan Siew Sin in August 1970 that a new airstrip capable of accommodating Boeing

737s would be built in Tebrau, Johor, added to the air of resentment (Low 1971, p. 107).

Ismail had been involved in air transport matters before his retirement, and since he was now chairman of the Cabinet Committee on Communications, the matter of splitting the airline landed on his table. He put G.K. Rama Iyer, who was with the General Planning Unit in the Prime Minister's Department, in charge of realizing the split with as little disadvantage to Malaysia as possible. Others involved were the Kuok brothers and Ismail Ali (Razaleigh, interview 28 June 2005; Rama Iyer, interview 11 April 2006).

The infrastructural challenges were forbidding. For example, a new airport — Senai — had to be built in Johor Bahru to serve East Malaysian flights that would soon be bypassing Singapore. Ismail personally gave instructions for the airport to be completed by July 1973 (*MM* 18 March 1972).

On 31 March 1971, Ismail announced that the Malaysian Government would invest M$100 million in building its own airline, tentatively called Malaysian Airlines Limited (MAL), the original company name. It would ply domestic routes as well as regional ones to Singapore, Hong Kong, Bangkok, Medan, Jakarta and Bali, and later include destinations in Australia, India and Japan (*ST* 1 April 1971). The final launch was planned for 1 January 1973, or earlier if possible. Singapore's Finance Minister Hon Sui Sen had, however, announced earlier in March that the two separate airlines should be ready to fly by 1 January 1972 (*MM* 24 March 1971). This put more unwanted pressure on those in charge of the separation process on the Malaysian side.

Ismail was generally optimistic about Malaysia's nation-building process. At a four-day conference held by the ACA on 12 April 1971, for example, he claimed that corruption in the civil service had been practically eradicated, but warned officers against "indecision", calling it "an evil comparable to corruption" (*ST* 13 April 1971).

The following week, Ismail took a nine-man delegation to Singapore to study its housing projects, and to attend the official opening of the first Shangri-la Hotel by Singaporean Finance Minister Goh Keng Swee. This was the first trip to the island neighbour by a Malaysian minister since the Razak administration came into being. Ismail told reporters that his trip would help his ministry formulate a housing policy (*ST* 23 April 1971). The idea, he said, was to generate more visits on both sides by officials involved in housing matters. "Don't let us live in a dream and think that we have no problems. We should solve our difficulties in a neighbourly manner. We have got co-operation in defence. We are inseparable" (*ST* 24 April 1971).

According to Abdul Rahman Hamidon, Ismail was very impressed by Singapore's Housing Development Board projects, and Malaysia's Urban Development Authority, which was founded on 12 November 1971, evolved from the interest Ismail had shown in them (A.R. Hamidon, interview 9 September 2005). Ismail was also very interested in Singapore's Jurong industrial area, and wished to create something similar in Malaysia (Abdullah Ali, interview 8 September 2005).

He wrote to Philip Kuok about how impressed he was by "the detailed planning of housing which goes right down the line from the top to the bottom and the success with which the Singaporean government managed to turn the Island into a garden city" (Letters 22 April 1971). When leaving Singapore two days later, Ismail took the opportunity at the airport to inform pressmen that Malaysia was seeking contact with China's leaders, "which you will hear about very soon" (*ST* 25 April 1971). China had in February shown its approval of Malaysia's support for Beijing's entry into the United Nations by donating relief supplies worth 625,000 MYR to help flood victims in West Malaysia, and through a highly appreciated visit that same month by the People's Republic's Silver Star Cultural Troupe to raise money, also for the flood victims (Tan and Yong 1971, p. 106).

Ismail went for a visit to Sarawak and Sabah soon after returning from Singapore. He had been worried that measures taken against communist subversion in East Malaysia might go too far and hamper economic development. He told journalists that his basic strategy was two-sided — economic development and successful prevention of communist subversion. During his week-long stay, he asked to be briefed on the detainee situation in the two states, as well as the issue of low-cost housing. He also announced that after having seen how Singapore tackled its housing problems, he thought that Malaysia should follow the republic's concept of planning (ST 1 May 1971). While in Sabah, Ismail was honoured, as was Razak in absentia, with Sabah's highest honour, the Sri Panglima Darjah Kinabalu (ST 6 May 1971).

On 6 May, a two-week, nineteen-man trade mission led by Tengku Razaleigh Hamzah, then president of the Association of Malay Chambers of Commerce and chairman of Pernas (Perbadanan Nasional, or the National Trading Corporation), left for Beijing. Besides trade agreements being reached, invitations were extended for Chinese table tennis and badminton teams to visit Malaysia (Jain 1984, pp. 159, 163; ST 7 May 1971). Although the mission was privately sponsored, the potential benefits were clearly connected to Malaysia's larger plan for regional neutralization. Ismail, who returned to Kuala Lumpur from East Malaysia the day the mission left, said that if the Chinese wished to reciprocate with a similar visit, they would be welcome (ST 7 May 1971). On 17 May, Ismail arrived in Bangkok for the Twelfth Thai-Malaysia Border Committee Talks, and told pressmen that Malaysia's condition for recognizing the communist regime in China was "if it stopped subversion in this part of the world". He reiterated that Malaysia would in the meantime support China's entry into the United Nations (*ST* 18 May 1971).

At a conference held on 19 June at Singapore's Institute of Southeast Asian Studies (ISEAS), Mahathir Mohamad — who had been expelled from UMNO — told participants that the ongoing change in Malaysia's foreign policy was a sustained effort by Ismail to cultivate friends outside the Commonwealth model of foreign relations, especially with the Soviet Union and China.* The Five Power Defence Pact, according to Mahathir, had proved itself incapable of dealing with Malaysia's biggest defence problem, which was communist guerrilla warfare. A foreign policy based on Southeast Asian neutrality, and which allowed for independence from Commonwealth forces, must in principle reject the assumption shared by the five powers that some common enemy, or enemies, existed (Mahathir 1971, p. 38). Incidentally, Ismail had a couple of months earlier told visiting journalists from New Zealand that the Five Power Defence Pact was "necessary until the neutralisation of Southeast Asia was made effective" (*ST* 20 April 1971).

> Perhaps the most significant change in trends in Malaysia's foreign policy lately is her relationship with the People's Republic of China. Without doubt this change is due to the new leadership. It was Tun Ismail who first suggested the then preposterous idea that China should guarantee Malaysia's security (Mahathir 1971, p. 38).

---

* Incidentally, a statement issued by UMNO headquarters at the end of June announced that the door was open for Mahathir to return to the party, despite his earlier pronouncements that he would not come back as long as the party was under Razak and Ismail (ST 29 June 1971).

Ismail had on 23 January 1968, when he was a retired cabinet minister and parliament backbencher, put forward his neutralization proposal for Southeast Asian neutrality before parliament (Sopiee 1973). This caused excitement in some quarters. For example, two days after that, former Singaporean Chief Minister David Marshall sent Ismail a telegram supporting his "concept of peace and security in Southeast Asia": *"May seed you have sown flourish stop bless you"* (DM221/7). However, in a letter to Philip Kuok, Ismail said that his proposal, "although it expresses the wish of the people, is, I am afraid, not making much headway". In a letter written that same day to Lee Moke Sang at the Malaysian High Commission in London, Ismail took on a more optimistic tone, saying that the proposal "seems to have been well received in the country and by the foreign Ambassadors in Kuala Lumpur". He even had a round of golf with the Russian ambassador "in order to explain to him the concept". At the same time, he tried "not to push too much on the proposals and embarrass the government" (Letters 15 July 1968).

The idea had met with little enthusiasm from the Tunku in the beginning. Ghazali Shafie, who was permanent secretary to the Ministry of Foreign Affairs when the proposal was made, remembers thinking that the idea as Ismail presented it then was somewhat "incomplete" (Interview 7 September 2005). Only after Razak had taken over the top post in September 1970 was the concept of neutralization adopted and propagated "as a viable response to the precarious balance of power in Southeast Asia" (Lau 1971, p. 27). Razak considered it "wise, imaginative and far-sighted" (Sopiee 1973, p. 5). A proposal was presented to the Non-Aligned Movement, the United Nations, the Commonwealth, ASEAN, and individual countries such as Japan, France and Germany, that a neutral Southeast Asian region should be created and guaranteed by the United States, the Soviet Union and

China. In line with this, Ismail also recommended that Southeast Asian countries jointly declare a policy of peaceful co-existence and non-interference in each other's affairs.

Among measures taken at that time to prepare the way for better ties with China were the curbing of the Taiwan lobby in Malaysia and a show of "readiness to back China's admission into the UN" (Mahathir 1971, p. 38). Ismail had earlier stated that Malaysia's stand in support of China's entry into the UN was "definite":

> We cannot ask Communist China to guarantee the neutralisation of Southeast Asia and at the same time say we do not approve of her. [...] If we do not get Communist China into the UN then we are paying lip-service to this new policy (*ST* 4 October 1970).

Ismail's argument that a neutral Southeast Asia was the region's long-term solution to its many security problems thus germinated within three years into the ideological cornerstone of Malaysia's foreign policy.

At the UMNO Silver Jubilee general assembly in May 1971, the party decided to revive its motto of "Unity, Loyalty, Service". Ismail disagreed with a suggestion that was also put forward at the meeting that "*Merdeka*" [Independence] should be made a permanent slogan. He argued that "the communists do not accept our independence, [and if] we still cry *Merdeka*, it would mean that we are still not a sovereign independent nation". The assembly accepted his reasoning (*ST* 10 May 1971).

The following week, while in Bangkok for the Malaysia-Thai General Border Committee meeting, he told pressmen that the border war would be an extended and changing one, and argued for the tactic he had earlier said should be used in East Malaysia, that is, economic development alongside a successful containment of subversion (*MM* 16 May 1971). Insurgents in the border areas were "on the run", he claimed. At the same time, he reiterated Malaysian support for China's entry into the United Nations, and told the Thais that the neutralization policy could work only if all parties in the region were behind it (*MM* 18 May 1971; *Sunday Times* 23 May 1971).

Ismail did not waste time tackling the housing problem and six weeks after his visit to Singapore, he called for a broad-based National Consultative Council on Housing to be formed. This two-tier body would consist of officials connected with housing as well as representatives from the private sector (*MM* 11 May 1971; *ST* 12 May 1971). He also urged state governments to build flats for sale, believing that flat-living would help ethnic integration in the urban areas (*ST* 18 June 1971; *ST* 23 June 1971).

Ismail, accompanied by Neno, was back in London on 24 October, again for a heart check-up. They stayed until 28 November. The British Foreign and Commonwealth Office, on the occasion of his visit that winter, appraised him in the following terms in an internally circulated report:

> Makes an important contribution to internal as well as external affairs. Firm believer in Malay/Chinese cooperation. Respected among non-Malay communities as a fair-minded and vigorous administrator. Well-disposed to Britain and the Commonwealth connection (FCO 24/824).

Although Ismail had at first intimated to British officials that he did not wish to see dignitaries, the satisfactory results of medical tests led him later to meet with the British prime minister and certain cabinet ministers. The British Foreign Office advised Britain's top leaders that it would be "very valuable" if they took time to meet Ismail and Neno, since "Tun Ismail is a likely future Prime Minister". The British also noted that Lee Kuan Yew called on Ismail on 10 November to discuss possible economic co-operation between Malaysia and Singapore, "but we have no details" (FCO 24/1187).

Ismail and Neno sent a pink tablecloth as a present to the British prime minister and his wife. Ismail also carried out field studies on the housing, urban renewal and prison reforms that were being carried out at that time in London.

Ismail analysed the latest X-rays of his own heart, and found no cause for concern. He treated himself to a week's recuperation in London's Lake District, and returned reportedly in very high spirits (FCO 24/1187).

Communist activities in Malaysia had been increasing in the meantime, and Ismail's earlier fears that the authorities might wind down anti-insurgency measures excessively early seemed well founded. In January 1972, Ismail presented a summation of operations against the guerrillas. He told parliament that three pro-communist organizations had been uncovered in Perak state, and 160 "Communist sympathisers" arrested. All three were aiding armed groups in the jungles. Over the preceding twelve months, there were 19 engagements with the insurgents, with four servicemen killed and 14 injured. This was a comparative improvement, but fresh operations had nevertheless been started in Kedah and Perlis. There was a case of a military patrol chasing three suspects and running into a group of 15, which seemed to be the average size for such units. One worry for the government was the condition of the New Villages into which the rural Chinese population had been moved in the early 1950s in an attempt to cut off supplies to the guerrillas. These settlements were now poor and congested. The situation at the Thai border was considered "well under control", and cooperation from the public and from the Thais was "excellent". The Thais now estimated the number of guerrillas active on their side of the border to be around 1,200, which was substantially larger than had been thought (*ST* 29 January 1972). Ismail remained optimistic throughout: "One thing is certain. There will be no Vietnam here. We will see that it does not happen" (*ST* 14 February 1976).

Later in the year, Ismail considered the situation at the Thai border to be "dangerous", though not "very dangerous". Operations in Sarawak, however, increased cooperation with Indonesian forces, and a vigilante corps system was being implemented (*ST* 20 May 1972). The Thais also managed to capture several camps along the border, but these turned out to be abandoned ones (*ST* 3 June 2006).

Intense communist activities would continue throughout the 1970s, and would involve the killing of policemen, especially Chinese detectives. More dramatic successes for the communists included the assassination of Inspector General of Police Haji Abdul Rahman, who was gunned down in early morning traffic in the heart of Kuala Lumpur in June 1974. In the early hours of 26 August 1975, members of a splinter group managed to blow up part of the National Monument, in close proximity to the Parliament Building (Shaw 1976, p. 230; *ST* 8 June 1974).

On 8 March 1972, Ismail visited Indonesia for talks with President Suharto and other leaders about Southeast Asian neutrality, border security and economic matters. His trip lasted eight days, during which the two governments agreed to reject a recent proposal by the Soviet Union to internationalize the Straits of Malacca (*ST* 8 March 1972; *ST* 17 March 1972). Ismail paid another visit to Indonesia later in the year, which resulted in the formation of two border committees aimed not only at fighting insurgents but also smugglers and pirates as well. Over a one-year period, Ismail visited no less than eight countries to discuss a wide range of issues ranging from ASEAN unity, regional security and foreign policy to housing and trade (*ST* 30 July 1972).

The process of dividing MSA into two was completed on 30 September 1972, and the resulting national airlines were called Malaysian Airline System (MAS) and Singapore Airlines (SIA). G.K. Rama Iyer, whom Ismail chose to realize the separation for Malaysia's part, became the first chairman of MAS. The Malaysian fleet consisted of seven Boeing 737s, nine Fokker Friendships and three Norman Islanders. As compensation for being kept out of Malaysia's domestic market, SIA was allowed twelve flights a day on the lucrative Kuala Lumpur–Singapore route (*ST* 2 October 1972).

The Malaysians thought MAL carried unhappy associations — *mal*function, *mal*aria, *mal*practice, etc. from the Latin *male*, meaning "badly" — and replaced it with something more clearly positive. MAS — the Malay word for gold — was chosen. Rama Iyer, who incidentally had been one of two joint secretaries to the NCC, remembers that Ismail had one day called him to his office:

> Tun Ismail was a man of few words, but he could certainly see the larger picture. Whatever had to take place had to take place. "Rama", he said to me, "I want you to set up the airline, and I want to see the planes in the air at such-and-such a date". And that was that. So we went ahead and quickly did what had to be quickly done (Interview 11 April 2006).

Between 30 March 1970 and 26 October 1972, Ismail did not make any addition to his autobiography. He was literally too busy for words. Fortunately, when he finally did have time to write down his private thoughts again, he allowed himself a calm and distanced look at recent Malaysian politics. These observations are worth presenting in their entirety (Drifting 26 October 1972):

> Tunku Abdul Rahman, the Father of the Nation, had finally agreed to retire and Tun Razak became the new Prime Minister

and I, his Deputy; Parliament had been reconvened to pass the act amending the Constitution, which had the effect of prohibiting "sensitive" issues being used in politics; I had gone to the Holy Land Mecca with my wife; a Second Malaysian Development Plan had been passed by Parliament and is now being implemented. Tun Razak's health had not deteriorated and he enjoyed being Prime Minister.

Tunku's departure from the scene was a drawn out affair. He used all the politician's skill to try to remain in power. He said at first that he wanted to retire. When there was no reaction to this statement, he made another that he would retire if the people wanted him to. Again there was no public response, but secretly people were cursing him for holding on to office when he had outlived his usefulness. Finally an opportunity came which allowed him to retire gracefully. He was offered the office of Secretary-General of [the] Islamic Conference.

The first act of Tun Razak as Prime Minister was to convene a meeting of divisional heads of UMNO. At this meeting he announced his future policy and also [named] me as his Deputy. This was the first time that my worth to the nation was admitted by a Prime Minister. The Tunku never acknowledged my worth publicly, although to a few chosen friends he admitted that I was indispensable to the nation, and he quoted especially my handling of the May 13th Affair and my defence of him in the period following this incident, when he was subjected to attacks of such obscenity by the Malays that one felt ashamed of them as a race.

By calling a meeting of UMNO and not the Alliance to make his first public stand, Tun Razak was serving notice to the Alliance and the country as a whole, that from then onwards the Govt. of the country was in UMNO's hands and the others were only supporters. It was a bold move and was unchallenged. It also marked the emergence of a new personality.

Tun Razak had been Tunku's Deputy since Independence. Tunku had used him recklessly, thereby enabling himself to live in style as a "happy Prime Minister". However Tun Razak has always been an astute [and] patient politician. He knew his ascension to the Prime Ministership was guaranteed so long as Tunku was Prime Minister. His main task therefore during his period of office as Deputy Prime Minister was to consolidate his position among the Malays, leaving the Tunku to look after the non-Malays. His political image during the period when he was deputy was that of a Malay leader, viewed with suspicion by some non-Malays and regarded as anti-Chinese by others. However, since becoming Prime Minister he has managed to change his image [to] that of a leader of a multi-racial country. The Malays accepted this new image and regarded it as a political strategy rather than a true change of personality and views; the Chinese sighed with relief at this metamorphosis. This general acceptance of his new political image coupled with the general improvement of his health, which confounded his medical advisers, including Dr. McPherson, has given him self-confidence and enabled him to shed off those fears and worries [that he lived with] as Tunku's Deputy.

Tun Razak is an able administrator and a shrewd politician. As an administrator he manages to get things done with little fuss and argument. He has laid down the infrastructure of Malay participation in the economic life of Malaysia and is now busy prodding them to take advantage of the facilities being made available to them.

As a politician, he is shrewd, cautious and has the ability to handle people. His main disability is his lack of charisma.

The three policies, which will determine the future of Malaysia, are:

1. The implementation of Malay participation in the commercial and industrial fields;
2. [The need to] maintain and if possible to decrease the rate of unemployment;
3. The neutralisation of South-East Asia.

The implementation of Malay participation in commerce
and industry

This was discussed in the National Consultative Council in
the days of [the] National Operations Council — (May 13th
1969–1970). Long debates on the policy of redressing economic
imbalance between the Malays and other Bumiputras took
place and many of the speeches were either inflammatory
because they were racially based, or academic. I foresaw that if
we were to get anywhere near to solving the problem, we must
paint a clear picture of what was going to be done for the
Malays without unduly frightening the non-Malays. I suggested
that there must be a target to aim at and that this target must
be reasonable and, what was more important, capable of being
implemented. I said that we should aim at a target period of
twenty years within which thirty percent of Malays would
participate in commerce and industry and that it should be
implemented in the context of a growing economy. This
proposal was unanimously accepted. At the time of writing,
the implementation of this policy has been going on for
almost two years. Although the policy is clear if it is seen in its
entirety, in the course of implementation various sectors of
our society chose to see it only from [a] sectional angle. It is
obvious that participation must mainly depend on new
activities in commerce and industry.

This should not be difficult to achieve in a developing
country like Malaysia, because new industries and new trading
opportunities are constantly and continually being established
and offered. Instead of trying to identify and promote new
industries for Malays to participate [in], Govt. and Govt.
sponsored agencies [and] officials used all sorts of strategy to
inject Malays into existing established industries and businesses.
The Chinese on the other hand, instead of accepting the fact
that new fields in industries and commerce must [benefit] the
Malays, use all commercial and business tactics to [prevent] this
from taking place.

The implementation [is] further distrusted by the Malays when they refuse to see the picture of implementation as a whole and rather choose to see details of implementation in isolation. The present Malay interest in capital accumulation when compared to that possessed by non-Malays is one example. They argue that the present rate of Govt. injection of capital into Malay commercial enterprises and trading institutions is so slow that in 20 years Malay capital accumulation will not only not achieve the target but the gap will widen. They forget or choose to forget the fact that capital accumulation can be achieved not only by means of injection of fresh capital but rather by the multiplication of existing capital through normal business activities. The Chinese, for example, achieved their present capital largely by business activities. Some of the big Chinese businesses achieve their success by this method. The Malays want the Govt. to restrict [the] business activities of the non-Malays while the Malays reach parity with them. If this philosophy is accepted then the whole concept of Malay participation in a growing economy is replaced by a policy of Malay participation in a standstill economy. This is neither politically possible nor is it practical from the Govt.'s point of view. Injection of capital into the Malay sector can only be done if Govt. taxes keep on increasing as the economy expands.

Another problem that is cause for concern is the manner by which the Malays want the Govt. to improve the quality of Malay manpower.

The Govt. policy of doing this is first of all in the existing seats of learning, where there are more qualified Malays seek[ing] to enter than there are places for them, to reserve [a] quota for Malays. This is a reasonable way, because all qualified Malays will be accommodated, and if there are surplus places they should be given to non-Malays. It is true that by this policy, the time taken to bridge the gap will [be] slower than if the Govt. were to deny surplus places to non-Malays, but this is a practical and just way of doing things in a multiracial society like Malaysia.

He did not jot down his ideas on the last two policies, although his general views on those matters were not unknown. Where unemployment was concerned, Lim Chong Eu revealed in a speech made much later (in September 2005) that Ismail gave his unreserved support to Penang's Gerakan government to build Penang Bridge to connect the new townships of Sebarang Jaya and Bayan Baru. This was to stem the social and economic imbalances that existed between the state's rural and urban populations. An outer ring road for Penang Island was already envisaged at that early stage (Lim 2005). The federal government finally agreed on 28 June 1971 to build the bridge that both the Alliance and Gerakan had promised Penang voters during the 1969 electoral campaign (*ST* 29 June 1971).

Lim Chong Eu worked closely with Ismail during the first years of the NEP. He held the latter in high esteem and until today, considers him Malaysia's Thomas Jefferson, referring generically to the astute mind that manages to place the cogent ideas and practicalities of an age in a cogent and practical pattern (Lim, interview 9 January 2006).

Where neutralization was concerned, China — with support from Malaysia — gained entry into the United Nations on 23 November 1971, replacing Taiwan in the Security Council in the process. Ismail did not live to see the establishment of full diplomatic relations between Malaysia and China. This occurred on 21 May 1974 and Razak paid a much-publicized six-day official visit to Beijing a week after that. Official ties with Taiwan were severed.

A preparatory trip by a Malaysian delegation made prior to the ties with Beijing — and which was arranged through Robert Kuok — had discussed and gained clarity on three major issues, namely, China's support for the MCP, mainland China's view on the status of Malaysians of Chinese origin, and Malaysia's defence arrangements with Britain. According to one of the delegates, Razali Ismail, who was assistant secretary for Southeast Asia in the Foreign Affairs Ministry at that time, Chinese Premier Zhou Enlai tried to ease Malaysian anxiety over the first issue by stating that the relationship between Beijing and the MCP was but "an aspect of history" (Razali, interview 13 September 2005). Zhou told the leader of the delegation, Raja Mohar bin Raja Badiozaman, who was economic adviser to the prime minister, that China could not possibly reject the MCP: "It's like Islam. One cannot ask Muslims in one country to reject other Muslims in another country" (Mazlan 2005, p. 226). On the second issue, Zhou kept to the stand taken at the Bandung Summit in 1955 that Chinese who were citizens of other countries should remain loyal to their own countries. Malaysia's neutralization policy seemed sufficient in counter-balancing its defence relations with Britain as far as Beijing was concerned.

Through these changes in international relations, Malaysia's neutralization policy began to attain visible contours. Regionalism remained the foundation stone. Ismail said just a month before he passed away that "when countries declare non-alignment individually, they usually suffer [...] but if all of us pursue this policy together — and it is guaranteed by all the big powers — then I think it will work" (*Sunday Mail* 5 August 1973).

In January 1973, Ismail agreed to take on the extra portfolio of trade and industry, with Musa Hitam as his deputy. Musa remembers:

> It was the greatest thing to happen to me. He called me in and told me I was responsible for this and that, and then left me alone. I learned a lot from him. The funny thing was that he allowed me to sit in at Cabinet meetings, which was not strictly constitutional. I think he was training me (Musa, interview 26 October 2006).

Ismail, being deputy prime minister, was also chief whip, and Musa was the assistant whip representing the UMNO component of the Alliance. Once, Musa was absent on an errand, but despite the fact that nothing went wrong while he was away, he was served with a letter a week later written in bold characters from the chief whip admonishing him for being absent, and warning him that "this should not happen again".

> You could happily receive a letter from anybody, but not from Tun Ismail. You shivered when that happened. That was the terror of the man. He would just tell you — behave yourself! That was the only time I was scolded by him, and it left an indelible mark on me. When I became Deputy Prime Minister I tried to adopt his style (Musa, interview 26 October 2006).

Musa also remembers how Ismail would not bow to pressure, even from relatives. For example, one of Ismail's nieces who had married an Englishman once asked for him to be awarded Malaysian citizenship. Ismail flatly refused since her husband did not fulfil the necessary requirements (Interview 26 October 2006).

Daud Ahmad, who was a staff member at the Home Affairs Ministry, remembers how Ismail once dismissed the Tunku's request for an entry permit for the daughter-in-law of a cabinet minister. She was from the People's Republic of China. Ismail merely sent a note back to the prime minister: "I think you know the rules". The Tunku did not pursue the matter further (Interview 27 June 2005).

Despite being a stickler for rules, there were instances when Ismail allowed for some leeway. Lawyer Dominic Puthucheary remembers an occasion when Ismail had to make a decision in a case where details provided in a successful citizenship application had turned out to be incorrect. Although the applicant was obviously eligible for citizenship, the fault in the application meant that his citizenship had to be withdrawn. Ismail's solution to the problem was to grant the man a permanent resident permit until he properly reapplied for citizenship (D. Puthucheary, interview 4 September 2006).

Once, Ismail's office boy Roslan was arrested for involvement in the burning down of a temple in Sentul. The boy's state assemblyman, an important figure within UMNO, came to Ismail's office to ask that the boy be released and not be sent to Pulau Jerejak. Ismail angrily told him off: "Look here! I am here not as a representative of UMNO but as Minister of Home Affairs. Whatever I do is based on the rule of law. I am closer to this boy than any of you, but this is something that must be done."

Daud noticed that party people did not normally drop in on Ismail for a chat, although one could not really say that he was not popular. Ismail was not one for small talk, and his efficiency was seen in the fact that he seldom had to work past office hours (Daud, interview 27 June 2005).

Cabinet Secretary Shahriman Sulaiman recalls an occasion in February 1972 when Razak's attention was called to the corrupt practices of a top official at Pernas, who was also one of Razak's trusted supporters. This body had only recently been created as a part of the NEP to benefit Malay businesses. This official had allegedly directed a British deal meant for Pernas to his own company. Razak was greatly disappointed, and sent Shahriman to Ismail for advice. Ismail thought the best thing to do was to confront the person with the allegation. If he freely admitted to the offence, then he had to resign at once. Should he choose not to do that, then the ACA would be directed to investigate the matter. Shahriman informed Razak of what Ismail had said, but Razak was afraid that he might weaken when faced with a repentant and crying friend, and hesitated. Shahriman took it on himself the next morning to approach the official with Ismail's ultimatum, letting the man assume that it was Ismail who had sent him. Luckily for Shahriman, who was fearfully aware that he had exceeded his authority, the official recognized that his game was up and chose to resign (Interview 6 September 2005).

Wahab Majid, who became Ismail's secretary after the latter's return to politics in 1969, remembers the time when the *New Straits Times Press* was being introduced on the Kuala Lumpur Stock Exchange. This was to take place on 14 April 1973, and several members of Ismail's personnel were excited about attaining an allotment. Since each 5,000-share lot cost a staggering $25,000, twenty to twenty-five of them got together to approach their boss at what they thought was a well-chosen moment to ask for his help in acquiring some shares. Razak had after all already given them his blessing. Ismail however considered it inappropriate, and refused. This disappointed them, at least until 14 April, when they were relieved to see that the market price for the share stayed below the introductory price (Wahab, interview 6 July 2005).

Abdullah Ali, who later became high commissioner to the United Kingdom, claims that no minister of the time, including Razak, enjoyed the high level of respect that civil servants had for Ismail.

> He believed fully in the oneness of Malaysia, and worked on that belief. He did not care whom he had to fight. He was absolutely neutral; no one could deny that. When you had to deal with him, you knew you would get fair treatment (Abdullah Ali, interview 8 September 2005).

In keeping with his reputation as "moderate" and "principled", Ismail never seemed to have invested time or effort into cultivating any loyal group of followers. His style of politics, infused with the reluctance he had felt about going into politics, did not involve populist tactics and normal "politicking" practices. Dragged away from his family back into politics by his sense of duty, his intolerance of incompetence and irrelevance appeared to grow to such an extent that most of his subordinates and colleagues came to fear him.

Robert Kuok describes Ismail thus:

> He was a lovely man with strength of character, high principles, and a great sense of fairness. In my opinion, he was probably the most non-racial, non-racist Malay I have met in my life. And I have met a very wide range of Malays from all parts of Malaysia. Doc was a stickler for total fair play, for correctness; total anathema to him to be anything else. Every Malay colleague feared him because of this, including Mahathir (Interview 10 February 2006).

Tengku Razaleigh Hamzah, who was one of the few young talents who got on comfortably with Ismail, recalls that although Ismail did not have a group of followers, people did follow him because they respected him: "You cannot say that he was a popular man. He wasn't even approachable, you know, so how can one say he was popular?" (Razaleigh, interview 28 June 2005).

Din Merican, who was chairman of the caddies committee, played golf with Ismail regularly on Sundays at the Subang National Golf Club. Ismail was then president of the club. He remembers that Ismail was a strong and meticulous golfer, and was in the habit of warning other players that he did not indulge in "diplomatic golf" but played to win. Ismail would always pay for the drinks, regardless of whether he won or lost (Merican, interview 4 September 2006).

Ismail's older children remember that he used to query them at meals about school, and particularly about what their schoolmates and teachers were saying in class or at recess. He would also regularly ask Neno about what people on the street — and at cocktail parties — were concerned and chatting about. It was apparently one of his ways of keeping his finger on society's pulse (Tawfik, interview 21 July 2006; Zailah, interview 23 March 2005).

Ismail's son, Tarmizi, who was a young boy when his father died, had few contacts with his busy father. Some of his lasting impressions include memories of how he would come over to Ismail's office after school, and would observe with amusement how important people coming to see his father would look very nervous, stop outside the door and adjust their ties before going in. On the other hand, Tarmizi also noticed how Ismail would on occasion return home with Dr Tan Chee Khoon, the influential oppositional parliamentarian with whom he had memorable quarrels in parliament, for a friendly drink (Interview 28 June 2005).

His third son, Zamakhshari, who was but nine years old in 1973, remembers that his father was always busy and he hardly saw him. In the mornings, Ismail would practise his golf swing and putt in his bedroom. At lunch, he tended to eat a lot of rice and always with his hands. His dinners were light, taken after a short swim in the garden pool, sometimes after a short game of golf at the Royal Selangor Golf Club. He had a preference for cheese and bread in the evenings. On weekends when not golfing, he would settle down to read with a pipe by his side, taken from his veritable collection. His favourite books were on espionage and detective work especially those about Sherlock Holmes (Zamakhshari, interview 28 June 2005; Tawfik, interview 21 July 2006).

In March 1973, Ismail took a delegation, which included Neno and their daughter Zailah, to Australia and New Zealand for talks on investments in Malaysia and Southeast Asian neutralization. Both those countries had new Labour Party administrations, and Ismail thought it a good time to discuss foreign policy matters, tourism, the exchange of skills, and trade agreements with them. Australia under Premier Gough Whitlam had recently severed ties with Taiwan and extended diplomatic recognition to Beijing.

The delegation's hectic journey took them to Canberra, Sydney, Melbourne, Hobart and Armidale. In Canberra, Ismail suggested to the Australian Defence Ministry, which had earlier announced that Australian forces should be withdrawn from Southeast Asia, that the Australian airbase in Butterworth, Penang, would be getting "a little crowded as a result of Malaysia's expansion of its own air force" (*ST* 17 March 1973).

An Australian suggestion for a large regional body that would include China and Japan was also discussed. Malaysia's reaction was that ASEAN needed to be consolidated before a wider forum could be considered. Indonesia had announced a stand similar to Kuala Lumpur's (*ST* 12 March 1973).

Ismail's family also visited Queen's College. It was the doctor's first return to his alma mater after almost thirty years, and the college made him an honorary Doctor of Laws. He also visited the University of New England in Armidale, where his eldest son Tawfik was studying.

New Zealand's Labour government under Norman Kirk had on several occasions stated its support for Ismail's neutralization policy (*MM* 27 March 1973). On 22 March, while in Wellington, Ismail addressed the New Zealand Institute of International Affairs:

> Malaysia firmly believes that an extensive network of meaningful bilateral and multilateral relations should be and must be established among the countries of Southeast Asia so that misunderstanding and mistrust will not arise, and regional cooperation [will be] enhanced and intensified. Politically, there

is no acceptable alternative to the development of a strong natural Southeast Asian region, particularly in view of the fast changing international situation (Jain 1984, pp. 198–99).

On 9 June, the new Universiti Sains Malaysia in Penang awarded its first honorary doctorate to Ismail. Vice-Chancellor Hamzah Sendut explained that the award was for Ismail's contribution to the establishment of the university, his readiness to return when his country needed him, and for "his upright and objective views on matters of national concern" (*ST* 11 June 1973).

Press Secretary Wahab Majid still considers the speech Ismail made on that occasion at USM as one of his most memorable (Interview 6 July 2005). In it, Ismail provided a post-colonial historical context for his government's policies.

> The struggle for independence was in the hands of two groups, one convinced that independence could only be achieved by revolutionary means, the other that it could be achieved by constitutional means. [...] The British decided to cooperate with the moderate nationalists. [...] But although independence was won by the moderates, history also shows that the radical nationalists also played a role in attaining independence. [...] The application of the New Economic Policy [...] will change from time to time to suit the situation and the circumstances and the geographical setting. But its aim and its fundamentals are the same and that is to close the gap between the rural and the urban, to destroy poverty without regard to background or race (Letters 9 June 1973).

Unlike most other leaders of that time and since, Ismail was prepared to admit the contributions made by the radicals to the cause of independence. In that speech, he also declared himself an "optimist" who believed that under a pragmatic form of government, "a Malaysian Race" that was "progressive" would develop.

On 28 June, Harun Idris submitted an UMNO Youth executive committee resolution to Razak. Cabinet Secretary Shahriman Sulaiman, who later became the first director-general of the Implementation Coordination Unit (ICU), remembers that the resolution proposed that since the NEP was in its early stages, the prime minister should refrain from any reshuffling of the cabinet. Ismail immediately told Razak that Harun was challenging his authority, and personally vowed that he would accept the challenge in Razak's stead if the resolution were not immediately withdrawn. The following morning, a stunned and "shivering" Harun apologized to Razak and said that it was never his intention to challenge the prime minister. Razak warned him to be careful in the future, or he would go after him as he had recently done with Trengganu's chief minister (Shahriman, interview 6 September 2005).

About six weeks before he passed away, Ismail asked Robert Kuok to fly over for a game of nine-hole golf. Kuok's plane was badly delayed and he arrived late:

> Ismail was seething, really seething. I had to apologize, saying that things were beyond my control. He finally accepted my excuse, and we got on with the game. If it had been anyone else but me, he would have exploded. That day he played extraordinarily well. I still remember it clearly. He managed 35 strokes, a boogie here, and par there, a birdie after that. At the end of it, he had played par golf. He had never played so well in all his life! However, I must say I sensed that danger was in store for him to be in such a heightened state. He was of course on Cloud Nine when he went off for his next meeting.

Kuok further recalls that about three weeks before Ismail's death, "Doc" asked him to come over to Maxwell Road. He had an earlier engagement and arrived late that evening. The house was in darkness and the door was unlocked. He hesitantly went in, whispering "Doc? Neno?" Neno appeared out of the darkness, welcomed him and directed him to the back of the house.

> Doc was by the pool, sitting in the patio. Something was bothering him that he would not burden his wife with. That was the kind of considerate person he was. He had champagne waiting, and he asked me to pour myself a glass. He then said: "I had three heart attacks in the last two weeks, Robert, quite serious ones. I have young children, and Neno is expecting. If anything happens to me..."
>
> I quickly replied: "No, no, no, Doc. Don't talk like that. I promise you, to put your mind at ease, that should anything happen to you, God forbid, my people and I will look after your family, and make sure that they get a good education. Let's tackle the problem at hand first. Can you hand in your resignation tomorrow?"
>
> Doc said: "No, I can't. I do want to resign, but Razak is leaving for the Commonwealth meeting in Ottawa soon, and I have promised him that I would act in his absence. I will resign when he comes back".
>
> What could I say to that? Duty bound him. Then he let off one of those sighs that we Chinese advise against: *Aaaaaaaaahh*. One of those deep sounds of dejection that the dying emits. The Chinese forbid it because it is supposedly injurious to one's health. Doc then said: "You know us Malays. If the Prime Minister wants things his way, no one tries to turn him around. Nothing has changed. I told Razak to use Musa, and not Mahathir, but he will not listen" (Kuok, interview 26 October 2006).

Corroborating the latter sentiments, Maurice Baker remembers Ismail telling him: "Musa is OK, we simply have to send him away out of the Tunku's way, but it is impossible to forgive Mahathir" (Interview 9 June 2005). Mahathir had, in the eyes of those most able to appreciate the Tunku's contributions, gone too far in his criticism of the old man.

According to lawyer Dominic Puthucheary, his brother James was asked by Razak to speak to Mahathir Mohamad about rejoining UMNO. Razak was hoping that Mahathir would counter-balance the opposition that existed within the party. A meeting was held at Syed Nasir's house at which the question of re-admitting Mahathir was discussed. Ismail was the only one who opposed Mahathir's return, but said that he would not stand in the way if Razak really wished it (D. Puthucheary, interview 4 June 2006).

Ismail frequently showed concern for the young and their influence on politics. Abdullah Badawi, who was then director of youth at the Ministry of Culture, Youth and Sports, recalls that about two or three days before he died, Ismail talked at length about how necessary it was for the government to maintain a dialogue with the young, and how important it was that they should not feel alienated (Interview 14 May 2006).

On 27 July, Ismail was among those at the airport to send Razak off to Ottawa. Shahriman Sulaiman remembers that Ismail stood next to him, and complained about the unbearable heat. The younger man suggested to Ismail that he should perhaps go on holiday and treat himself to a good rest. Shahriman thought Ismail looked like he needed it (Shahriman, interview 6 September 2005).

Ismail had the habit of playing a round of nine-hole golf after work, almost always with a partner. On 1 August, he had a game at the Royal Selangor Golf Club with one of his regular partners, Leslie Eu Peng Meng. On the fourth hole that day — now the par-four thirteenth hole — Ismail managed an eagle, which put him in a very good mood, and he bought his golfing partner a beer before going off to visit his wife in hospital (Eu, interview

9 September 2005). That was the last time he played the game he loved so dearly, and that had been such a source of inspiration for him. Incidentally, his official golf handicap — as the club certified on 21 October 1969 — was 15. Once, in November 1970, he even managed a hole-in-one at the same venue and was awarded a Ronson "Windlite" Gas Lighter (Letters).

He did not play golf on 2 August, being busy with the GPMS celebrations in Kampung Baru. Once that was over, he went to Lady Templer Hospital to visit his wife. He then went home for dinner. After seeing that all was well with his young sons, he went upstairs to rest. Soon after that, a massive heart attack killed him.

Ismail's failure to have a heart operation proved fatal, and also showed that his decision in 1967 to retire for health reasons was a sound one. After re-entering politics, the knowledge that Razak did not have long to live made it difficult for him to contemplate going back into treasured retirement.

Ismail's death left Razak without the one person with whom he could discuss his own impending death. Razak knew about Ismail's autobiography, and was certainly worried that his own illness was mentioned therein. Details about how Razak's ailment was diagnosed are indeed given in Ismail's autobiography:

> Shortly after this incident of my heart [being found to be deteriorating in September 1969], an unexpected and far-reaching occurrence, if it were made known publicly, occurred. For a long, long time, Tun Razak's personal physician was Dr MacPherson, who has been and still is my personal physician, and close friend for a much longer time. However, for political reasons, Tun Razak dropped Dr MacPherson and used the medical services of Govt doctors, who were all Asians. Lately Tun Razak's appearance gradually began to change. He began to lose weight and his face has a sickly unpleasant pallor and the total effect

made him look really an old man, although he was only 47 years old. It was, of course, a common joke among Tun Razak's friends that he always liked to look an old man and tried his best to achieve this in his College days but this time he did look old. One day at a party in my house, both he and Dr MacPherson were among the guests and they started talking together at one corner. It resulted in his asking Dr MacPherson to examine him medically, which the latter did the next day. The results were a shock to Dr MacPherson and myself. I had been taken into confidence by the expressed wish of Tun Razak himself. The results gave clear indications that he was suffering from an incurable blood disease, akin to cancer. The only people who knew of this besides Tun Razak, were Dr MacPherson, myself, the haematologist at the hospital and an expatriate research worker who was at the University of Malaysia. All these people were sworn to top secrecy (Drifting 30 March 1970).

When Ismail passed away, his 22-year-old eldest son Tawfik inherited the memoirs, and learned the terrible truth that Razak was dying. He had to bear that adult secret in silence and with trepidation for the next three years. Razak suspected that Tawfik had access to the state secret and on one occasion, he despondently told Tawfik that he knew about Ismail's memoirs, "but I don't want to know what is in them" (Tawfik, interview 13 May 2006). What these two did not know was that both Robert and Philip Kuok had separately been taken into Ismail's confidence on the matter (Kuok, interview 10 February 2006; Kuok 1991, p. 228). Razak found on rushing home from Ottawa that his instructions for Ismail's funeral had not been followed. In despair, he exclaimed to Ismail's widow, Neno: "Who am I to trust now?" (Tawfik, interview 13 May 2006). On Robert Kuok's suggestion, Leslie Cheah was chosen to help Ismail's family with paperwork. Cheah in turn brought in their childhood friend James Puthucheary and chartered accountant Hew Kiang Meng to help out as trustees for the estate (Tawfik, interview 6 September 2006).

The death of Ismail on 2 August 1973 inevitably altered Malaysian politics. Razak's choice of Hussein Onn, a recent addition to the cabinet, to succeed Ismail as his deputy, surprised many. Hussein also took over Ismail's position as minister of trade and industry. Ghazali Shafie became the new minister of home affairs on 13 August.

Abdul Rahman Hamidon suspects that Hussein Onn was chosen because he was the least controversial figure, and Razak did not wish to play into the hands of any of the ambitious and opposing factions within UMNO (Interview 9 September 2005).

Shahriman Sulaiman, Razak's aide, recalls how Tan Siew Sin was deeply disappointed on being told on 12 August that Hussein Onn was to be Razak's new deputy. He asked in disbelief: "What about me?" (Shahriman, interview 6 September 2005). The MCA continued to push for its president to be appointed as second deputy prime minister but met strong resistance from UMNO. In disappointment over this failure, Tan considered resigning as finance minister. He was persuaded to stay on by Philip Kuok, with some prodding from behind the scenes by Razak. Nevertheless, ill health forced Tan to resign in February 1974, and to take on the specially created post of financial adviser to the government instead (Kuok 1991, pp. 234–36).

With Tan's departure, Razak's regime evolved further. It left Tunku Abdul Rahman's brand of inter-communal politics behind and critics of Tunku Abdul Rahman, such as Mahathir Mohamad and Musa Hitam, were successively placed in positions of power. The latter had already been appointed, apparently with Ismail's blessings, as deputy minister of trade and industry in January 1973, and the former, whose attempt to rejoin UMNO was rejected in 1971 but who became a member of the party's Supreme Council already on 7 March 1972, was appointed Senator in 1973. Razak had personally asked the Chief Minister of Kedah state, Syed Ahmad Shahabuddin, to choose Mahathir as Kedahan representative to the upper house (Zainuddin 1994, p. 41). After an uncontested victory at the general elections held on 24 August 1974, Mahathir was immediately made minister of education, a portfolio that, given the traditional teachers-based support structure of UMNO, tended to propel the holder to higher political positions.

Musa Hitam, who had hoped for a promotion, remained deputy minister of trade and industry after Ismail's death. Hussein Onn, knowing that Musa was deeply disappointed, took upon himself the job of consoling the younger man. However, he quickly noticed that Musa's presence at cabinet meetings was not constitutional, and so put a stop to it (Musa, interview 26 October 2005). Musa nevertheless became a full minister after the 1974 elections, taking over the portfolio of primary industries.

Shahriman Sulaiman remembers discussing the future of UMNO with Razak, and getting the distinct impression that the prime minister considered Mahathir Mohamad as having most leadership potential ahead of other contenders such as Tengku Razaleigh Hamzah, Musa Hitam and Ghazali Shafie (Interview 6 September 2005).

The three-party Alliance thus collapsed after the 1969 elections, and was replaced by a new format — Barisan Nasional (BN, National Front) — that exhibited a strongly enhanced UMNO dominance. The government paved the way for this new power constellation when it managed in February 1972 to recruit Gerakan under Lim Chong Eu as an ally. The PPP of Perak joined three months later. When the PMIP also accepted the new formula soon afterwards, the stage was set for the declaration on 1 January

1973 that the Alliance would be replaced. On that New Year's Day, Kuala Lumpur — where the 13 May violence had started — was also carved away from Selangor state to create a centrally controlled federal territory.

These moves considerably altered the electoral balance of inter-ethnic power, pushing the percentage of Malay-majority constituencies in Peninsular Malaysia to 69.3 per cent, up from 57.7 per cent in 1969. Such delineation exercises had been and remain a constant factor in the country's electoral politics.

> The 1974 re-delineation restored the Malay delineation advantage to about the 1955 level and thus enabled the Malays to regain some of the overall advantage they had lost, mainly from increased non-Malay enfranchisement, since independence. This restored level of delineation advantage has been generally maintained in subsequent re-delineations (Lim 2002, p. 130).

On 1 July 1974, the new consociation officially came into being, followed on 24 July by new delineations in electoral constituencies passed by parliament (Lal 1982, p. 84). In the BN elections manifesto introduced on 25 July, besides expected points about maintaining peace and security in the country, protecting the lives and property of the people, and strengthening and consolidating social and political stability, BN aimed to "implement fully the New Economic Policy" and "establish a just, united and prosperous society in accordance with the *Rukunegara*". Furthermore, it vowed to pursue "a free, neutral and active foreign policy" (Lal 1982, p. 126).

In the elections of 24 August, the BN — by then a collection of nine parties — harvested 135 of 154 parliamentary seats, retaining control over all thirteen states and gaining a firm grip over Pahang, Kelantan and Perlis. It won 345 of the 392 state seats. Since Sabah's legislative assembly was not due to be dissolved until 1976, there was no contest there on that occasion (Shaw 1976, pp. 243–44).

Thus, four years after the trauma of 1969, the country was remade and democracy was practised once again. Ismail did not live to see democracy's resurrection in the new form that he had helped to shape. What was impressive was that the re-enactment of parliamentary rule took less than twenty-one months and democratic elections, though restricted, could be held without postponement. Between 1969 and 1974, a new structure for inter-ethnic balance and power-sharing came into being that has since given the country relative peace, if not harmony.

A more sobering review suggests that the new democracy was imposed overly heavy-handedly, and thus succeeded in burning the wariness and divides of a more violent time into the national psyche, seriously limiting the country's ability to achieve proper closure.

Where foreign policy was concerned, Malaysia granted recognition to Communist China soon after Ismail's death. On 24 February 1976, ASEAN members signed the Treaty of Amity and Cooperation to guarantee non-interference in each other's internal affairs.

A thorough understanding of Ismail's contributions has traditionally been made difficult by the fact that he was always the third or the second most powerful man in the country. Historiographic convention has always allowed the Tunku and Razak to overshadow Ismail's achievements, and his name is often mentioned in combination with the other two, and with Tan Siew Sin. This has meant that latter-day Malaysians have not learned to know him, and what is worse, they have not had opportunity to understand the ideas behind the deeds. His legacy has yet to be discovered.

But for now, perhaps the proudest heritage that he left behind — that any person could hope to leave behind — is his reputation. According to his children, the mention of the second part of their name — bin or binte Tun Dr Ismail — so many years after his death, still brings forth immediate expressions of respect and gratefulness, especially from older Malaysians and Singaporeans.

For those who worked with or under Ismail, he is remembered for his deep dislike of incompetence and bigotry, his strict adherence to the virtues of hard work and honesty, and his belief in the principles of national independence and multi-racialism.

That is a legacy for his children, and for Malaysians in general, to contemplate with pride.

LIST OF ABBREVIATIONS

AAS	Association of Asian Studies
ACA	Anti-Corruption Agency
ASA	Association of Southeast Asia
ASEAN	Association of Southeast Asian Nations
BMA	British Military Administration
BN	Barisan Nasional; National Front
BSP	Barisan Socialis Parti
Cantab	*Cantabrigiensis*, Latin for "of Cambridge"; Cambridge University
CEC	Central Executive Committee
CEO	Chief Executive Officer
CIA	Central Intelligence Agency, USA
CLC	Communities Liaison Committee
CPM	Communist Party of Malaya; see MCP
DAP	Democratic Action Party
DNU	Department of National Unity
Felda	Federal Land Development Agency
GATT	General Agreement on Tariffs and Trade
Gerakan	Gerakan Rakyat Malaysia Party; Malaysian People's Movement
GH	General Hospital
GLU	General Labour Unions, Singapore
GPMS	Gabungan Pelajar-pelajar Melayu Semenanjung; Peninsular Malaysia Malay Students Foundation

GPU	General Planning Unit
IBRD	International Bank of Reconstruction and Development
ICC	Information Coordinating Centre
ICU	Implementation Coordination Unit
IMF	International Monetary Fund
IMP	Independence of Malaya Party
ISA	Internal Security Act
ISC	Internal Security Council
ISEAS	Institute of Southeast Asian Studies, Singapore
JB	Johor Bahru, written as Johore Baru in earlier times
MAL	Malaysian Airlines Limited
MAS	Malaysian Airline System
MCA	Malayan, later Malaysian, Chinese Association
MCACECC	MCA Chinese Education Central Committee
MCP	Malayan Communist Party; see CPM
MIC	Malayan, later Malaysian, Indian Congress
MIM	Malaysian Institute of Management
MISC	Malaysian International Shipping Corporation
MP	Member of Parliament
MSA	Malaysia-Singapore Airline
MSC	Malaysian Solidarity Convention
NEP	New Economic Policy
NOC	National Operations Council
NCC	National Consultative Council
NGC	National Goodwill Committee
NSTP	New Straits Times Press
PAP	People's Action Party, Singapore
PMIP	Pan-Malayan Islamic Party
PPP	People's Progressive Party
Pernas	Perbadanan Nasional; National Trading Corporation
QCSSC	Queens College Sports and Social Club, Melbourne University, Australia
RMAF	Royal Malaysian Air Force
SAP	Singapore Alliance Party

Seato	Southeast Asian Treaty Organization
SIA	Singapore Airlines
SOAS	School of Oriental and African Studies, London University
SPA	Singapore People's Alliance
SSM	Seri Setia Mahkota; Grand Commander
SUPP	Sarawak United People's Party
UAR	United Arab Republic
UDP	United Democratic Party
UM	Universiti Malaya
UN	United Nations
UMNO	United Malays National Organization
USCSCA	United Chinese School Committees' Association
UCSTA	United Chinese School Teachers Association
USM	Universiti Sains Malaysia
WHO	World Health Organization

BIBLIOGRAPHY

The Tun Dr Ismail Abdul Rahman Papers, marked IAR at ISEAS Library, Singapore

Drifting — *Drifting into Politics.* Unpublished memoirs (Folio 12*a*). Chapters 1 to 16.

Letters

— *Letters 10 February 1938 – 3 March 1946.* (Folio 3/1);

— *Letters 3 March 1946 – 15 May 1969.* (Folio 3/2);

— *Letters and Speeches from 16 May 1969.* (Folio 3/3)

Notes — *Notes by the Ambassador.* 30 December 1957 – 26 August 1958. (Folio 5)

TS — *Top Secret.* (Folio 14; IAR/14).

Diverse (Folio 11, *etc*).

Public Documents
(from the British National Archives and the Internet)

CO — Colonial Office, Information Department, UK
1. CO 1027/563: "Counter Communist Propaganda — Federation of Malaysia".
2. CO 537/7297: "Political Developments — Influence of Dato Onn and UMNO in Malayan Politics".

CRO — Commonwealth Relations Office, UK.
1. "Malaysia's Formation"

FED — Far Eastern Department, UK.
1. 175/3/02 — "Independence of Malaya Movement".

FCO — Released files of the South-West Pacific Department, British Foreign and Commonwealth Office (FCO).
1. FWM1/1: "Malaysia: Political Affairs (int): East Malaysia: Internal Situation".
2. FWM1/3: "Malaysia: Internal Affairs: West Malaysia: Internal Situation".
3. FWM1/4: "Malaysia: Internal Affairs: Sabah: Internal Situation".
4. FWM1/6: "Malaysia: Political Affairs: Political Parties: United Malays National Organization (UMNO)".
5. FCO 24/484: "Malaysia: Internal Affairs: Civil Disturbances following General Elections".
6. FCO 24/485: "Malaysia: Internal Affairs: Civil Disturbances following General Elections".
7. FCO 24/486: "Malaysia: Internal Affairs: Civil Disturbances following General Elections".
8. FCO 24/487: "Malaysia: Internal Affairs: Civil Disturbances following General Elections".
9. FCO 2/2: "Visit of Deputy Prime Minister of Malaysia to United Kingdom".
10. FCO 24/824: "Visit of Deputy Prime Minister of Malaysia to London and UN".

MOD — Released files of the British Ministry of Defence.
1. Dissec/22/1/16: "Intelligence General — Commonwealth Countries: Malaysia".
2. D8-11/6/5/1/9: "Malaysian Internal Security".

SEAD — Southeast Asia Department, UK
1. "Constitution and functions, etc. of United Malays National Organization" (UMNO).

RC (Reid Commission) — Federation of Malaya Constitutional Commission 1956

1. "Confidential Memorandum submitted to the Reid Commission by the Pan-Malayan Federation of Chinese Associations". Group CO; Class 889; Piece 8/6.
2. "Memoranda submitted by individuals and various organizations 2000–2040".
3. "Memoranda submitted by individuals and various organizations 2041–2090".
4. "Memoranda submitted by individuals and various organizations 2091–2140".
5. "Memoranda submitted by individuals and various organizations 2141–2170".
6. "Minutes of Meetings No. CC 1000".

UC — Library archives of the University of Canterbury, New Zealand. <http://library.canterbury.ac.nz/mb/archives/mb367organ.shtml>

CIA — "Prospects for the Proposed Malaysian Federation". Number 54-59/1962.

Other Unpublished or Classified Documents

DM — David Marshall Papers Collection, Singapore: Institute of Southeast Asian Studies.

ISEAS VCD — Chin Peng, "My Views on the Emergency", 7 November 2004.

Ismail Iskandar Wildan (grandson of Ismail). School paper 2004.

Minutes of the meetings of the Queen's College Sports and Social Club (QCSSC), Melbourne University, 8 March 1939 to 10 June 1942.

Mohammad Abu Bakar 1978: *The Escalation of Konfrontasi (June–September 1964). Malaysia's Response to Indonesia's Confrontation Policy in the Aftermath of the Abortive Tokyo Summit.* Kertas Seminar Jabatan No. 2. Jabatan Sejarah Universiti Malaya.

Mohd Suffian, Tan Sri 1974: *Tun Dr Ismail Oration*. First address in the series delivered Friday 6 September in Kuala Lumpur.

Zakaria Haji Ahmad 1974(?): *Police Forces and Their Political Roles in Southeast Asia: A Preliminary Assessment and Overview*. Archived at ISEAS Library.

Mass Media Reports and Press Releases

Berlingske Tidende. "Malaysia indenrigsminister besøger Kopenhavn: Vi går ind for demokrati. Krisen i Malaysia overvundet, siger indenrigsminiseren" [Malaysia's Minister for Home Affairs Visits Copenhagen: We are for Democracy. The crisis in Malaysia has been surmounted, says the Minister], 3 October 1969.

Daily Telegraph, 26 March 1951.

FEER — Far Eastern Economic Review 81, no. 32. 13 August 1973. "Malaysia: Tun Dr Ismail (1915–1973)" by M.G.G. Pillai.

New Straits Times Press (NSTP) archival collection on Tun Dr Ismail Abdul Rahman (consisting of clippings in folders, arranged in chronological order)

— *MM (Malay Mail)*
— *NST (New Straits Times)*
— *ST (Straits Times)*
— *SM (Sunday Mail)*
— *Sunday Times*

Siaran Akhbar, news releases from *Jabatan Penerangan Malaysia* (Information Department of Malaysia), Kuala Lumpur:

— PEN. 6/69/44.
— PEN. 6/69/263.
— PEN. 7/69/67.
— PEN. 8/69/22.
— PEN. 8/69/305.
— PEN. 10/69/59.
— PEN. 8/73/8.

The Star, Joceline Tan "Tun Ismail — A Model for Politicians", 2 August 2004.

Utusan Melayu, 8 August 1970.

Warta Negara (Government Gazette) 13 June 1969. Jil. 13, Bil 12, Tambahan no. 36. Perundangan (A).

Interviews

Encik Daud Ahmad, former official of the Secrets Registry of the Ministry of Home Affairs under Ismail, on 28 June 2005 in Petaling Jaya.

Datuk Abdullah Ali, former chief of protocol, former high commissioner to the United Kingdom, relative of Ismail, and president of the Malaysian Branch of the Royal Asiatic Society, on 8 September 2005 at Promet Tower in Kuala Lumpur.

Tan Sri Zakaria Ali, former ambassador to the United Nations, and Canada, on 12 April 2006 at his residence in Petaling Jaya.

Datuk Dr Hussein bin Tun Dr Awang, nephew to Ismail, on 30 March 2006 in Petaling Jaya.

Datuk Seri Abdullah Badawi, former secretary to the National Operations Council and Prime Minister of Malaysia (2003–), on 14 May 2006 at Seri Perdana in Putrajaya.

Mr Maurice Baker, close friend of Tun Abdul Razak Hussein, and former Singaporean high commissioner to Malaysia, 1971–73 and 1980–88, on 9 June 2005 at his residence in Singapore.

Mr Tom Critchley, former Australian high commissioner to Malaysia and Singapore (1956–65) on 22 March 2005 at the Australian high commissioner's residence, Kuala Lumpur.

Tun Abdul Ghafar Baba, former deputy prime minister of Malaysia, on 16 June 2005 at his office in Tan & Tan Building, Kuala Lumpur.

Ungku Bakar, relative of Ismail and expert on family relations within Johor's aristocracy, on 7 July 2005 at Bawang Merah Restaurant, Subang Jaya.

Mr Leslie Eu Peng Meng, golf partner to Ismail and first director of MISC, on 9 September 2005 at the Royal Selangor Golf Club.

Tan Sri Dato Aishah Ghani bt Abdul Ghani, former head of UMNO's Women's Wing and member of the National Consultative Council, on 7 July 2005 in Kampung Baru, Kuala Lumpur.

Datuk Abdul Rahman Hamidon, former secretary to the National Operations Council, on 9 September 2005 at the Royal Selangor Golf Club, Kuala Lumpur.

Tengku Tan Sri Razaleigh Hamzah, former chairman of Pernas and former finance minister, on 27 June 2005 at his residence in Kuala Lumpur.

Tan Sri Musa Hitam, deputy prime minister of Malaysia (1981–86), chairman of Guthries Group and Lions Land, on 26 October 2005 at his residence in Kuala Lumpur.

Mr Mohamed Ariff, fourth son of Ismail, on 28 June 2005 at family residence in Kuala Lumpur.

Ms Badariah, second daughter of Ismail, on 23 March 2005 at family residence in Kuala Lumpur.

General Tun Ibrahim Ismail, former chief of staff of the Malaysian Armed Forces, CEO of the National Operations Council, on 23 March 2005 at his residence in Kuala Lumpur.

Tan Sri Razali Ismail, former under-secretary at the Foreign Affairs Ministry, on 13 September 2005, at Hotel Nikko, Kuala Lumpur.

Encik Mohamed Tarmizi, second son of Ismail, on 28 June 2005 at family residence in Kuala Lumpur.

Encik Mohamed Tawfik, eldest son of Ismail, series of informal conversations and discussions between March 2005 and May 2006.

Ms Zailah, eldest daughter of Ismail, on 23 March 2005 at family residence in Kuala Lumpur.

Encik Zamakhshari, third son of Ismail, on 28 June 2005 at family residence in Kuala Lumpur.

Tan Sri Rama Iyer, first head of Malaysian Airlines System, on 11 April 2006 at the Selangor Club, Kuala Lumpur.

Datuk Khoo Kay Kim, Professor Emeritus in History, on 6 July 2005 at the University of Malaya.

Tan Sri Robert Kuok, founder of Malaysian International Shipping Corporation, etc., and close friend of Ismail, on 11 February 2006 at Citic Towers, Hong Kong.

Mr Lee Kuan Yew, Minister Mentor of Singapore, and Prime Minister of Singapore 1965–90, on 7 February 2006 at the *Istana*, Singapore.

Tun Dr Lim Chong Eu, Chief Minister of Penang 1969–90, on 9 January 2006 at Berjaya Towers, Penang.

Datuk P.G. Lim, former ambassador to Yugoslavia, and the United Nations, and member of the National Consultative Council, on 14 May 2006 in Kuala Lumpur.

Tan Sri Lim Taik Choon, first secretary to Ismail in 1957 at the Malaysian Embassy in New York, and former ambassador to Japan and Australia, on 13 May 2006 at the Petaling Jaya Hilton.

Encik Wahab Majid, former press secretary at the Ministry of Home Affairs, 1970–73, on 6 June 2005 at the Petaling Jaya Hilton.

Encik Din Merican, golf partner to Ismail and former under-secretary (political) at the Ministry of Foreign Affairs, on 4 September 2006 at Holiday Villas, Subang Jaya.

Tun Mohd Hanif B. Omar, former inspector-general of police, on 13 September 2005 at his residence in USJ.

Dato' Noordin Omar, former aide-de-camps to Ismail, on 6 September 2005 at Bangsar Shopping Arcade, Kuala Lumpur.

Dato' Dominic J. Puthucheary, former opposition politician and left-wing activist, on 6 September 2006, at his residence in Damansara Heights, Kuala Lumpur.

Mr Francis Puthucheary, brother of James and Dominic, on 6 September 2006, at his residence in Damansara Heights, Kuala Lumpur.

Tengku Ahmad Rithauddeen, former minister of foreign affairs, on 6 September 2006 at the Royal Selangor Golf Club, Kuala Lumpur.

Tun Ghazali Shafie, former minister of foreign affairs, on 7 September 2005 at his residence in Subang Jaya.

Datuk Chet Singh, former assistant secretary (Police) to Ismail at the Ministry of Home Affairs 1962–67, and general manager of Penang Development Board 1971–90, on 10 January 2006 and 2 February 2006 at Penang's Hotel Equatorial.

Brother Lawrence Spritzig, former headmaster of St John's Institution, Kuala Lumpur, on 11 April 2006 at St John's Seminary, Kuala Lumpur.

Tunku Tan Sri Shahriman Tunku Sulaiman, former high commissioner to the United Kingdom, on 6 July 2005 at Millennium Tower in Kuala Lumpur.

Tan Sri Abu Bakar bin Dato Suleiman and Puan Sri Sukarnya, son and
daughter-in-law of Ismail's brother, 30 March 2006 at their residence
in Petaling Jaya.

Dato A.S. Talalla, former principal assistant secretary for the Commonwealth
and Europe, and Under-secretary (political), Ministry of Foreign
Affairs, on 31 March 2006 at the Lake Club, Kuala Lumpur.

Datuk Tan Chin Nam, businessman and friend of Tun Abdul Razak
Hussein, on 19 June 2006 at the Institute of Southeast Asian Studies,
Singapore.

Prof. Wan Arfah binti Tan Sri Wan Hamzah, niece to Ismail, on 30 March
2006 in Petaling Jaya.

Wan Hussein bin Tan Sri Wan Hamzah, nephew to Ismail, on 30 March
2006 in Petaling Jaya.

Datuk Mohd Annuar bin Zaini, treasurer-general of Gabungan Pelajar-
pelajar Melayu Semenanjung (GPMS), and chairman of *Bernama
News Agency*, on 20 April 2006 at his office in Petaling Jaya.

Puan Sri Razimah Zakaria, wife of Tan Sri Zakaria Ali, former ambassador
to the United Nations and Canada, on 12 April 2006 at their
residence in Petaling Jaya.

Secondary Sources

A. Karim Haji Abdullah (1974) *Amanat Tun Dr Ismail*. Pahang: Pustaka
Budaya Agency.

Abdullah Ali, Datuk (1986/2002) *Malaysian Protocol. Correct Forms of
Address*. Singapore and Kuala Lumpur: Times Books International.

Alias Mohamed (1993) *Ghafar. A Biography*. Petaling Jaya: Pelanduk.

Allen, Richard (1968) *Malaysia. Prospect and Retrospect. The Impact and
Aftermath of Colonial Rule*. London, New York and Kuala Lumpur:
Oxford University Press.

Andaya, Barbara Watson and Leonard Y. Andaya (1982) *A History of
Malaysia*. Macmillan Asian Histories Series. Basingstoke and London:
Macmillan Press.

Bass, Jerome Ronald (1973) *Malaysian Politics, 1968–1970: Crisis and
Response*. University of California, Berkeley: University Microfilms.

Bloodworth, Dennis (1987) *An Eye for the Dragon. Southeast Asia Observed, 1954–1986.* Singapore: Times Books International.

Chin, Aloysius (1995) *The Communist Party of Malaya. The Inside Story.* Kuala Lumpur: Vinpress.

Chin Peng (2003) *My Side of History* (as told to Ian Ward and Norma Miraflor). Singapore: Media Masters.

Chung Choo Ming (2002) "Our Queen's Scholars" <http://viweb. freehosting.net/QSchol.htm>.

Columbia World of Quotations (1996) <http://www.bartleby.com/66/70/ 9970.html>.

Comber, Leon (1983/2001) *13 May 1969. A Historical Survey of Sino-Malay Relations.* Singapore: Graham Brash.

Croissant, Aurel, ed. (2002) *Electoral Politics in Southeast and East Asia.* Singapore: Friedrich-Ebert-Stiftung, Office of Co-operation in Southeast Asia.

Crouch, Harold (1996) *Government & Society in Malaysia.* New South Wales: Allen & Unwin.

Dee, Maureen (2005) *Australia and the Formation of Malaysia 1961–1966.* Series: Documents on Australian Foreign Policy. Australian Department of Foreign Affairs and Trade.

Dennis, Peter and Jeffrey Grey (1996) *Emergency and Confrontation. Australian Military Operations in Malaya and Borneo 1950–1966.* The Official History of Australia's Involvement in Southeast Asian Conflicts 1948–1975 series. NSW, Australia: Allen & Unwin.

Emerson, Rupert (1937/1970) *Malaysia. A Study in Direct and Indirect Rule.* Kuala Lumpur: University of Malaya Press.

Fernando, Joseph M. (2002) *The Making of the Malayan Constitution.* MBRAS Monograph no. 31. Kuala Lumpur: The Malaysian Branch of the Royal Asiatic Society.

Fletcher, Nancy McHenry (1969) *The Separation of Singapore from Malaysia.* Data Paper: Number 73. Southeast Asia Program. Department of Asian Studies. New York: Cornell University.

Gagliano, Felix Victor (1967) *Political Input Functions in the Federation of Malaya.* Doctoral thesis. Ann Arbor, Michigan: University of Illinois.

————— (1971) *Communal Violence in Malaysia 1969: The Political Aftermath.* Papers in International Studies. Southeast Asia Series no. 13. Ohio University Center for International Studies. Southeast Asia Program.

Ghazali Shafie (1998) *Ghazali Shafie's Memoir on the Formation of Malaysia.* Bangi: Penerbit Universiti Kebangsaan Malaysia.

Goh, Cheng Teik (1971) *The May Thirteenth Incident and Democracy in Malaysia.* Kuala Lumpur and Singapore: Oxford University Press.

Gullick, J.M. (1992) *Rulers and Residents. Influence and Power in the Malay States 1970–1920.* Southeast Asian Historical Monographs. Singapore, Oxford and New York: Oxford University Press.

Han, Fook Kwang, Warren Fernandez and Sumiko Tan (1998) *Lee Kuan Yew. The Man and His Ideas.* Singapore: Times Private Ltd and Singapore Press Holdings.

Harper, T.N. (1999) "Power and the People: The End of Empire in Malaysian History", pp. 203–14. In *Rethinking Malaysia*, edited by Jomo K.S. Malaysian Studies I. Kuala Lumpur: Malaysian Social Science Association.

Hatton, Tim (2004) *Tock Tock Birds. A Spider in the Web of International Terrorism.* Sussex: The Book Guild.

Heng, Pek Koon (1988) *Chinese Politics in Malaysia. A History of the Malaysian Chinese Association.* Singapore, Oxford, New York: Oxford University Press.

Heng, Pek Koon (1997) "The New Economic Policy and the Chinese Community in Peninsular Malaysia", in *The Developing Economies*, vol. XXXV, September: 262–92. Tokyo: Journal of the Institute of Developing Economies.

IBDB — Internet Broadway Database <http://www.ibdb.com/show. asp?ID=9114>.

Ibrahim bin Ismail (1984) *Have You Met Mariam?* Johor Bahru: Westlight.

Ismail bin Mohamed Ali (2005) "Spearheading the Administration". In Yayasan Tun Razak, *Tun Abdul Razak. A Personal Portrait.* Kuala Lumpur: Utusan Publications, pp. 167–72.

Jain, R.K., ed. (1984) *China and Malaysia, 1949–1983.* New Delhi: Radiant Publishers.

Josey, Alex (1968/1980) *Lee Kuan Yew. The Crucial Years.* Singapore and Kuala Lumpur: Times Books International.

Kwok, Kian-Woon (1999) "The Social Architect: Goh Keng Swee", pp. 45–69. In *Lee's Lieutenants. Singapore's Old Guard*, edited by Lam Peng Er and Kevin Y.L. Tan. New South Wales, Australia: Allen & Unwin.

Jabatan Penerangan Malaysia (1971) *Chatitan riwayat hidup Tun Dr. Ismail Dato Haji Abdul Rahman.* Kuala Lumpur: Kementerian Penerangan.

Keith, Patrick (2005) *Ousted! An Insider's Story of the Ties that Failed to Bind.* Singapore: Media Masters.

Khong, Kim Hoong (2003) *Merdeka! British Rule and the Struggle for Independence in Malay 1945–1957.* Petaling Jaya: Strategic Information Research Development (SIRD).

Khoo, Kay Kim (1991) *Malay Society. Transformation & Democratisation.* Selangor: Pelanduk.

Koh, Swe Yong (2004) *Malaysia. 45 Years Under the Internal Security Act.* Translated by Agnes Khoo. Petaling Jaya: Strategic Information Research Development (SIRD).

Kua, Kia Soong, ed. (2002) *K. Das & the Tunku Tapes.* Kuala Lumpur: Strategic Information Research Development (SIRD).

Kuok, Hock Khee, Philip (1991) *Philip Kuok Hock Khee* (privately published and circulated autobiography). Landmark Books Pte Ltd.

Lal, Shiv (1982) *Malaysian Democracy: An Indian Perspective.* New Delhi: The Elections Archives.

Lau, Teik Soon (1971) "Malaysia and the Neutralisation of Southeast Asia". In *Proceedings and Background Paper of Seminar on Trends in Malaysia*, edited by Patrick Low. Trends in Southeast Asia no. 2. Singapore: Institute of Southeast Asian Studies, pp. 27–32.

Lam, Peng Er and Kevin Y.L. Tan (1999) *Lee's Lieutenants.* St. Leonards, NSW: Allen & Unwin.

Lee, Hock Guan (2001) "Political Parties and the Politics of Citizenship and Ethnicity in Peninsular Malay(si)a 1957–1968". ISEAS Working Papers on Social and Cultural Issues No. 2. Singapore: ISEAS Publications, pp. 1–37.

Lee, Kuan Yew (1998) *The Singapore Story. Memoirs of Lee Kuan Yew.* Singapore: Singapore Press Holdings.

—— (2000) *From Third World to First. The Singapore Story: 1965–2000. Memoirs of Lee Kuan Yew.* Singapore: Singapore Press Holdings.

Lim, Chong Eu 2005 (10 Sept): "Building on Penang's Strengths: Going Forward". Penang Lecture <http://www.seri.com.my/Penang%20 Lecture%202005%20-%20Speech%20Text.pdf>.

Lim, Hong Hai (2002) "Electoral Politics in Malaysia: 'Managing' Elections in a Plural Society". In *Electoral Politics in Southeast and East Asia,* edited by Aurel Croissant. Singapore: Friedrich-Ebert-Stiftung, Office of Co-operation in Southeast Asia, pp. 101–48.

Lim, P.G. (2005) "A Balance of Interests". In Yayasan Tun Razak, *Tun Abdul Razak. A Personal Portrait.* Kuala Lumpur: Utusan Publications, pp. 109–14.

Low, Patrick, ed. (1971) *Proceedings and Background Paper of Seminar on Trends in Malaysia.* Trends in Southeast Asia no. 2. Singapore: Institute of Southeast Asian Studies.

Mahathir bin Mohamad (1971) "Trends in Foreign Policy and Regionalism". In *Proceedings and Background Paper of Seminar on Trends in Malaysia,* edited by Patrick Low. Trends in Southeast Asia no. 2. Singapore: Institute of Southeast Asian Studies, pp. 33–41.

Matsui, Kazuhisa (2003) *Decentralisation in Nation Building of Indonesia.* IDE Research Paper no. 2, August. Institute of Developing Economies, Japan External Trade Organization.

Mazlan Nordin (2005) "Footsteps on the Sand". In Yayasan Tun Razak, *Tun Abdul Razak. A Personal Portrait.* Kuala Lumpur: Utusan Publications, pp. 215–28.

Memorandum on Malaysia by the Malaysia Solidarity Consultative Committee, 23 February 1962. Appendix to Zainal Abidin bin Abdul Wahid (1984) "The Formation of Malaysia: The Role of the Malaysia Solidarity Consultative Committee". In *Historia. Essays in Commemoration of the 25th Anniversary of the Department of History, University of Malaya,* edited by Muhammad Abu Bakar, Amarjit Kaur and Abdullah Zakaria Ghazali. Kuala Lumpur: The Malaysian Historical Society, pp. 129–451.

Mid-term Review of the Second Malaysia Plan 1971–1975. 1973. Kuala Lumpur: Government Press.

Milne, R.S. and Diane K. Mauzy (1978) *Politics and Government in Malaysia*. Singapore: Times Books International and ISEAS.

——— (1990) *Singapore. The Legacy of Lee Kuan Yew*. Boulder, San Francisco and Oxford: Westview Press.

Minchin, James (1986/1990): *No Man is an Island. A Portrait of Singapore's Lee Kuan Yew*. Sydney: Allen & Unwin.

Ministry of External Affairs (MEA) (1965) *Malaysia's Case in the United Nations Security Council*. Documents reproduced from the official record of the Security Council Proceedings. Kuala Lumpur: Ministry of External Affairs, Malaysia.

Mohd Hazim Shah, Jomo K.S. and Phua Kai Lit, eds. (2002) *New Perspectives in Malaysian Studies*. Bangi: Persatuan Sains Sosial Malaysia.

Mohd Tajuddin bin Haji Abdul Rahman (1987) *Tun Dr Ismail — Negarawan Berjasa*. Petaling Jaya: Pelanduk Publications.

Morais, J. Victor (1981) *Portrait of a Statesman*. Singapore and Johor Baru: QUINS.

Mustapha Hussain (2005) *Malay Nationalism Before UMNO. The Memoirs of Mustapha Hussain*. Translated by Insun Sony Mustapha and edited by Jomo K.S. Kuala Lumpur: Utusan Publications.

National Operations Council (1969) *The May 13 Tragedy. A Report.* 9 October. Kuala Lumpur.

Nehru, Jawaharlal (1934) *Glimpses of World History: Being Further Letters to His Daughter Written in Prison and Containing a Rambling Account of History for Young People*. India: Penguin Books.

Ong, Kee Hui (2005) "Enticing Sarawak". In Yayasan Tun Razak, *Tun Abdul Razak. A Personal Portrait*. Kuala Lumpur: Utusan Publications, pp. 203–16.

Ongkili, James P. (1985) *Nation-building in Malaysia 1946–1974*. Singapore: Oxford University Press.

Oong, Hak Ching (2000) *Chinese Politics in Malaysa 1942–55. The Dynamics of British Policy*. Bangi: Penerbitan Universiti Kebangsaan Malaysia.

Owen, Norman G. (2005) *The Emergence of Modern Southeast Asia*. Honolulu: University of Hawai'i Press.

Puthucheary, Dominic and Jomo K.S., eds. (1998) *No Cowardly Past: James Puthucheary — Writings, Poems and Commentaries*. Kuala Lumpur: INSAN.

Puthucheary, J.J. (1960/2004) *Ownership and Control in the Malayan Economy — A Study of the Structure of Ownership and Control and its Effects on the Development of Secondary Industries and Economic Growth in Malaya and Singapore*. Afterword by Jomo K.S. INSAN: Kuala Lumpur. First edition by Donald Moore for Eastern Universities Press, Singapore.

Puthucheary, Mavis and Norani Othman, eds. (2005) *Elections and Democracy in Malaysia*. Bangi: Penerbit Universiti Kebangsaan Malaysia.

Rukunegara (1971) Government of Malaysia. Kuala Lumpur: Jabatan Chetak Kerajaan.

Selvan, T.S. (1990) *Singapore the Ultimate Island. Lee Kuan Yew's Untold Story*. Victoria, Asutralia: Freeway Books.

Shaw, William (1976) *Tun Razak*. Kuala Lumpur: Longman.

Shariff Ahmad (2001) *Tun Razak. Prince of Titiwangsa*. Kuala Lumpur: Utusan Publications.

Simandjuntak, B. (1969) *Malayan Federalism 1945–1963. A Study of Federal Problems in a Plural Society*. East Asian Historical Monographs. Kuala Lumpur: Oxford University Press.

Sodhy, Pamela (1991) *The US-Malaysian Nexus*. Kuala Lumpur: Institute of Strategic and International Studies.

Solidum, Estrella D. (2003) *The Politics of Asean. An Introduction to Southeast Asian Regionalism*. Singapore: Eastern Universities Press.

Sopiee, Mohamed Noordin (1974) *From Malayan Union to Singapore Separation. Political Unification in the Malaysia Region 1945–65*. Kuala Lumpur: Penerbit Universiti Malaya.

——— (1973) "The 'Neutralisation' of Southeast Asia". Paper for Session 2 from the conference "Asia and the Western Pacific: Internal Changes and External Influences", at Canberra, 14–17 April 1973, organized by the Australian Institute of International Affairs.

Stockwell, A.J. (1979) *British Policy and Malay Politics During the Malayan*

Union Experiment 1945–1948. Monograph no. 8. Kuala Lumpur: Council of the Malaysian Branch of the Royal Asiatic Society.

Stockwell, A.J., ed. (1995) *Malaya*. British Documents on the End of Empire. Series B Volume 3. London: HSMO.
— Part I: The Malayan Union Experiment 1942–1948;
— Part II: The Communist Insurgency 1948–1953;
— Part III: The Alliance Route to Independence 1953–1957.

Tan, Chin Nam (2006) *Never Say I Assume*. Kuala Lumpur: MPH Group Publishing.

Tan, T.H. (1957) "How Independence was won", in *Malayan Mirror*, 22 August.

Tan, Kevin Y.L. (1999) "The Legalists: Kenny Byrne & Eddie Barker". In *Lee's Lieutenants. Singapore's Old Guard*, edited by Lam Peng Er and Kevin Y.L. Tan. New South Wales, Australia: Allen & Unwin, pp. 70–95.

Tan, Liok Ee (1997) *The Politics of Chinese Education in Malaya 1945–1961*. Kuala Lumpur, Oxford, Singapore and New York: Oxford University Press.

Tan, Ta Sen and Yong Mun Cheong (1971) "Background Paper for Seminar". In *Proceedings and Background Paper of Seminar on Trends in Malaysia*, edited by Patrick Low. Trends in Southeast Asia no. 2. Singapore: Institute of Southeast Asian Studies, pp. 88–119.

Thajunnisa Mohamed Ibrahim (2004) *Tun Dr Ismail. Kejora Timur yang Mengerdip*. Kuala Lumpur: Utusan Publications.

The American Heritage Dictionary of the English Language (2000/2003). Fourth edition. Boston: Houghton Mifflin Company.

Tjoa, Hock Guan (1978) "Chinese Malaysians and Malaysian Politics". In *Southeast Asian Affairs*. Singapore: Institute of Southeast Asian Studies.

Tunku Abdul Rahman Putra al-Haj (1969) *May 13: Before and After*. Kuala Lumpur: Utusan Publications.

——— (1977) *Looking Back. The Historic Years of Malaya and Malaysia*. Kuala Lumpur: Pustaka Antara.

——— (1978) *Viewpoints*. Kuala Lumpur: Heinemann.

————— (1981) *As a Matter of Interest.* Kuala Lumpur: Heinemann.

————— (1984) *Malaysia. The Road to Independence.* Petaling Jaya: Pelanduk.

————— (1986) *Political Awakening.* Petaling Jaya: Pelanduk Publications.

UBC Reports Vol. 4, no. 5, May 1958. Canada: University of British Columbia. <http://www.library.ubc.ca/archives/pdfs/ubcreports/UBC_Reports_1958_05_00.pdf>.

von Vorys, Karl (1976) *Democracy without Consensus. Communalism and Political Stability in Malaysia.* Kuala Lumpur and Singapore: Oxford University Press.

White, Nicholas J. (2004) *British Business in Post-colonial Malaysia, 1957–70. 'Neo-colonialism' or 'disengagement'?* London and New York: RoutledgeCurzon.

Winstedt, R.O. (1932/2003) *A History of Johore (1365–1941).* Kuala Lumpur: Malaysian Branch of the Royal Asiatic Society Reprint no. 6.

Yayasan Tun Razak (2005) *Tun Abdul Razak. A Personal Portrait.* Kuala Lumpur: Utusan Publications.

Zainuddin Maidin (1994) *The Other Side of Mahathir.* Kuala Lumpur: Utusan Publishers.

Zakaria Haji Ahmad and Harold Crouch (1985) *Military-Civilian Relations in Southeast Asia.* Singapore: Oxford University Press.

INDEX

4th Meeting ASEAN Foreign
Ministers, 243
12th Malaysia-Thai Border
Committee Talks, 246
Abdul Hamid, Justice, 84
Abdul Kadir Shamsuddin, 195
Abdul Rahman bin Yassin, 14,
15, 16, 41, 63, 221
death of, 224
gifts of land to children, 17
retirement from Senate, 179
secretary of UMNO, 51
State Commissioner of Muar,
promotion to, 28
suspension from civil service, 43
Abdul Rahman Hamidon, 195,
203, 243
Abdul Rashid Maidin, 73
Abdullah Ali, 174, 262
Abdullah Badawi, 195, 211, 240,
269
Abu Bakar bin Dato Suleiman,
13, 178
Abu Bakar Hamzah, 163

Afghan ambassador
visit to, 92
Ahmad Badawi bin Abdullah
Ibrahim, 196
Ahmad Rithaudeen, Tengku, 203
Aishah Ghani, 211, 219
Akihito, Crown Prince, 223
Akron rubber world, 100
Algeria
issue of, 112
Ali Sastrowidjojo, 90
Alliance, 57
boycott by, 66, 68
delegation to England, 64
faith in the Commonwealth, 64
MCA's departure, 188
push for elections, 59
reforming of, 235
trouble with PAP, 159
weaknesses, analysis of, 236, 237
Alliance formula, 49, 57, 58
test of internal resilience, 81
Alliance National Council, 126
Alsagoff, Brigadier S.M., 158

Ambassador
  life as an, 86–136
American academic degrees
  acceptance in Malaya, 99
American capitalism
  views on, 100, 101
Anderson College, 98
Annuar Zaini
  view on effect of Ismail's
    retirement, 170
Anti-Corruption Agency (ACA),
  171
Anwar Ibrahim, 209
Ariff, 7, 10
Association of Malay Chambers
  of Commerce, 246
Association of Southeast Asia
  (ASA), 164
Association of Southeast Asian
  Nations, 169
Athisagam, John, 30
Australia
  arrival in, 21
  delegation to, 264
  final days in, 44
  first journey to, 31
  end of military aid from, 142
  return from, 3, 43, 44
Australians
  views on, 31

B. Malik, Justice, 84
Badariah, 7
Bahaman Samsuddin, 50

Baker, Maurice, 203, 210, 227,
  229, 268
Balai Muhibbah, 223
Baling talks, 73
Bandung Summit, 259
Bangkok Declaration, 169
Bank Negara, 105
Bank of China
  closure of, 119, 120
Barisan Sosialis Party (BSP), 138
  preventive arrest of leaders,
    139
Barisan Nasional, 273
  election win, 274
Barker, E.W.
  drafting of separation
    agreement, 156
Barnes Report, 79
Bass, J.R., 207
bonus
  for service on the cabinet,
    174
Brigden, Dr., 165
Briggs, Sir Harold, 55
Briggs Plan, 55
Britain
  arm sales to South Africa, 232
British Advisers, 77
Brockett, Emily, 18
Brockway, Gilbert, 65
Brooks, Keith G., 40
Brunei, 137
Brussels
  official visit to, 171

Bumiputera
  dislike of term, 225
burial, 9, 10

Cabinet Committee on
    Communications, 244
Caccia, Sir Harold, 112
cancer, 3, 175, 214, 220
capitalism
  views on, 11–101
Catterall, Dr., 8
Central Bank Ordinance of
    Malaya, 105
Central Executive Committee
    (CEC)
  first meeting, 53
  nominations for, 52
Central Intelligence Agency
    (CIA), 138
Chan Chia Chow, 22, 28
Cheah, Eileen, 18, 172
Cheah, Leslie, 271
Cheah, Joyce, 18, 172
Cheah Tiang Earn, 18
China
  backing of Malaysia for bid to
      UN, 249, 258
  entry into United Nations,
      245, 247, 258
  recognition by Malaysia, 275
  views on, 141
Chin Peng, 47, 72, 73
  calls to surrender, 141
Chinese education, 78

Chinese middle schools
  arrest of students from, 144
Civil Service Committee, 76
citizenship
  issue on, 81, 82
  grant of, 154
Commonwealth commission
  formulation of Constitution, 3
communalism
  fear of, 133
communists
  activities increasing, 251
  meeting with, 72
Communities Liaison
    Committee (CLC), 63
Conference of Law Ministers, 165
Conference of Rulers, 64
Confrontation, 142, 168, 214, 236
Constitution, 154
  amendment of, 254
  formulation of, 83
  review of, 65
constitutional monarchy
  Johor, 14
Cordner, Donald, 213
corruption
  views on, 173
"corrupt practice"
  definition, 222
Critchley, Tom, 146, 155, 171
  report regarding Separation, 156, 157
  trip to islands of Johor, 165
curfew
  racial riots, 196

Darjah Yang Mulia Setia Mahkota
    Malaysia, 166
Daud Ahmad, 260, 261
death
    effect on politics, 272
declaration of peaceful co-
    existence, 175
delineation exercises, 274
Delson, Robert, 112
democracy
    views on, 131, 132, 218
Democratic Action Party (DAP),
    185
Department of National Unity
    (DNU), 205
depression
    during cancer treatment, 224
diary
    keeping of, 89
Dillon, Clarence Douglas, 109,
    111
Din Merican, 263
directorships, 178
doctor
    life as one in Australia, 41, 42
Doyle, Arthur Conan
    reading of books by, 24
Dugan, Lady
    wife of governor of Victoria, 36
Dulles, John Foster, 107

early life, 15
East Malaysia
    balloting, 200

economy
    views on, 177, 178
education
    admission to Melbourne
        University, 21
    medical school in Singapore,
        20, 21
Education Committee, 79, 80
Education Ordinance, 79, 80
elections
    1959
Elections (Amendment) Bill, 122
Elections Ordinance, 223
Emergency, 47, 55, 72
    end of, 130
    expenditure on, 108
    push to end, 127
Emergency (Essential Powers)
    Ordinance, 222
Emergency Regulations
    Ordinance, 130
Emerson, Rupert, 30
English College (in Johor Bahru),
    16
Executive Council, 60
    members, 61
    see also Federal Executive
        Council

family
    large in number, 15
    uniqueness, 17
Far Eastern Economic Review, 8
faulty heart valve, 3, 58

Federal Elections Committee
announcement of formation,
60
Federal Executive Council, 128
Federal Land Development
Authority (FELDA), 63
Federal Legislative Council, 79,
122, 127
Federal War Council
elimination, 56
Federation of Malay Teachers'
Organization, 125
Federation of Malaya Agreement,
46
preamble, 55
Federation of Malaya Agreement
(Amendment) Bill, 66
Federation of Malaysia
objections from Indonesia, 142
Finance Committee, 76
First Malaya Plan, 108
First Malaysia Plan, 163
Five Power Defence Pact, 152,
247
Fong Swee Suan, 142
foreign capital
government's policy on, 118,
119
Foreign Correspondents'
Association of Southeast
Asia, 168

Gagliano, Felix, 202, 229
Gamal Abdel-Nasser, 78

general elections
1969, 4
10 May, 185
General Adviser, 13
General Agreement on Tariffs
and Trade (GATT), 122
General Labour Unions (GLU),
46
General Planning Unit (GPU),
228
Gerakan, 273
Ghafar Baba, 52, 143, 187, 188,
211, 226
Ghana
self government, 54
Ghazali Seth, 10
Ghazali Shafie, 139, 195, 205,
215, 228, 248, 272
Goh Keng Swee, 155, 227, 245
golf with, 135
keeping seperation decision
secret, 157
golf, 135, 267, 269
Governor's Advisory Council, 46
Grand Order of the National
Order of Vietnam, 163
Griffiths-Jones, Eric, 186, 188, 198
Gromyko, Andrei, 162
Gurney, Henry, 51
death, 55
Guthrie Corporation
directorship of, 171
Guthrie Corporation's Group
Planting Conference, 181

Hamzah bin Abu Samah, 195
handicap, 217, 270
Hanif Omar, 193, 212
Harcourt Guest House, 27
Hari Raya Puasa
    open house, 233
Harun Hashim, 222
Harun Idris, 189, 194, 239
    resolution to prevent Cabinet
        reshuffling, 267
Hatton, Tim, 130
health problems, 214
heart attack, 4, 270
heart operation
    postponement, 223
heart valve
    faulty, *see* faulty heart valve
Heath, Edward, 232, 234
Heroes' Mausoleum, 9, 11
Herter, Christian, 107
Hidup Melayu slogan, 47
hikes
    Dandenong, 29
    Warrandyke District, 25
    Yarra Valley, 24
HKS *Alert*, 66
Hogan, Michael, 66
hole-in-one, 270
Holmes, Sherlock, 264
Home Affairs Minister, 193
hometown, 3
Hon Sui Sen, 244
Housing Development Board
    projects, 245

housing issues
    low-cost housing projects, 131
Horsham Base Hospital, 41, 42
Hussein bin Tun Dr Awang, 13
Hussein Onn, 53, 228, 229, 272

Ibrahim Ismail, 191, 195
illness, 3, 58
independence
    date set, 77
    granted, 78
    negotiations, 78
Independence Day, 86
Indonesia
    arguments against federation,
        149
    forces attacking Malaysia, 146
    moral pressure to behave, 151
    relations with, 123
    visit to, 252
Information Co-ordinating
    Centre, 196
invitations
    speeches at dinners and
        conferences, 101
Institute of Southeast Asian
    Studies (ISEAS), 74
    speech by Mahathir
        Mohamed, 247
inter-ethnic tensions, 154
Internal Security Act, 130, 131
Internal Security Council
    Singapore, 142
Internal Security portfolio, 130

International Bank of
Reconstruction and
Development (IBRD), 97, 122
International Monetary Fund
(IMF), 97, 122
Ismail Ali, 88, 105, 118, 119,
120, 121, 172, 234
Italy
trip to, 121, 122

Ja'afar ibni Almarhum Tuanku
Abdul Rahman, 93, 96, 97,
102, 110
Jennings, Sir Ivor, 83
Johnson, Lyndon B., 169
Johor, 13
commercial agriculture, 14
constitutional monarchy, 14
economy, 18
independence of royal family, 14
population growth, 18
Johor Bahru, 3
moving back to, 66
unaffected by racial riots, 199
Johor Bahru Town Council
elections, 58
Johor Timor, 185
Jones, A. Creech, 65
Josey, Alex, 158
journey to Australia, 21
Jurong Industrial area, 245

Kaiser Aluminium Factory, 95
Kamariah, sister of Onn Ja'afar, 16

Keith, Patric, 158
Khaw Kai Boh, 168, 228
Khir Johari, 178, 185, 187, 210, 239
Kia Ora, 26
Kirk, Norman, 265
Kocher, Eric, 102, 103, 111
Konfrantasi, 146, 147, 152
Kuala Lumpur Flying Club, 52
Kuok, Eileen, 10
see also Cheah, Eileen
Kuok, Philip, 10, 129, 166, 172,
189, 194, 217, 226
knowledge of Razak's ailment,
271
letter to, 178, 179, 197
Kuok, Robert, 6, 49, 171, 172,
192, 221, 258, 263, 267
founding a local shipping
company, 179
knowledge of Razak's ailment,
271
Kuok, William, 19
Kuok Keng Kang, 19
Kwane N'krumah, 54

Labour Party, 70, 219
language
issue of, 82
Le Cain, John, 158
Lee, H.S., 57, 60, 78
Lee Kuan Yew, 134
birthday, 143
discussion concerning national
language, 145

golf with, 135
postponement of goodwill
    visit, 227
questions over Malay special
    status, 153
views on Ismail, 136, 137,
    171, 172, 17
Lee Moke Sang, 169, 176
Lee Siew Choh, 138
Lee Tiang King, 63
legacy of clean reputation, 276
Lennox-Boyd, Alan, 71
Leong Yew Koh, 71, 78
Lim Chia Seng, 30
Lim Chin Siong, 138, 140, 141, 142
Lim Chong Eu, 9, 80, 125, 126,
    163, 258, 258, 273
Lim Kean Chong, 38
Lim Kean Siew, 175
Lim Kim San, 155
Lim Kit Siang, 202, 219, 231
Lim, P.G., 169, 219
Lim Taik Choon, 88, 93, 95, 105,
    111
Lim Yew Hock, 134
Lions Club, 98
loans
    Malaya's request for, 107, 108,
        109
London
    visit for health check up, 250,
        251
Lowson, 29
Lyttleton, Oliver, 65

MacDonald, Malcolm, 54, 63
MacGillivray, Sir Donald, 66, 68,
    69, 84
MacMichael Agreement, 45
Mahathir Mohamad, 188, 206,
    210, 239, 268, 272
    fear of Ismail, 172
    rejoining UMNO, 269
    statement at ISEAS conference,
        247
Maimunah Latiff, 172
Malaya ethno-nationalists, 206
Malay Graduate's Association,
    50, 51, 52, 54
Malay language
    common language, 82
    official language, 85
Malay manpower
    raising standards of, 257
Malay schoolteachers
    dissatisfaction, 125
Malaya
    announcement of founding of,
        85
    independent line, keeping of,
        123
    relations with Indonesia, 123
Malayan Banking
    directorship of, 178
    mismanagement, 164
Malayan Chinese Association
    (MCA), 55, 56
    in defence of Chinese
        education, 78

member seeking cooperation
    with UMNO, 57
position taken re 1959
    elections, 126
Malayan Communist Party
    (MCP), 46, 47
    armed units, 74
    official recognition, 73, 74
    support of China, 128
Malayan Democratic Union, 46
Malayan Indian Congresss
    (MIC), 68
Malayan Labour Party, 116
Malayan Medical Service, 43
Malayan National Party, 58
Malayan Party, 127
Malayan Special Branch, 140, 141
Malayan Students Association,
    99
Malayan Union, 42, 45
Malays
    special position of, 82, 83, 217
Malaysia
    making and partitioning, 137–81
Malaysia Act, 154
Malaysia-Thai Border
    Committee, 249
Malaysia-Singapore Airlines
    (MSA), 243
    process of breaking up, 253
Malaysian Airlines Limited
    (MAL), 244
Malaysian Airline System (MAS),
    253

Malaysian International
    Shipping Corporation
    (MISC), 179
Malaysian Police
    improvements to, 163
Malaysian society
    restructuring of, 242
Malaysian Solidarity
    Convention, 153, 161
Malaysian Special Branch, 161
Malaysian-American Society,
    178, 180
Marella, The, 44
Marshall, David, 73, 128, 248
Martin, Sir John, 76
Masjid Negara, 9
Maxwell Road
    residence in, 169, 170
MCA Chinese Education Central
    Committee (MCACECC),
    79
McKell, Sir William, 84
McKittrick, Thomas H., 106
McPherson, Stuart C., 6, 8, 9,
    165, 255
medical graduate, 3, 41
medical practice, *see* private
    medical practice
medical student
    fear of war spreading to
        Malaya, 35
    graduation, 41
    homesickness during Hari
        Raya in Australia, 25

life as a, 23–40
summer vacation, 26
Melbourne, 23
Melbourne University's Queen's
    College, 3
    see also Queen's College
"member system", 56
Menon, V.K. Krishna, 90
Mercury Singapore Airlines, 243
Merdeka slogan, 47
Middle East, 114, 115, 116
military cooperation
    with Singapore, 162
military coup
    fears of, 230
Mohamed Din, Dr., 109, 110
Mohamed Yassin bin Ahat, 14
Mohamed Suffian Mohamed
    Hashim, 54
Mohammad Sopiee Sheik
    Ibrahim, 102, 112, 116, 119
Marcos, Ferdinanc
    inauguration, 164
Morozov, Platon D., 147
municipal elections
    Penang, 57
Musa Hitam, 50, 58, 176, 193,
    208, 210, 239, 259, 260,
    272, 273
    study leave, 206
Mustapha Hussain, 48

Nair, C.V. Devan, 163
Nanyang University
    arrest of students from, 144

National Association of Perak, 70
national bank
    creation of, 104, 105
National Consultative Council,
    219, 256, 257
    Housing, on, 250
National Day 1970, 227
National Goodwill Committee,
    205
national language
    implementation period, 225
National Language Bill, 168, 170
National Operations Council
    (NOC), 191, 195, 201, 222,
    256
    Information Co-ordinating
        Centre (ICC), 204
National Monument, 252
National Security Council, 241
National Unity Council, 241
natural resources, 63
Naval Air Taining School, 96
Nehru, Jawaharlal,
    influence of, 212, 213
neck cancer, 3, 175, 214, 220
neo-colonialism, 149
neo-diplomacy, 149
neo-imperialism, 150
neutralization policy, 265
New Economic Policy (NEP), 215
    class structure of Malays, 217
New Treasury Hotel, 27
New Zealand
    delegation to, 265
New Zealand Embassy, 92

Nik Ahmad Kamil, 75, 121, 124
Non-Aligned Nations
    Second Conference, 152
Noordin Omar, 211
Norashikin (Neno), 6
    busy life as an ambassador's
        wife, 91
    first meeting with Ismail, 52
    love of sports, 213
Norway
    draft resolution, 150, 151

offsprings, 7
Ogmore, Lord, 65
Ong Kee Hui, 199
Ong Yoke Lin, 57, 71, 78
Onn Ja'afar, 46, 47, 58, 59, 63,
    85
    departure from UMNO, 48
Operation Cold Store, 142
Osman Jewa, Tunku, 195, 230

Pakistan
    severing diplomatic ties, 162
Palestine
    liberation of, 240
Palmer, Norman, 101
Pan-Malayan Islamic Party
    (PMIP), 69, 70, 127, 139
Pangkor Island
    racial fighting, 127
Parti Negara, 58, 69, 127
Penang
    municipal elections, 57
Penang Bridge, 258

Peninsular Malaysia Malay
    Students Foundation
    silver jubilee celebrations, 5
People's Action Party (PAP), 134
    elections win, 139
People's Progressive Party, 127
People's Republic's Silver Star
    Cultural Troupe, 246
Perak Malay League, 70
Perak Progressive Party, 70
Pernas, 246
Petronas, 179
Pepys, W.E., 17
Philippines
    normalisation of ties with,
        168
Pillai, Dr., 8
pilgrimage to Mecca, 240
pipe
    preference for, 25
politics
    decision to enter into, 51
post-colonial historical context
    of policies, 266
poverty
    eradication, 242
Poynton, Sir Hilton, 76
Prevention of Corruption
    Ordinance, 222
private medical practice, 43, 49
Proctor, W.T., 65
Pulau Jerejak, 203
punctuality, 211
Puthucheary, Dominic, 19, 142,
    202, 269

Puthucheary, James, 19, 216
Puthucheary, Joseph Chako, 19

Queen's College, 22
  family's visit to, 265
Queen's College Sports and
  Social Club (QCSSC), 25

race-based politics, 49
racial riots, 4
  13 May 1969, 189–97
  casualties, 197
  explanation to the public,
    224
  political changes in the
    aftermath, 238
  Singapore, in, 144
Railway Service Commission, 77
Raja Mohar bin Raja
  Badiozaman, 259
Rajaratnam, S., 169
Razak Report, 79
Razaleigh Hamzah, Tengku, 206,
  2, 24620, 240, 263
Razali Ismail, 259
reading
  love for, 16, 17, 24
regionalism, 259
Reid, Lord, 83
Reid Commission, 84, 138
Republic of Indonesia Medal
  Second Class, 224
retirement, 3, 4, 167–81
  forced out of, 185–218
rheumatic heart, 93

road transport, 63
Robertson, 35
Rodyk & Davidson, 15
Roosevelt Day Dinner
  attendance of, 93
Royal Malaysian Police, 163
Royal Selangor Golf Club, 5
Rubber Manufacturers
  Organization, 100
Rukunegara, 220, 227, 242
Rumah Tawakkal, 14
Rusk, Dean, 162

Sabah, 137
Sambanthan, V.T., 71, 78
Sarawak, 137
Sarawak United People's Party
  (SUPP), 199
Sardon Jubir, 11, 48, 71, 78
Second Malay Congress, 85
Second Malaysia Plan, 242, 254
Seenivasagam, S.R., 170
self-government
  preparation for, 56
Senn, Sammy, 172
Senu Abdul Rahman, 123, 178
Separation
  official announcement, 157
Separation Agreement, 154
Separation Bill, 157
Seri Setia Mahkota, 166
Seth Said, 77
Seow, Eugene, 52
Shahriman Sulaiman, 50, 261,
  262, 267, 269, 273

Shangri-la Hotel, 245
Shell oil refinery
    visit to, 95
Silver Jubilee General Assembly,
    239, 249
Singapore
    air attack by Japanese, 37
    declaration as part of
        Malaysia, 143
    elections as part of Malaysia, 144
    housing projects, 245
    incorporation into Malaysia, 137
    Internal Security Council, 128
    racial riots, 145
    security matters, 131
    separation from Malaysia, 154
    views on relations with, 159,
        160
Singapore Airlines, 253
Singapore Alliance Party, 144
Singapore People's Alliance
    (SPA), 134
Singapore Special Branch, 139
Singh, Chet, 132, 193
Skids Row (Chicago), 99
Smallwood, 35
Socialist Front, 141
South Africa
    racial conflict in, 113
    views on, 232
South Korea
    visit to, 165
South Korean Central
    Intelligence Service, 164
Spencer, Oscar A., 88

sports
    interests in, 17
Socialist Front, 127
Southeast Asian Treaty
    Organization (Seato), 98
Sports Pool, 180
Sri Panglima Darjah Kinabalu,
    246
student demonstrations, 227
Straits of Malacca
    Russian proposal to
        internationalise, 252
Suara Merdeka, 53
Subang National Golf Club, 180
Suffian, Chief Justice, 160, 192
Sukarno, 142
    destabilizing Malaysia, 146
Suleiman, 45, 51, 78, 121
    death, 167
Sultan Abu Bakar, 13
Sultan Ibrahim, 13, 77
Sultan of Johor, 9
super powers
    distrust of, 168
Swezey, Anthony C., 111
Syed Ahmad Shahabuddin, 273
Syed Hussein Alatas, 205
Syed Ja'afar Albar, 153, 158, 211
Syed Nasir Ismail, 187, 211

Taiwan
    replaced by China at the UN, 258
Talalla, A.S., 176, 228
Tan Chee Khoon, 205, 264
Tan Chin Nam, 107

Tan Cheng Lock, 56, 57, 59, 73,
79, 84, 125
Tan Siew Sin, 59, 102, 118, 174,
187, 191, 228, 243, 272
MCA's departure from
Alliance, 188
Tan Soo Bing, 33
Tang Mong Lan, 12, 19
"Tango King"
nickname, 39
Tarmizi, 7, 8, 264
Tawfik, 7, 10, 11, 13
inherited father's memoirs, 271
Templer, Sir Gerald, 56, 60
Texas
tour of, 107
Thailand
relations with, 133
security matters with, 131
The Wyvern, 39
Thuraisingham, E.E., 63
Tokyo Summit, 146
trade
cooperation with Singapore, 159
Trudeau, Pierre, 234
Tun Abdul Razak, 9
education minister, 78
effect of Ismail's death, 270
leukaemia, 4, 220, 271
obituary, 194
partnership with Ismail, 228
prime minister, 253, 254
trip to Ottawa, 269
views on, 254, 255

Tunku Abdul Rahman, 3, 48, 59,
120, 191
aftermath of racial riots, 193,
194, 201
calls for resignation, 208
chief minister, 78
China, recognition of, 128,
129
direct notes from Ismail, 89
fascination for, 53
Federation of Malaysia talks in
Britain, 140
letter to Ismail, 62
meeting with Oliver Lyttleton,
65
nominating Ismail for
Executive Council, 60
retirement, 200, 228, 253
separation of Singapore,
announcement of, 154
Tunku Abdul Rahman College,
177
Turnbull, Constance Mary, 118

United Chinese School
Committees' Association
(UCSCA), 79
United Chinese School Teachers
Association (UCSTA), 79
UMNO Wanita, 219
UMNO Youth, 239
United Malays National
Organization (UMNO), 3
beginnings, 46, 48

Central Executive Committee,
see Central Executive
Committee (CEC)
elections in 1956, 83
headquarter building, 239
institutional changes, 235
uniform, 60
United Nations
25th Commemorative Session,
231
China's entry, 245
first appearance at, 89, 90
first permanent representative,
86
special delegation to, 147, 148,
149
United Nations Economic
Commission for sia,
(ECAFE), 108
United Nations Film Unit, 97
United States of America
first ambassador to, 86
Mutual Security Programe,
124
seeking loans from, 102, 103
Universiti Kebangsaan Malaysia,
177
University Sains Malaysia, 233,
266
University of British Columbia,
118

Veerapan, V., 205
Victorial Institution, 57
Victoria League, 35
von Vorys, Karl, 191

Wahab Majid, 5, 194, 212, 224,
235, 262, 266
Wan Arfah binti Tan Sri Wan
Hamzah, 215
Wan Hussein bin Tan Sri Wan
Hamzah, 13
Warrandyke District, 25
"Whites only"
views on, 95, 96
wife
relationship with, 32
World Health Organization
(WHO), 109
world politics
views on, 114, 115, 116

Yahya Abdul Razak, 57
Yang di-Pertuan Agong, 85
Yarra Valley, 24
Yong, S.M., 57

Zahara binte Abu Bakar, 14
passing away, 15
Zailah, 7, 9, 13
Zakariah Ali, 9, 91, 121, 147
Zamakhshari, 7, 264
Zhou Enlai, 259